the popular images of th
American film is includ
reading.

By educating the publi
"pretend Indian" when it
book can help to break a
doctrination that begins in early childhood
and harms us all.

GRETCHEN M. BATAILLE is Assistant
Professor in the Department of English and
chairs the American Indian Studies Program
at Iowa State University, Ames. She teaches
courses in American Indian literature.

CHARLES L. P. SILET is Associate Professor in the Department of English, Iowa State
University, Ames. He teaches film courses
and has published extensively in the areas
of American literature and film.

**THE WORLDS BETWEEN TWO RIVERS: Per-
spectives on American Indians in Iowa.**
   Gretchen M. Bataille, David M. Gradwohl, and
Charles L. P. Silet, editors. Focuses on the history
and education of the American Indian in the
Hawkeye State. Attempts to correct many
misconceptions about the Native Americans who
inhabited the state and those who remain. 1978.
156 pp., ill., 6x9, cloth. CIP. ISBN 0-8138-1795-1.

WESTERN IOWA PREHISTORY.
   Duane Anderson. In a simple, entertaining
fashion, tells what archeologists think western
Iowa's early inhabitants were like by means of text
and drawings of artifacts. Traces the cultures of
nomadic hunters, pottery makers, and village
farmers. 1975. 85 pp., ill., 8½x11, cloth. CIP. ISBN
0-8138-1765-X.

**INSIDE THE CIGAR STORE: Images of the
American Indian.**
   Prepared by Gretchen M. Bataille. Produced by
Media Resources Center, Iowa State University.
This instructional package focuses on the con-
tradictory stereotypes of the American Indian that
have been perpetuated by mass media and text-
books. Includes 140 slides, audio cassette, script,
teacher's guide, bibliography, map of reservation
lands. For ordering information write to: Media
Resources Center, 121 Pearson Hall, Iowa State
University, Ames, Iowa 50011.

THE PRETEND INDIANS
IMAGES OF NATIVE AMERICANS IN THE MOVIES

THE PRETEND INDIANS
IMAGES OF NATIVE AMERICANS
IN THE MOVIES

EDITED BY **GRETCHEN M. BATAILLE**
CHARLES L. P. SILET

THE IOWA STATE UNIVERSITY PRESS / **AMES**

Gretchen M. Bataille, Assistant Professor, Department of English, Iowa State University

Charles L. P. Silet, Associate Professor, Department of English, Iowa State University

Composed and printed by The Iowa State University Press, Ames, Iowa 50010

First edition, 1980

Library of Congress Cataloging in Publication Data

Main entry under title:

The Pretend Indians.

    Bibliography: p.
    Includes index.
    1. Indians in motion pictures—Addresses, essays, lectures. 2. Western films—History and criticism—Addresses, essays, lectures. I. Bataille, Gretchen M., 1944–   II. Silet, Charles L. P.
PN1995.9.I48P7   791.43´09´093520397   79–27432
ISBN 0-8138-0925-8
ISBN 0-8138-0715-8 pbk.

CONTENTS

FOREWORD / AMERICAN FANTASY

During the first three centuries of contact between Indians and whites, the image of the Indian, although confused and fictional, nevertheless had an empirical reference point—the experiences of the people on the frontier who encountered Indians—and the correlation between reality and symbol was not difficult. Beginning with the Wild West shows and continuing with contemporary movies, television, and literature, the image of Indians has radically shifted from any reference to living people to a field of urban fantasy in which wish fulfillment replaces reality.

Visual images, of course, hold much more potential for communication than does the printed word. A vivid scene will do more to impress long-standing images than the most clever aphorism or slogan. The story lines remain the same and the plots continue to project the same familiar images, serving neither the viewer nor the producer. In the postwar period as the American conscience was continually grated over the coals of historical substance, Indians have not gained nearly as much ground as other minorities. If anything, Indians have become the great unknown to which can be attached almost any current concern that cannot be expressed in other parabolic and fable format.

Consider the movie *Billy Jack*, better titled "Bully Jack." Bully Jack is a pacifist who demonstrates his commitment to nonviolence by riding around an obscure western Indian reservation and breaking people's necks. He is smitten with the local schoolmarm who runs a "Freedom School" for psychologically disturbed white youngsters, primarily refugees from the Haight-Ashbury scene who have returned home, pregnant with feelings and other things. The Freedom School features nonsensical psychodramas in which the students are encouraged to give vent to their most sentimental feelings. Almost everyone at the school spends time writing songs and poems but has to be encouraged to recite or sing in public.

Billy Jack apparently shares the primordial mysteries of the tribe and this wisdom gives him the ability to pass instant moral judgment on everyone. In one dreadful scene he dances in an abandoned ruin while a rather angry rattlesnake uses his leg as a target. Billy, however, is the blood brother of the snake, an exalted position he probably achieved while a Green Beret, and he is sincere, so the snake venom, ordinarily nothing to be casual about, has no effect. Eventually Billy breaks one too many necks and is surrounded by the local posse and state police. He is a much better bone crusher than a negotiator since his surrender hinges upon the promise that the Commissioner of Indian Affairs will allow the students of the Freedom School to hold a press conference each year on the anniversary of Bill's surrender and report on the progress of the school. As the fuzz are taking Billy away to prison, he is saluted by students of the Freedom School who line the road, fists alert and militant in the Black Power gesture of defiance.

Insofar as this film has anything to do with Indians, it is tied with Lawrence of Arabia for accuracy and relevancy. Even the snake dance, thought by many urban youths to be an accurate recapitulation of a tribal ceremony, has nothing to do with Indians. We are no more immune than whites to rattlesnake venom. The theology of the scene, if one wishes to trace it, is pure Martin Luther—justification by faith alone—modified, of course, by traditional American mediocrity, to the belief that sincerity conquers all.

The technical adviser of this movie is apparently one "Rolling Thunder," an alleged Cherokee who once wandered into the lands of the Western Shoshone and emerged years later as their "medicine man." Rolling Thunder has a book of the same name written about him by a young man named Doug Boyd who has written a lot of books about contemporary gurus. In the book, Rolling Thunder apparently spends his mornings stalking snakes in the desert and staring them down before they can strike. Need it be said that few Indians devote their waking hours to this kind of activity.

At any rate, Billy Jack has nothing to do with Indians of any stripe but it is a map par excellence of what antiestablishment young whites thought the world was like circa 1970–71. A dash of Indian religion, some karate, blatant racism, a mystical mountain treasure which was an inscribed tablet that told us to love each other, and the persisting identity problem of individuals raised in American society who are afraid to dance, sing, and recite poetry—these are the elements of the world as perceived by the American white as the decades changed. The same complex of elements can be found about halfway through an hour's speech by a flying saucer enthusiast. It apparently takes a great deal of preaching to get whites to love each other and the message has to be repeated many times using every conceivable medium of communication.

Billy Jack is merely a symptom of a much deeper problem in which the image of the Indian seems to form a familiar boundary. Americans are really aliens in North America and try as they might, they seem incapable of adjusting to the continent. Indians, the original possessors of the land, seem to haunt the collective unconscious of the white man and to the degree that one can identify the conflicting images of the Indian which stalk the white man's waking perception of the world one can outline the deeper problems of identity and alienation that trouble him. A review of the various images and interpretations of the Indian, therefore, will give us a fairly accurate map of the fragmented personality that possesses the American white man. One can start at almost any point and list the collective attributes, attitudes, and beliefs about the Indian and then strip away the external image to reveal the psyche of the American white.

Let us examine a few of the traditional conceptions of the Indian and probe beneath the surface to discover what they say about the Americans. My favorite, to be sure, is the "old chief." We see this image in numerous examples. The old chief is a weathered veteran of literature and movies. He contains the classic posture of mysterious earth wisdom. He speaks primarily in aphorisms and rarely utters a word that is not wise and sentimental. He is always in favor of love and understanding and never advocates that we take up violence against those who have wronged us. The old chief recognizes the futility of opposition to progress and he sadly relates this wisdom in every movie scene where the younger men council for war. John Ford used him sparingly, perhaps the old man of *She Wore a Yellow Ribbon* is the classic personality here, but we can find him represented in other films, *Little Big Man,* for example, fairly well developed as a personality type.

Writers are much more shameful in their exploitation of this personality. The great fraud of recent times in this respect, of course, was McGraw-Hill's ridiculous *Memoirs of Chief Red Fox.* This old man was allegedly over a hundred years old, had been born in three different places on three different occasions, was regarded, according to the publicity release as a "historic and respected figure" by the Oglala Sioux, a tribe who had never heard of him, and from the platform of ageless wisdom he had copied James MacGregor's account of the Wounded Knee massacre, written in the late 1930s but reprinted only a year before the chief's memoirs hit the bookstands. The chief emerged just as the American Indian Movement was beginning its activities and he, of course, counseled against protests and violence. No one cared to investigate the chief's authenticity because everyone knew it was impossible that such a creature could exist. More important, he was badly needed as a symbolic figure who would counteract not only the Indian activists but the antiwar protestors, the Black Power advocates, and all who would disturb the domestic tranquility.

T. C. McLuhan, in *Touch the Earth,* an anthology containing reprints of Curtis photographs, warmed-over Indian surrender speeches, and a crafty use of italics, exploited this image also. *Touch the Earth* relies upon disembodied voices which repeat earth-derived sayings confirming the inevitability of progress while reminding us that the earth is our true home. Carlos Castaneda parlayed the old man image into a series of best-sellers that have much more relationship with an LSD travel tour than with Indians. Whatever Don Juan is, he is far from a recognizable Indian except to confused and psychically injured whites who have a need to project their spiritual energies onto an old Indian for resolution. Doubleday is resurrecting this image once again with a book, *Hanta Yo,* in which the Indian claims to be the last youth trained by the elders of the Santee Sioux. Hanta Yo apparently waited for over forty years until a younger white lady arrived to take down his words of wisdom. She then spent years translating his message from English to Dakota then back to English and produced the perfect text about how life was before the coming of the white man.

The most common feature of these resurrected chiefs and old-timers is that for all the publicity they receive not one, ever, dares to come before an Indian audience where he might be exposed. Rather they strut before white audiences in faraway cities where their aphoristic nonsense can pass for primordial wisdom without anyone becoming the wiser. Apparently the images of wisdom of the white man have all been exhausted and so the Indian is pressed into service. Each culture needs this figure, if we read Carl Jung correctly, and what European figure could conceivably convey the accumulated wisdom of the North American? None—so we have to bring forth caricatures of Indians to accomplish this task.

Behind the image of the old chief resides the firm conviction of the American white that expropriating the continent was not really a bad act. Natural law of some sort had already decreed that the agriculturalist would replace the hunter, and the old chief, as he describes his tribe marching into the sunset, gives this belief validity. Very few of the sayings in *Touch the Earth* and other anthologies, or in the movies, during the old chief scene feature the old chief saying, "You dirty sons-of-bitches, you lying bastards, you gave your promise and then when we were weak and disarmed, you betrayed us. If I had my ax here I would take a few of you treacherous bastards with me when I go." No, rather the old chief explains that one tribe follows another and the white man himself will vanish. (We all know that ain't true but it does sound cosmically comforting, huh?)

Now, you see, if the old chief, who represents the collective wisdom that this continent possesses, tells us that it is all much bigger than we are, we are released from all responsibility—which is what we desperately need some older person to tell us—the old Jehovah of the Bible isn't much good here because he wants us to be "good." And if the cosmic process has already determined the demise of the people who would stand in the way of progress, then we can wash our hands of ethical questions and revert to the true American moral stance: "If I don't do it someone else will" and "Don't blame me, I'm only doing my job." Once these attitudes can be cosmically justified, anything is possible—and moral.

The archetype of the old chief has one very important component which almost always follows it in tandem and makes the figure a complete one. The white—be he Stan Steiner, Carlos Castaneda, Cash Asher,

Thomas Mails, or T. C. McLuhan—has always been eagerly awaited by said chief. The chief is always about ready to pass to the Happy Hunting Grounds and has been anxiously awaiting someone who will put his words on paper that they may not be lost to the generations who will follow. The chief never has found a tribal member who is worthy of receiving this message and passing it along. But the first white who sticks his or her head inside the tipi door seems to trigger a compulsion by the chief to reveal secrets that nearly a hundred generations of Indians have kept close to their hearts and enshrined in their memories.

While the faithful white informant is an important part of the old chief archetype, it is also an important item of belief of Western people. Thinking that they have corralled the world in their scientific doctrines, they believe that all secrets, not just the secrets of nature, should be given up to them easily and that they should be recognized as the only impartial priests of human knowledge. When this informant figure reaches the silver screen it is altered somewhat but remains in an identifiable form if you know how to interpret it. Revealing ancient truths is not designed to move the action along very swiftly. So the informant is transformed into the Indian's most cherished friend. "Don't go in there, Jimmy (or John, or Kirk, or Burt), those Indians are mad and have sworn to kill all white men they see." But our hero does ride into the canyon, content in the knowledge that if he can get to see Cochise (or Geronimo, or Sitting Bull, or Red Cloud, or Crazy Horse) the war chief will remember their friendship and refuse to continue the war against the whites—remembering perhaps our hero's warning to the chief a decade ago that war is bad for people.

Recognition of the informant-confidant by the chief immediately antagonizes the chief's leading rival for the chieftainship, a rather scurvy individual whom no one, white or Indian, would trust, and a knife fight generally ensues between the white hero and the chief's political rival. This rival is never killed—he is always empirical evidence of the innate savagery of the Indian which the chief's benevolence seems to undermine. Since this rival is always in tandem with the good chief, he must represent the other members of the tribe who are never worthy enough to be trusted with the tribe's secret lore. Since he is not killed in the initial scene but continues until the end, there is every indication that he does represent the tribal tradition and membership which is unworthy of continuing. He becomes the same threat as do contemporary tribal members who might blow the whistle on the white confidant if he or she should appear before an Indian audience.

With few exceptions and many variations, this is the image of the Indian in contemporary American society. It has nothing to do with Indians, of course, but it is not supposed to represent the contemporary Indian since he is a pale imitation of the real Indians of the American imagination. Contemporary Indians confront this demon of the past whenever they attempt to deal with the various institutions that make up American society. In almost every instance we are forced to deal with American fantasies about the Indians of white imagination rather than the reality of the present. At a recent conference dealing with the subject of the emerging alternative world view, I made my presentation and then opened the floor for questions. The first question, entirely predictable, concerned how the lady querying me would be able to recognize that I was an Indian if she followed me around the streets of Tucson, Arizona, for a week. What could I say in response? That I would be dressed in buckskin, be carrying bow and arrows, have a deer slung over my shoulder, and be carrying some pottery? That picture would have been absurd, of course, but it was precisely the image that I was expected to present which would enable her to correctly identify me as an Indian.

There are, of course, other logical sequences in which we could discuss the image of the Indian. They would, almost universally, begin at some obscure point on the circumference of the circle and work their way toward a convergence with the figures I have outlined above. And, almost universally, they would concern and articulate some attitude about the world held by whites but made objective by attributing it to the Indian as a personality characteristic. Once the emotional complex has been attributed and someone has achieved either the chief or informant status, whites seem to close their minds deliberately to any critical effort by Indians to correct the situation.

I doubt if the Indian image will be any better a century from now. Publishers will still be digging up old chiefs, although their directors of publicity will be increasingly hard pressed to explain the existence of old chiefs who are nearly a century and a half in age. But the Indian survives because whites have many unanswered questions about who they are and they have no real authority figures or personalities to answer these questions. Insofar as they can construct a venerable figure, vest him with the happy slogans that they feel are true, and be allowed to sit at his feet in wonder, they have recaptured not only the precious memories of the YMCA Indian Guides program but have received verification that everything they have done is proper, historically and cosmically.

Indians, I must admit, intuited this subconscious drive for authenticity decades ago and adopted certain techniques in order to survive. When we are confronted with zealous but uninformed people who think they have solved the "Indian problem," we send out the most Indian-looking people we can muster to deal with them. Realizing that many whites worship money, we try to find someone who could have modeled for the buffalo nickel. No white man, no matter how callous, can resist this classic figure since it has been burned into his subconscious during those formative years when that profile would get him an ice cream cone or a box of popcorn. You just don't argue with the face on the coin—maybe that's why we place only the most cherished and pristine American heroes on the coins.

During the early OEO days when government agencies and private foundations were seeking Indian organizations to fund, we used to pick out the handsomest of representatives. People give funds more readily if they are giving to a young man who looks like Tonto or a young woman who resembles Pocahontas. The technique worked perfectly; it was an appeal to imagination and not to the relevancy of the project under consideration. Only as the granting process became a well-beaten path did the Indian representatives begin to take themselves seriously and screw up what had been the perfect scam. Politics? Find an Indian with a nice haircut who could be the Indian Bobby Kennedy and you have the Democrats lusting after you; get an Indian princess who can do either the Lord's Prayer or the Twenty-third Psalm in sign language (or who can at least wave her arms in some sequential manner that looks like it might be sign language) and you gain admittance to any Republican meeting, convention (or even the Cotton Bowl), or caucus you want to attend. Church meetings—find either a young militant or a fundamentalist elder Indian minister (preferably a Baptist or Methodist) and you get whatever you want from the churches. The list, if you think about it, is endless and is limited only by the almost inexhaustible fantasies of the whites.

Now, is this Indian response to white fantasy proper? Should Indians scam whites who are sincere? Well, the answer is complex in an abstract sense but very simple in a practical, everyday context. The whites are sincere but they are only sincere about what they are interested in, not about Indians about whom they know very little. They get exceedingly angry if you try to tell them the truth and will only reject you and keep searching until they find the Indian of their fantasies. So if you have to deal with them to get the job done, that comes with the job. The first ones, if you remember, were convinced that Seven Cities of Gold existed somewhere in northern Arizona and even when the Indians told them that no such cities existed they refused to believe them. Instead they tortured countless Indians in an attempt to find the Seven Cities. The next expedition we saw was convinced that a "Fountain of Youth" existed somewhere in the Florida-Louisiana-Mississippi area. They also tortured Indians in the mistaken belief that we were trying to keep them from learning the secret. As long as the white suspects that he does not know the whole story and that we are trying to keep our secrets—whether gold, history, religion, or lands—from him, he will find one torture or another to plague us with until we tell him something.

The obvious solution to the whole thing would be for the white to achieve some kind of psychological and/or religious maturity. But the whole psychological posture of American society is toward perpetual youth. Everyone believes that he or she must be eternally young. No one wants to believe that he or she is getting or will ever get old. Somehow only Indians get old because the coffee table books are filled with pictures of old Indians but hardly a book exists that has pictures of old whites. A strange thing, perhaps, for a vanishing race—having one's pictures on display every-

where—but therein lies the meaning of the white's fantasy about Indians—
the problem of the Indian image. Underneath all the conflicting images of
the Indian one fundamental truth emerges—the white man *knows* that he is
an alien and he *knows* that North America is Indian—and he will never let
go of the Indian image because he thinks that by some clever manipulation
he can achieve an authenticity that cannot ever be his.

VINE DELORIA

ACKNOWLEDGMENTS

WE would like to thank the following people for their kind forbearance and many courtesies with this project: Donald Benson, former Chairman, and Frank Haggard, Chairman, Department of English at Iowa State University, who provided us with much needed released time from academic duties; Daniel J. Zaffarano, Dean of the Graduate College and Vice-President for Research at Iowa State University, who granted us research support; Deans Wallace A. Russell and Nathan W. Dean of the College of Sciences and Humanities, who helped us with the manuscript preparation; Donald S. Pady, English Librarian, and Millie McHone and Sue Rusk of Interlibrary Loan of the Iowa State University Library, who furnished much information in the early stages of this work; Charmian Nickey, Sheryl Kamps, Sandi Wright, and Sue Gordon, who typed portions of this manuscript; and Bobbi Farrell, who assisted with the research and the final preparation of the volume.

Portions of the editors' work were published elsewhere and we wish to thank the following people for permission to reprint that material: Ronald Gottesman, editor of *The Quarterly Review of Film Studies*, who published our "The Indian in the Film: A Critical Survey"; Michael T. Marsden, editor of *The Journal of Popular Film*, who printed "The Indian in the American Film: A Checklist of Published Materials on Popular Images of the Indian in the American Film"; and Randall M. Miller, who included our "The American Indian Image" in *The Kaleidoscopic Lens: Ethnic Images in American Film*.

Finally some personal thanks are due to our students in the course "The American Indian Image in Film" for their insights into film and the portrayal on film of the Native American; the discussions were challenging as well as informative. One of our students put it this way:

As a Native American viewing movies, I tended to see the Indians on the screen as not being real. I knew better. I lived with "real Indians."

To Gertrude Burrell, our editor, who tackled our manuscript with good sense and grace, we owe a generous measure of gratitude. Also to Kay, who put up with our frustrations and lengthy telephone calls and through it all remained supportive, and to our children, who did not always understand but who nevertheless contributed in their unique fashion to this collection, we owe more than this acknowledgment can say.

GRETCHEN M. BATAILLE

CHARLES L. P. SILET

INTRODUCTION

BECAUSE the medium of film is so pervasive in our society and so influential in molding our perception of the world around us, it has become increasingly urgent that we examine the kinds of screen images we have been subjected to and determine how those images shape our world. Film functions strongly in our culture as a purveyor of national ideologies, values, and trends. This is especially true of our understanding of minorities, and in particular the Native American. For a generation or more Hollywood, and now increasingly television, has presented the viewing public with a rather badly distorted picture of American Indian peoples. From childhood we have been bombarded by cartoons, television serials, and old movies that tell us the Indian is the "bad guy" or, at best, a tragic anachronism. For both Indians and non-Indians this celluloid version of the culture of the Native Americans has had devastating results.

The image of the Native American that is a part of the history of the motion picture evolved from stereotypes created by the earliest settlers and chroniclers of this country. The contradictory views of the Indian, sometimes gentle and good and sometimes terrifying and evil, stem from the Euro-American's ambivalence toward a race of people they attempted to destroy. The screen images we have today have descended from the captivity narratives of the eighteenth century, the romances of James Fenimore Cooper, and the Beadle dime novel tradition. The treatment of the Indian in the movies is the final expression of white America's attempt to cope with its uneasiness in the face of a sense of cultural guilt.

I

When the Western Europeans initially came to this continent they were faced with a dual problem: first, what to do with the wilderness, and second, what to do with those who inhabited that wilderness. Not only did those early Renaissance Englishmen inherit what they believed to be uncivilized environment but uncivilized people as well. Their task, and they felt it keenly, was to subdue the wilderness and to bring order to this newly found chaos. They wanted to create a civilized Anglo-Saxon society much like the one they had just left. One of the impediments to this progress was the Indian, so these early colonists set about civilizing the "savage." In the end, the Native American was all but destroyed.

Initially, the impulses of the colonists, however finally disastrous, were at least well intentioned. They wanted to Christianize the Indians into part of their social order. But the Native Americans were not easily assimilated. As Roy Harvey Pearce has pointed out in his seminal study, *Savagism and Civilization: A Study of the Indian and the American Mind,*[1] by the end of the 1770s the American Revolution demanded a commitment on the part of the colonists to a new world vision of a glorious civilization, one in which the Indian would play no part. The original notion of the noble savage, a product of what Pearce calls Anglo-French primitivistic thinking, gave way to the realization that the Native American was bound inexorably to "a primitive past, a primitive society, and a primitive environment, [one which was] to be destroyed by God, Nature, and Progress to make way for Civilized man."[2] Pearce notes that first the colonists tried to understand the savage and to bring him into civilization; however, after the dawning of the Republic, the Indian became an unfortunate obstacle in the path of progress.

The transition in mental attitudes from assimilation to annihilation was not an abrupt one and its various permutations need not concern us here. The point is that by the beginning of the nineteenth century there was public recognition of both the failure in theory and in practice of the white attitude toward the Indian. Since the Indian would not conform to the way of life of the new society, and since he could not or would not be civilized, then he must be destroyed. As Pearce writes, the whites could pity the Indian and still censure him for his failure to adapt, and in the end this pity and censure would be the "price Americans would have to pay for destroying the Indian, . . . the price of the progress of civilization over savagism."[3]

The new society of which Americans felt themselves a part craved the assurances of progress and superiority—the Indian became the obvious point of comparison. The Europeans who settled this continent brought with them all the trappings of Western culture including its need to know the past and the future. The Native American's "historyless antiquity," as Leslie Fiedler calls it, was beyond their comprehension.[4] The Indians had no past and no future in Western terms and thereby fell out of society and out of history. Despite the wanton destruction of the native environment and of the native cultures, Americans remained fascinated by what they regarded as savagism. By the beginning of the nineteenth century, the Native American was no longer a threat to white expansionism, and became a curious object for study.

The primitive life was not all bad. From Rousseau, Europeans had learned about the inherent goodness of natural man and the simple life, and Americans inherited the noble savage as part of their literary tradition. With the rise of an indigenous literature, however, writers were forced to modify the noble savage to fit with the preexisting image of the Indian in America—one to be pitied and censured, and the doomed noble savage became a part of American culture. It was easy enough to pity the Indian, especially after his fall from grace, but it was necessary to undercut his nobility as well. One could not wipe out a noble race without justification, and so the bloodthirsty noble savage was created. Writers were also forced to admit, albeit hesitantly, white guilt as well as hatred for the Indian. Hatred and guilt mixed with celebration; the noble savage was given a peculiarly American view. He was reduced to a set of contradictions: noble and ignoble, pitied and praised, censured and celebrated. In such a way Americans justified and bolstered their own barbarism. White Americans could become savage, too, to crush savagism to save civilization.

This ambivalence toward the Native American was reflected in the earliest accounts of life in the New World. In the journals of explorers such as Christopher Columbus and John Smith, and later in histories by government officials such as William Byrd and William Bradford, descriptions of the Indians depicted varying qualities of generosity, barbarousness, or piety.[5] During the seventeenth and eighteenth centuries, the captivity narratives reinforced the existing Puritan explanation of the Indians as subhuman or inspired by the devil. One of the strongest influences on later similar works as well as on the frontier romances was Mrs. Mary Rowlandson's story, *The Sovereignty and Goodness of God . . . Being a Narrative of the Captivity and Restoration of Mrs. Mary Rowlandson* (1682). The Puritan view of the Indian remained a pervasive theme and, although the hope of "civilizing" the Indian was often expressed, ultimately religion demanded that the confrontation between Indian and white result in Indian capitulation to white domination. Individual Indians could be "good," but the group had to be depicted as "bad" to justify the existing philosophies of government and religion. Relying on existing documents and stories, James Fenimore Cooper created both the noble and ignoble savages as stock characters in American literature. However, Cooper's *The Leatherstocking Tales* were preceded by a number of other nineteenth-century works that drew on the conventions of the English historical romance of Walter Scott as well as the prototypes created in earlier frontier accounts. Robert Montgomery Bird's *Nick of the Woods* (1837) and William Gilmore Simms's *The Yemassee* (1835) reinforced existing attitudes. These works of fiction were bolstered by the epic sweep of such historical studies as Francis Parkman's *Oregon Trail* (1849) which solidified white attitudes about manifest destiny and the role of the Indian in the expanding nation. By the late nineteenth century the bloodthirsty savage had become a staple of the popular dime novel and pulp weekly. Such thrillers as *Massacre!* and *The Fighting Trapper* became favorites during the same time that the enormously popular Wild West shows were playing across the country and were being exported to France and England.

Buffalo Bill was not only the most popular of the dime novel heroes but he was also an extremely successful showman and his Wild West show toured all over the world. His show even had a crown performance before Queen Victoria; presumably she was amused. Included among the exhibits in the show were real live Indians whom Buffalo Bill paraded around in front of the audience and used in the mock battle scenes he staged between the white settlers and the savages. By the time Buffalo Bill was through, the Indians were firmly established as figures of entertainment like the stage Irishman and the comic Jew.[6]

II

Since the Indian had high entertainment value, it seemed only natural that Edison should have shot film vignettes of Indian dances for his early penny arcade peep shows.[7] Edison's machines showed such films as the *Sioux Ghost Dance* (1894) and the *Parade of Buffalo Bill's Wild West* (1898). As Ralph and Natasha Friar put it in their book *The Only Good Indian . . . : The Hollywood Gospel*, "The filmic cultural genocide of the Native American begins with such commercialization as *Sioux Ghost Dance*."[8] There is no historical evidence that what was filmed was the Ghost Dance but filmmakers, always eager to take advantage of ready-made publicity, were probably relying on the memory of Wounded Knee only four years before. From those earliest dim flickerings of the motion picture, there continued the process of miscreating the Native American's culture and way of life. What followed for the next few years was a conscious reworking of history through the filming of the battles of the Indian wars. Audiences were treated to a series of films that touted the mythical, often falsified, exploits of such legendary frontier figures as Kit Carson and Daniel Boone, plus a number of cowboys, including the ever-present Buffalo Bill Cody. The white heroes got the billing, and the Indians got the pratfalls.

D. W. Griffith, Thomas Ince, Cecil B. DeMille, all of the greatest of the early filmmakers contributed to this stereotype. Despite the talent of these directors, the image of the Native American did not become any clearer or more historically accurate. One still saw Sioux-bonneted actors selling Navajo blankets. Even actor-writer-director William S. Hart, who prided himself on the authenticity of his Westerns, spewed forth bilge about the white man's supremacy over the Indian in such films as *The Aryan* (1916). One title of this epic read: "Oft written in letters of blood, deep carved in the face of destiny, that all men may read, runs the code of the Aryan race: 'Our women shall be guarded.' "[9] The threat of miscegenation was powerful.

By the time of World War I the image of the Native American was well established in the popular film and for the next three decades, with some minor exceptions, that image remained constant. The moviemakers expressed the same ambivalence toward the Indian that the dime novelists had. The ignoble, noble savage was still with us. There was one major difference though; because of the visual nature of the new medium,

Hollywood had more opportunity to distort the image of the Native American. The writers of pulp fiction sketched in the settings and described the "red men," but Hollywood actually showed them. The resulting confusion was symptomatic of white ignorance of the people they had dispossessed. Indians of the Northeast were shown wearing clothing of the Plains Indians and living in dwellings of tribes of the Southwest. Hollywood created the instant Indian: wig, warbonnet, breechclout, moccasins, Hong Kong plastic beadwork. The movie men did what thousands of years of social evolution could not do, even what the threat of the encroaching white man could not do; Hollywood produced the homogenized Native American, devoid of tribal characteristics or regional differences. As long as an actor wore fringed pants and spoke with a halting accent he was an Indian.[10]

The Indian had a multiple image and at the same time a partial image. *The Indian*—no tribe, no identity, almost always male—was either noble (still savage, but noble nevertheless) or bloodthirsty and vicious. There were variations of the stereotypes—the drunken Indian, the heathen, the lazy native—but still it was a picture of a creature less than human without religion and lacking in morality or virtue. Usually he was viewed apart from wife or children or any family relationships; he was an isolated figure, one with a pinto pony, gliding across the plains of America, viewed always as an Indian first and an individual last. He combined all the noble virtues expressed in a Catlin painting with the savagery of a Beadle novel.

III

From the beginning of the twentieth century with the publication of reviews in daily newspapers, the Indian in the film has been the subject of a wide variety of articles. Even early articles were ambiguous about the portrayal of the American Indian on the screen, some lamenting the inaccuracies and others justifying the views as accurate. Among the first articles dealing specifically with the Indian and the movies are several appearing in *Moving Picture World* between 1909 and 1914. The concerns voiced in these essays echo down to us through the years. They are pleas grown mute with repetition. An article published in 1911, "The 'Make-Believe' Indian," notes that movies do not accurately portray Indians as a "noble race of people, with their splendid physique and physical prowess." The article mentions that a number of Indians resented the "untrue, unreal, and unfair representations of themselves and their habits." The notice concludes with the hope that a series of films of "real" Indian life will be forthcoming.[11]

Unlike the pattern that developed later, American Indian people were often included as actors in the early films. This led to such reactions as Ernest Alfred Dench's in "The Dangers of Employing Redskins as Movie Actors."[12] Because American Indians were forced to act out the image the white director had of them, they played the roles of "savages" or "stoics," many unwittingly perpetuating the stereotyped inaccuracies.

In the developing years of the movies, Indian material provided exciting drama on the screen. The Indian conflicts of the nineteenth century had been settled to the advantage of the United States, and American Indians were condemned to reservations. The use of the Indian as a subject for the films was successful and, even as film audiences grew and changed, the popularity of the subject continued. The Western came to be a metaphor for American life—triumph over the land and the people who had once inhabited it, success of the immigrant who had sought and gained new economic and social status, and a visual representation of a colorful past of what was now perceived to be a growing nation.

These earliest critical views of the Indian on the screen suggest some of the confusion that existed from the very beginning about the portrayal of Indian people by Hollywood producers.[13] Although there was a recognition of the lack of accuracy, critics were unsure about solutions to the problem. By mid-century Indians had become a staple in Saturday afternoon serials and necessary to the myth of the West and its portrayal on the screen. Audiences did not generally know the difference between a Navajo and a Cheyenne, so they certainly would not know the differences among tribal traditions or clothing. Producers knew this and knew also that the films would be popular despite the lack of accuracy. Because the Indian's voice has always been an isolated one, his pleas went unheeded. The few critics who spoke out on behalf of the misrepresentation during the first half of the century were equally isolated voices. Politically and socially it was all right to stereotype minority groups and women, the film industry seemed to be saying; it was, after all, entertaining and profitable. And that was what the movies were all about.

And so popular films of the last seventy years have represented the Native American as an entertaining anachronism. In spite of the sympathetic representations of Indians by photographers such as Edward Curtis and the white culture's long tradition of scientific curiosity about the Indian, it has been this distorted popular image that has dominated.

IV

In the early 1960s filmmakers began to exhibit a changing attitude about portraying Native Americans, and the industry's concerns were reflected in the reviews of those movies.[14] Increasingly reviewers called into question the stereotypes and misconceptions appearing on the screen. Contemporary reviews demonstrate this heightened awareness as well as the persistence of the Hollywood images. Unfortunately, many films that have presented a more balanced view of the Native American have not been received as films about Indians. For example, *One Flew Over the Cuckoo's Nest* was reviewed almost entirely for Nicholson's performance, with occasional references to the film's obvious use of religious metaphor. The fact that Kesey's novel was narrated by an Indian was totally missing from the film version. The reviewers of *Jeremiah Johnson* made little of the Indian elements in that film as did the reviewers of *Hombre,* a film that did some interesting things with the image of the half-breed. Even a movie so obviously about relations between Indians and whites such as *Tell Them Willie Boy Is Here* brought forth more copy about the return of its director, Abraham Polonsky, to film work after a long forced absence because of blacklisting in the 1950s. Many films that should have been reviewed for their progressive treatment of Indian stereotypes have not received that emphasis.

It was not until the aftermath of the Vietnam debacle in the early seventies that we were treated to a series of pro-Indian films, the most famous of which were *A Man Called Horse, Soldier Blue,* and *Little Big Man.* Sympathetic viewers eagerly grabbed on to what they perceived as a major shift by filmmakers in their attitudes toward the Indian. Unfortunately, the films did little to correct the popular stereotypes. What the films did provide was a fascinating study of white America, via the movies, trying to come to grips with itself and, in some measure, with its past.

A Man Called Horse, for all its anthropological detail, became for some critics a dissatisfying study in sadism. Although the film boasts scenes graphically depicting the central character's ritualistic self-mutilation, it resolves into what one critic called just another chapter of Indian romance in a museum diorama. The interest of the film lies in director Eliot Silverstein's concern for its tone. If it was not authentic, at least it tried to be, which was something new in American popular films. The problem was that although the film began to *look* authentically Indian, it did not "feel" Indian.

For many critics Ralph Nelson's *Soldier Blue* became a theater-of-cruelty Western based on a proto–My Lai, the Sand Creek, Colorado, massacre. The problem with all its slaughter, however, was that it portrayed the Indian as pretty much the stereotyped savage given to blood lust that we have seen on the movie screen for years. In response to the whole problem of American self-hate, Pauline Kael, in her review of *Tell Them Willie Boy Is Here,*[15] used the term genosuicide to describe the apparent zeal with which the American audience was applauding the brutal exploitation of our collective guilt to be found in movies dealing with relations with the Native American.

The one film that has done consistently well with a large number of critics is Arthur Penn's *Little Big Man.* The emergence of Chief Dan George as a film personality helped to quiet the traditional complaints about the absence of Indian actors. In spite of the blood bath in the massacre scenes, the reversal of traditional Western roles seems to have provided a rationale for the action of the Indians in ways that *A Man Called Horse* and *Soldier Blue* did not. The slaughter of Custer and his men was seen as a perfectly justifiable revenge for atrocities committed by the cavalry on a peaceful people. Although the perspective is decidedly mid–twentieth century, the film works. In *Little Big Man* Penn contrasts the organic culture of the Cheyenne with the confusing and destructive Anglo-Saxon Protestant society that is engulfing it. Civilization becomes disordered, hypocritical, self-seeking, and nihilistic with people living in constant fear and tension. The culture projects all its hatred and insecurity onto its enemies. The character who bears the main burden of the destructive and death-seeking impulse of the white society is George Armstrong Custer. It is through Custer, here figuring as a vainglorious psychopath, that Penn strikes out at American society, but it is unfortunate that Custer bears so much of the burden because it tends to dilute the charge against American society by emphasizing one crazy individual.

That same appeal, however, provided Robert Altman with the subject matter for *Buffalo Bill and the Indians.* The starring role was given to Paul Newman, which automatically focused attention on the single individual, but the debunking of national heroes has been an American pastime for years and Buffalo Bill as well as George Armstrong Custer in their absurdity and megalomania make perfect marks for the debunking film. Because the reassessment of the Native American in the movies necessitates a revision of the entire myth of the West, broadening the scope of analysis offers the most fruitful possibilities for the future.

It becomes clear after reading the criticism on the Indian in film that reactions differ depending on the expectations of the critic or viewer. Some look for accuracy in the portrayal of cultural ways and artifacts; others are more concerned with the ethnicity of the actors and actresses. But what they are all saying amounts to the same thing—the American Indian has been and continues to be stereotyped. The stereotypes will no doubt continue as long as the Indian is portrayed only in his adversary role in nineteenth-century America. The most recent hope for a change in the portrayal may be with films such as *One Flew Over the Cuckoo's Nest* in which Bromden's Indianness, although significant symbolically, is somewhat accidental. Kesey suggests in this twentieth-century version of "cowboys and Indians" that there are many victims of the American myth, and they do not all have feathers or straight black hair.

Certainly the political and social moods of the country during the 1960s and 1970s had been changing. At the same time, American Indian people were visible in the news media with the takeover at Wounded Knee, the Trail of Broken Treaties, and The Longest Walk. Perhaps producers realized that they could no longer portray the old images, that the public was becoming aware of what Stan Steiner called "the new Indians." At a time when "flower children" were searching with Don Juan and Carlos Castaneda for spiritual awakening and protesters were decrying the genocide of Vietnam, new aspects of Indian existence became significant.

In this country it will be a long time before the major studios have many American Indians as employees or technical advisers. And financial backing for Native American film companies is sadly lacking. The film version of N. Scott Momaday's *House Made of Dawn* is available, but it has been shown only to limited audiences. Based on a Pulitzer Prize–winning novel written by a Kiowa Indian, directed and produced by an Indian film company, and featuring many new Indian actors, this film demonstrates what can be done despite a low budget and a lack of "Hollywood" experience. Although the film may receive criticism on selected technical issues or resentment from some Native Americans who would have preferred that the religious peyote ritual be omitted, it is generally a fine film which visually presents Native American experience as something other than the usual fare of "cowboys and Indians." Perhaps if there were more Native Americans "in the business," we would begin to receive something other than an outside view of Indian experience. The probability of this is unlikely at this time, however.

V

What is the current "mythology" of the American Indian? Certainly there are many "mythologies" about the people who were the first to walk the forests, climb the mountains, and plant corn in what is now America. The savage of Beadle dime novels, the romantic nomad of the forest created by Rousseau, the Indian princess with roots in Jamestown and branches as far as Dame Judith Anderson's portrayal in *Little Big Man,* the drunken Indian, the stoic cigar store vender, the old chief with the secrets of the ages in ancient mythology and oral tradition—all have remained as variants of the myth.

What better place to portray these fantasies of Americans than on the wide screen? Hollywood has managed to distort and stereotype almost every ethnic and religious group, but American Indians seem frozen in time as far as film is concerned. Although a few recent films use a twentieth-century setting, by and large the Indian of the film exists in a world somewhere between the landing of the Pilgrims and the end of the nineteenth century, the primary focus being on the period between 1850 and 1900, the time when Indian people were desperately trying to hold on to their land and were fighting for their lives. But because this period represents for non-Indian Americans a time of victory, of overcoming an obstacle in the way of progress, it is a glorified time. To justify mass slaughter and land grabbing, white producers were forced to portray Indians as savage, illiterate, and not suited for "modern" civilization. The few who were no doubt descendents of Chingachgook, Pocahontas, or Squanto were "good" Indians. They either "vanished" or were transformed into the Tontos who knew their role in the changing society.

The images of early historians and writers still exist in the twentieth century. The Noble Savage who appeared as Natty Bumppo's companion was resurrected with Tonto. The scenes reproduced in Catlin paintings later appeared in *A Man Called Horse.* The drunken Indian of 1846 signing a worthless treaty was recreated in *Flap* during the 1960s. The feathered chief of Remington was still around in the 1970s, appearing as the reincarnated shaman in *Manitou.*

What will happen to the image of the Indian in film in the future is impossible to predict. If past history is any guide, films will find or develop a new stereotype, one that will accommodate a new popular image. Mass arts tend to the allegorical, preferring surfaces and types to essences and individuals, which allows them a broader or more universal appeal. And while we can expect to see Native Americans portrayed more sympathetically and with greater historical accuracy, the Indian in the popular film nevertheless will remain as one-dimensional as all other types.

The cultural distortions that have been perpetuated by the motion picture industry reflect the moral obtuseness and ethical myopia technologically advanced peoples have generally exhibited toward those less advanced. After all, it was the early Greeks, the most civilized of Western cultures, who coined the word barbarian for those peoples who could not speak Greek and were therefore presumably denied access to the Greek way of life. So, too, the English tramped around the globe bearing their white man's burden with admirable tenacity, despite the reluctance of many of the peoples they conquered. It is not surprising then that white Americans allowed their sense of superiority and their allegiance to the idea of a manifest destiny to blunt their sensitivity. Unfortunately, films and television have not done much in the last few years to correct the misconceptions that were created. It would suggest an enormous insensitivity on the part of our culture to continue to produce the old films in the same old way. A reassessment is now in order.

NOTES

1. Baltimore, Maryland: Johns Hopkins University Press, 1965.

2. Ibid., p. 4.

3. Ibid., p. 53.

4. *The Return of the Vanishing American* (New York: Stein and Day, 1969).

5. The earliest graphic depictions of American Indians are contained in travel narratives dating back to 1505 and portray the Native American as a seminaked savage. See Frank Weitenkampf's "How Indians Were Pictured in Earliest Days," *The New York Historical Society Quarterly* 33(October 1949):213–21. Also see Robert F. Berkhofer, Jr., *The White Man's Indian* (New York: Vintage Books, 1979).

6. For some interesting observations about the importance of the declining frontier, see George N. Fenin's "The Western—Old and New," *Film Culture* 2(1956):7–10. For discussion of the popular imagery of the Native American in the 1870s, see Robert A. Trennert's "Popular Imagery and the American Indian: A Centennial View," *New Mexico Historical Review* 51(1976):215–30.

7. Most of the following information about the images of Indians found in early films was gleaned from Ralph and Natasha Friar's excellent book *The Only Good Indian . . . : The Hollywood Gospel* (New York: Drama Book Specialists, 1972).

8. Ibid., p. 70.

9. Ibid., p. 137.

10. For a further discussion of this idea, see John C. Ewers, *The Emergence of the Plains Indian as the Symbol of the North American Indian* (Washington, D.C.: The Smithsonian Institution, 1964).

11. "The 'Make-Believe' Indian," *Moving Picture World* 7(March 4, 1911):473.

12. Alfred Ernest Dench, "The Dangers of Employing Redskins as Movie Actors," in *Making the Movies* (New York: Macmillan, 1915), pp. 92–94.

13. For a lengthy and comprehensive discussion of these images, see Charles L. P. Silet and Gretchen M. Bataille, "The Indian in the Film: A Critical Survey," *The Quarterly Review of Film Studies* 2(February 1977):56–74.

14. A variety of the reviews of the films discussed in this section are listed and annotated in Section 6. See also Richard Schickel, "Why Indians Can't Be Villains Any More," *The New York Times,* February 9, 1975, Section 2, pp. 1, 15.

15. See Pauline Kael, "Americana," *New Yorker* 45(December 27, 1969): 47–50.

1

THE NATIVE AMERICAN: MYTH AND MEDIA STEREOTYPING

W E HAVE INCLUDED in this section a number of articles that suggest the broad cultural bases for the stereotypes of the Native American and point out the enormous intellectual import of the conflict between the races as an integral part of the myth-building process in the New World. These selections trace the process of solidification that the image of the Indian has experienced over the last one hundred years both in literature and in the media, and the reasons why white Americans have demanded such a distortion.

The origins of such stereotyping predate the settlement of the North American continent and can be traced in part to the travel narratives written by the Portuguese and Spanish as well as English and Dutch sailors who first explored the New World. Often rather crude but lurid woodcuts illustrated their accounts of the new land and its people. Indians were frequently portrayed as savages who went naked and even resorted to cannibalism. Scenes of Indians dismembering their enemies and eating them, or of savage combat, were prevalent, as were portraits of seminaked native women, and they became in the European mind not only exotic objects but also objects of curiosity. Pocahontas, perhaps the most famous Native American of those early years, was taken to London where she had her portrait painted wearing a ruff and hat—just as any other Elizabethan gentlewoman. The step from oddity to adversary came when white Europeans decided to colonize the wilderness across the Atlantic.

Roy Harvey Pearce's *Savagism and Civilization: A Study of the Indian and the American Mind* traces the acceptance of the savagism/civilization duality that has characterized white attitudes toward Indians up to fairly modern times. One reason for its persistence, of course, is that the Native American was inextricably linked with the myth of the West which in many ways forms the central myth of the American experience. Embodied in the myth, the image of the red man as noble/ignoble savage has passed into the American consciousness through art and literature and, in our own time, the movies. This static, almost simple-minded, stereotypical view was far more appealing in mythic terms than a more dynamic and complex understanding of the plight of the Native American. As long as the collective consciousness of the nation could identify emotionally and historically with the myth, there was no need to modify it or alter its dimensions. It has been only in the last few years as a result of some fundamental reexamination of American ideals that the historical and anthropological information about the Indian, much of which had been available for years, was allowed to surface and enter into a restructuring of our historical and emotional perspectives on the Indian.

It is ironic that the ecology movement that focused on human relationship with the environment should have played such a big part in this process of redefinition. It was as part of the wilderness landscape that those first settlers saw the "savage" inhabitants of this virgin world, and it was this ability to see them not as human beings but as something else that allowed the white Europeans to slaughter them in the same way they would destroy the other natural resources of this continent. To call into question our forefathers' attitudes toward the world they lived in is to request a similar reexamination of their attitudes about the peoples they displaced.

Mythic stereotypes, however, die hard—especially if they are as ingrained in the national psyche as is the image of the Indian. The essays in this section suggest

3

that a revision of that image is underway. By a clear understanding of our past, both in fact and in fiction, we can better comprehend the present and, as these authors demonstrate, perhaps even begin to correct the misperceptions willed to us by preceding generations. ■

1

In this excerpt from his important study, *Regeneration Through Violence: The Mythology of the American Frontier, 1600-1860,* Richard Slotkin, professor of English at Wesleyan University, describes the process a nation goes through to formulate the myths by which it defines itself and its peoples. He applies this mythogenesis to the American experience to clarify how and why white Americans see the Indians as they do. He also offers some suggestions as to how this myth-creating process aided in distorting the images of the Indian in our culture.

MYTH AND LITERATURE IN A NEW WORLD

RICHARD SLOTKIN

THE mythology of a nation is the intelligible mask of that enigma called the "national character." Through myths the psychology and world view of our cultural ancestors are transmitted to modern descendants, in such a way and with such power that our perception of contemporary reality and our ability to function in the world are directly, often tragically affected.

American attitudes toward the idea of a national mythology have been peculiarly ambivalent. There is a strong antimythological stream in our culture, deriving from the utopian ideals of certain of the original colonists and of the revolutionary generation, which asserts that this New World is to be liberated from the dead hand of the past and become the scene of a new departure in human affairs. Nonetheless, we have continually felt the need for the sense of coherence and direction in history that myths give to those who believe in them. The poets of the early years of the republic—taught, as part of their classical education, that national mythologies are embodied in literature and begin with national epics in the manner of Homer—attempted to fabricate an "American epic" that would mark the beginning of a national mythology, providing a context for all works to come after. Their concept of myth was essentially artificial and typically American: they believed, in effect, that a mythology could be put together on the ground, like the governments of frontier communities or the national Constitution, either by specialists or by the spontaneous awakening of the popular genius.

Like the Constitution, such myth-epics would reflect the most progressive ideas of American man, emphasizing the rule of reason in nature and in human affairs, casting aside all inherited traditions, superstitions, and spurious values of the past. The freedom and power of man were to be asserted against the ideas of necessity, of historical determinism, of the inheritance of guilt and original sin. From Barlow's *Columbiad* and Dwight's *Greenfield Hill* in the late eighteenth century, through Whitman's "Song of Myself" and Melville's *Moby Dick* in the nineteenth, to Hart Crane's *The Bridge* and Williams's *Paterson* or the "great American novel" in the twentieth, American writers have attempted the Homeric task of providing, through epic poetry or epic fiction, a starting point for a new, uniquely American mythology. Even scholarly critics who address themselves to the problem of the "myth of America" have a marked tendency to engage in the manufacture of the myth they pretend to analyze in an attempt to reshape the character of their people or to justify some preconceived or inherited notion of American uniqueness. Such critics are themselves a part of this national phenomenon of myth-consciousness, this continual preoccupation with the necessity of defining or creating a national identity, a character for us to live in the world.

Works like the *Columbiad* and *The Bridge,* whatever their artistic merit, failed (at least in their authors' lifetimes) to achieve that quasi-religious power throughout the whole of a culture that is the characteristic attribute of true myth. The premises of such works do not take into account the facts that myth-making is a primary attribute of the human mind and that the process of mythogenesis in a culture is one of continuous activity rather than dramatic stops and starts. True myths are generated on a subliterary level by the historical experience of a people and thus constitute part of that inner reality which the work of the artist draws on, illuminates, and explains. In American mythogenesis the founding fathers were not those eighteenth-century gentlemen who composed a nation at Philadelphia. Rather, they were those who (to paraphrase Faulkner's *Absalom, Absalom!*) tore violently a nation from the implacable and opulent wilderness—the rogues, adventurers, and land-boomers; the Indian fighters, traders, missionaries, explorers, and hunters who killed and were killed until they had mastered the wilderness; the settlers who came after, suffering hardship and Indian warfare for the sake of a sacred mission or a simple desire for land; and the Indians themselves, both as they were and as they appeared to the settlers, for whom they were the special demonic personification of the American wilderness. Their concerns, their hopes, their terrors, their violence, and their justifications of themselves, as expressed in literature, are the foundation stones of the mythology that informs our history.

The failure of writers and critics to recognize and deal with the real mythological heritage of their time and people has consequences that go beyond the success or failure of their literary works. A people unaware of its myths is likely to continue living by them, though the world around that people may change and demand changes in their psychology, their world view, their ethics, and their institutions. The antimythologists of the American Age of Reason believed in the imminence of a rational republic of yeomen farmers and enlightened leaders, living amicably in the light of natural law and the Constitution. They were thereby left unprepared when the Jeffersonian Republic was overcome by the Jacksonian Democracy of the western man-on-the-make, the speculator, and the wildcat banker; when racist irrationalism and a falsely conceived economics prolonged and intensified slavery in the teeth of American democratic idealism; and when men like Davy Crockett became national heroes by defining national aspiration in terms of so many bears destroyed, so much land preempted, so many trees hacked down, so many Indians and Mexicans dead in the dust.

The voluminous reports of presidential commissions on violence, racism, and civil disorder have recently begun to say to us what artists like Melville and Faulkner had earlier prophesied: that myths reach out of the past to cripple, incapacitate, or strike down the living. It is by now a commonplace that our adherence to the "myth of the frontier"—the conception of America as a wide-open land of unlimited opportunity for the strong, ambitious, self-reliant individual to thrust his way to the top—has blinded us to the consequences of the industrial and urban revolutions and to the need for social reform and a new concept of individual and communal welfare. Nor is it by a far-fetched association that the murderous violence that has characterized recent political life has been linked by poets and news commentators alike to the "frontier psychology" of our recent past and our long heritage. The first colonists saw in America an opportunity to regenerate their fortunes, their spirits, and the power of their church and nation; but the means to that regeneration ultimately became the means of violence, and the myth of regeneration through violence became the structuring metaphor of the American experience.

The culture and literature we call American was born out of the confrontation between cultures that embodied two distinctly different phases of mythological evolution, two conflicting modes of perception, two antagonistic visions of the nature and destiny of man and the natural wilderness. The European cultures that sought to transplant themselves to these shores possessed a sophisticated, romanticized mythology, in which the land of what was to become the American West figured long before its actual discovery. The Europeans were met by native Indian cultures whose mythology was closer to the primary, Moira stage, whose vision of the American landscape was mythopoeic rather than conventional, whose values and mores (derived from their environment and their mythic vision) were in important respects antagonistic to those of Europe. Yet between European and Indian there was a fundamental bond of sympathy, a mutual recognition of a brotherhood of consciousness (or perhaps of the unconscious). The whites appreciated and envied what they took to be the Indian's ease of life and sexuality, the facility with which he adjusted to the land, the fidelity and simplicity with which he worshiped his wilderness gods, and the gratification of mind and body such worship brought him. The Indian perceived and alternately envied and feared the sophistication of the white man's religion, customs, and technology, which seemed at times a threat and at times the logical development of the principles of his own society and religion. Each culture viewed the other with mixed feelings of attraction and repulsion, sympathy and antipathy.

Human cultures on the North American continent, whether they were of European or Indian origin, have been shaped by the interaction of their migrant peoples with the American landscape, the wilderness. The one constant in the American environment has been the wilderness in its varying forms of forest, plain, mountain, and desert. The French and English settlers of Canada and the eastern seaboard of the United States confronted essentially the same physical environment as the Abnaki (Wabanaki), Iroquois, Algonkian, and Cherokee who preceded them in the land. As the American environment was the same for each of these cultures, one might reasonably expect that in the process of adjusting their lives to the wilderness, each of these cultures would acquire certain elements or qualities distinctly derived from and suited to that environment. Differences between them might be accounted for by considering their differing points of cultural and historical origin. Also, their presence together in the land, resulting in both violent and amicable cultural interaction, would affect the development of each culture, just as the constant of the wilderness would. If we are to understand the mythology and the cultures derived from this complex of interacting factors, we must have some understanding of the nature of the hostile cultures involved (Indian and European), of how they reacted to their environment, and of their vision of both their own role in the cosmos and that of their opposites. ●

2

Leslie Fiedler, professor of English and American literary critic, sees the Native American as the one element of the Western myth that has not been totally eradicated by or assimilated into the white culture. It is the presence of the Indian that gives reality to the Western idea. As he notes, ''Any piece of American space can become to the poet's imagination an authentic West.'' And it is precisely the confrontation between the white European and the Indian that forms the essential ingredients for the creation of the new American, a process still going on.

THE DEMON OF THE CONTINENT

LESLIE A. FIEDLER

> *The moment the last nuclei of Red life break up in America, then the white man will have to reckon with the full force of the demon of the continent . . . within the present generation the surviving Red Indians are due to merge in the great white swamp. Then the Daimon of America will work overtly, and we shall see real changes.*
>
> *D. H. Lawrence,* Studies in Classic American Literature

Fifty years ago, the demonic future which Lawrence foresaw seemed only the troubled dream of a foreigner never really at home on our soil, a fantasy for poets to exploit and serious scholars to ignore; but suddenly his *then* is our *now*, and all of us seem men possessed.

Toward the end of Allen Ginsberg's hilarious little poem ''America,'' for instance, the voice of that Jewish Walt Whitman from Paterson, New Jersey, mocking the fear of Russia which vexed the land in the mid-fifties, becomes suddenly the grunt of a stage Indian:

The Russia want to eat us alive. The Russia's power mad. She wants to take our cars
    from out our garages.
Her want to grab Chicago. Her needs a Red Reader's Digest. Her wants our auto
    plants in Siberia. Him big bureaucracy running our filling stations.
That no good. Ugh. Him make Indians learn read . . .

And at almost the same moment, Sebastian Dangerfield, J. P. Donleavy's alter ego in *The Ginger Man,* that joyous Irish-American extension

From *The Return of the Vanishing American* (New York: Stein and Day, 1969), pp. 11–14, 22–28. Reprinted by permission of Leslie A. Fiedler.

of the methods of James Joyce, is yelling at the top of his fool voice, "Did you know I'm part Mohawk? *Whoo hoo!*"

It seems to make no difference at all; descendants of East European Jews or Dublin Irish, at home and abroad, everyone who thinks of himself as being in some sense an American feels the stirrings in him of a second soul, the soul of the Red Man—about which, not so very long ago, only an expatriate Englishman, his head full of Natty Bumppo and Chingachgook, had nerve enough to talk seriously. Young poets sign themselves "tribally yours," and lovers send each other feathers from ancient headdresses as tokens of esteem.

To be sure, the Indian has not disappeared at all "into the great White swamp," but has begun to reinvent himself—in part out of what remains of his own tribal lore, in part out of the mythology and science created by White men to explain him to themselves. The Native American Church, whose rites combine the smoking of peyote and the beating of drums with the recitation of formulae inherited from evangelical Protestantism, moves the Indians of the Southwest and West as nothing else has moved them since the Ghost Dance. And meanwhile, the Iroquois begin to learn, however reluctantly, to turn their backs on booze and the Baptists alike, and to take up the almost forgotten ceremonial of the Long House Religion.

Fascinatingly, it is not as Utes or Cheyennes, Mohawks or Delawares, that aboriginal Americans are rediscovering their identity, though once such parochial definitions constituted their whole sense of themselves and provided sufficient occasions for endless warfare. The Vanishing Americans may have bowed out as Last Mohicans or Flatheads or Sioux, but they return as what they all seemed to invading White Europeans from the start, simply "Indians," indistinguishable non-White others.

That Tuscarora leader of the Indian nationalist movement, Mad Bear, for instance, expounds to all who will listen a vision of Red America which begins in the legendary past of Atlantis and ends in the perhaps equally legendary future of after-the-Chinese-invasion. He explains how the ancestors of the Indian people once lived on a great island in the midst of the ocean, how they were wicked and therefore overwhelmed by a flood, how a tiny remnant escaped destruction by escaping through underground tunnels and an underground river which brought them up in the High Mesa country of the Hopis, how *all* Indians are descended from that remnant (whatever lies the White anthropologists may tell of movement over a land bridge from Asia). And he goes on to prophesy that times of trouble are ahead, indicated by the return to this world of the "Big People," sixty-foot giants, fourteen of whom are already stalking the land. He urges that it is the moment to take to the woods for council and, after "burning much tobacco," to begin the riots and demonstrations which, along with those sponsored by the Negroes, will lead to the intervention of the Chinese Communists and the destruction of all White Americans. After this, he assures his Indian listeners, the Negroes will depart in peace for Africa, whence they came, and the whole continent will be left to the Red Men who have inhabited it since the disappearance of Atlantis.

And even as the Indian has become visible once more to himself, he has become visible to certain White writers, who think of themselves as being on his side. Within a couple of years, Ed Dorn, a Black Mountain poet and voice of the sixties, has written a book about the Shoshone, and Edmund Wilson, last spokesman for the twenties, one about the Iroquois.

An astonishing number of novelists have begun to write fiction in which the Indian character, whom only yesterday we were comfortably bidding farewell (with a kind of security and condescension we can no longer even imagine), has disconcertingly reappeared. Books with Indians are, as any small boy can tell you, "Western," and the Western we were sure, up to a decade ago, had vanished along with the Indian into a region where no "serious reader" ventured: the world of pulp magazines, comic books, Class B movies, and innumerable second-rate TV series, not even interesting as camp. And how certain we used to be, in that irrecoverable recent past, that the distinction between high literature and popular culture was final and beyond appeal: quite like that between White men and Indians, us and them.

But in the last several years, beginning somewhere around 1960, John Barth and Thomas Berger and Ken Kesey and David Markson and Peter Matthiessen and James Leo Herlihy and Leonard Cohen, as well as the inspired script writers of *Cat Ballou,* and I myself twice over, have, perhaps without being aware, been involved in a common venture: the creation of the New Western, a form which not so much redeems the Pop Western as exploits it with irreverence and pleasure, in contempt of the "serious reader" and his expectations.

Even Truman Capote's recent best-selling work of reportage, *In Cold Blood,* turns out to be an almost classic Western in theme, involving a White man and an Indian (Capote's Perry has a Cherokee mother, from whom he inherits his thick straight black hair and his "iodine-colored" skin) bound together in a homosexual alliance against the respectable White world around them; and the scene is westernmost Kansas, more Far West than Midwest, Capote himself remarks, with cattle and Stetson hats and Colorado just over the horizon. It is not just a lust for blood which has won a huge readership for that odd book, in which the author and history have so uncomfortably collaborated, but also a genuine hunger for the West.

The heart of the Western is not the confrontation with the alien landscape (by itself this produces only the Northern), but the encounter with the Indian, that utter stranger for whom our New World is an Old Home, that descendant of neither Shem nor Japheth, nor even, like the Negro imported to subdue the wild land, Ham. No grandchild of Noah, he escapes completely the mythologies we brought with us from Europe, demands a new one of his own. Perhaps he was only a beast of the wildwood, the first discoverers of America reassured themselves, not human at all; and at the end of the fifteenth century, Princes of the Church gravely discussed whether, being undescended from Adam, the Indian indeed had a soul like our own. It was a question by no means settled once and for all when the Church answered "yes"; for at the beginning of our own century, Lawrence amended that answer to "yes, but—" Yes, a soul, but *not* one precisely like our own, except as our own have the potentiality of becoming like his.

And in the five hundred years between, how the Indian in his ultimate otherness has teased and baffled the imagination of generation after generation of European voyagers and settlers. How they have tried to assimilate him to more familiar human types, to their own mythologic stock-in-trade. The name "Indian" itself memorializes the first misguided effort of Columbus to assure himself that he was in those other, those *East* Indies, after all, and confronting nothing but types known since Marco Polo, like the inhabitants of Cipango or Cathay.

After that delusion had collapsed, after the invention as opposed to the mere discovery of America, there were new explainers-away eager to identify the Red Men with the Welsh, the Irish—and especially the Semites, the lost Tribes of Israel.

Only the minority group comprising "scientific" anthropologists have clung in our time to the delusion of Columbus, postulating a migration from continent to continent which makes our Indians kin to the subjects of the Great Khan after all. And only a handful of nuts have been willing to identify the Indians as survivors of quite another world, another creation—refugees from Atlantis or Mu. Lawrence was tempted to the latter alternative, hinting somewhat mysteriously of an affinity between the western Indians, at least, and the priesthood of the lost Pacific civilization, "the world once splendid in the fulness of the other way of knowledge."

"They seem to lie under the last spell of the Pacific influence," he says of the Redskins of Cooper's *The Prairie;* "they have the grace and physical voluptuousness . . . of the lands of the great Ocean." But the deep imagination of Americans has sought stubbornly to link the Savages of the New World with the once-Chosen People of the Old.

From those apostles to the Indians of the seventeenth century who thought of themselves as penetrating the wilderness to restore the Old Testament to those to whom it properly belonged, through Fenimore Cooper in the early nineteenth, recounting the adventures of just such a deluded missionary in the form of Parson Amen in Oak Openings (to whom the bewildered Redskins object that, being Indians, they can never be *lost*), to the later Mormons, incorporating the wrong-headed myth in their homemade scriptures, and the rancher of *Cat Ballou,* baffled at the Indian who refuses to answer his Hebrew greeting of *"Shalom!"*—the tradition has never died.

It is, in fact, carried from door to door even now by missionaries for the Church of Latter Day Saints, who leave behind them the *Book of Mormon,* complete with a prefatory gloss that sends those eager to know the "Fate of Indians" to the fourteenth verse of the thirteenth chapter of *First Nephi:*

And it came to pass that I beheld multitudes of the Gentiles upon the land of promise; and I beheld the wrath of God, that it was upon the seed of my brethren; and they were scattered before the Gentiles and were smitten.

This may be, to true believers, a sufficient mythological explanation not only of the origin, but of the expropriation of the Indians. To the Indians themselves, however, though they may be in fact as stubborn and persistent witnesses as the Jews, it remains inconceivable that they can be anything so familiar to the three-thousand-year-old tradition of the White West as mere children of Israel, that they can be anything but their untranslatable selves.

Everything else which belongs to the Western scene has long since been assimilated: the prairies subdivided and landscaped; the mountains staked off as hunting preserves and national parks; fabulous beasts, like the grizzlies and the buffalo, killed or fenced in as tourist attractions; even the mythological season of the Western, that nonexistent interval between summer and fall called "Indian summer," become just another part of the White year. Only the Indian survives, however ghetto-ized, debased, and debauched, to remind us with his alien stare of the new kind of space in which the baffled refugees from Europe first found him (an unhumanized vastness), and the new kind of time through which, despite all our efforts, he still moves (a historyless antiquity). It is for this reason that tales set in the West seem to us not quite Westerns, unfulfilled occasions for myth rather than myth itself, when no Indian—"stern and imperturbable warrior" or lovely, complaisant squaw, it scarcely matters—appears in them.

The Western story in archetypal form is, then, a fiction dealing with the confrontation in the wilderness of a transplanted WASP and a radically alien other, an Indian—leading either to a metamorphosis of the WASP into something neither White nor Red (sometimes by adoption, sometimes by sheer emulation, but *never* by actual miscegenation), or else to the annihilation of the Indian (sometimes by castration-conversion or penning off into a ghetto, sometimes by sheer murder). In either case, the tensions of the encounter are resolved by eliminating one of the mythological partners—by ritual or symbolic means in the first instance, by physical force in the second. When the first method is used, possibilities are opened up for another kind of Western, a secondary Western dealing with the adventures of that New Man, the American *tertium quid*; but when the second is employed—our homegrown Final Solution—the Western disappears as a living form, for the West has, in effect, been made into an East.

But into what exactly is the transplanted European converted by the Western encounter when he resists resolving it by genocide? It is easy enough to name the aspects of Americans defined by the three other forms: the Northern, in which we become Yankees; the Southern, in which we are turned into Whitey; the Eastern, in which we are revealed as Tourists. But the transformation effected in the Western evades easy definition. Thinking of Natty Bumppo (that first not-quite-White man of our literature, for all his boasts about having "no cross in my blood") and his descendants, we are tempted to say that it is the woodsman which the ex-European becomes beside his Red companion: the hunter, the trapper, the frontiersman, the pioneer, at last the cowboy—or maybe only next-to-last, for after him comes the beatnik, the hippie, one more wild man seeking the last West of

Haight-Ashbury in high-heeled boots and blue jeans. But even as he ceases to be beatnik and becomes fully hippie, the ultimate Westerner ceases to be White at all and turns back into the Indian, his boots becoming moccasins, his hair bound in an Indian headband, and a string of beads around his neck—to declare that he has fallen not merely out of Europe, but out of the Europeanized West, into an aboriginal and archaic America.

It is tempting, at this point, to take the dilemma as the answer, and to settle for saying that, since this new kind of man came into existence only with the West, he is best called simply the "Westerner," that there is no way of moving beyond this. But we know, too, that at the moment of looking into the eyes of the Indian, the European becomes the "American" as well as the Westerner. And if we forget it for a moment, there is the title of Henry James's early novel to remind us: his account of a white barbarian from San Francisco, actually called—with a bow to Columbus—Christopher Newman. And who has more right than the man from the farthest West to be called both new and American, since before a single White man had set foot on American soil, the whole continent had been dreamed by Europe as "the West": a legendary place beyond or under the ocean wave, a land of the dead or those who rise from the dead. And it needed only the invention of the name America to set up the equation *America equals the West.*

Once the Atlantic was crossed, moreover, the name *West* was transferred, step by step, to whatever part of the continent lured men on just over the line of settlement, to the unexplored space behind the next natural barrier, past the Appalachians, the Mississippi, the Rockies. Vermont or Maine may define our North once and for all; Georgia, Alabama, or Louisiana may circumscribe our mythological South; the harbors of Boston and New York City, ports from which tourists embark for the adventure of returning to the Old World, can scarcely be thought of as anything but the East.

But where, geographically, is the elusive West? We know that first of all it was Virginia itself, the Old Dominion, then New England, Pennsylvania, Kentucky, Louisiana, Ohio, Missouri, Texas, the Oregon Territory, etc., etc.—always a bloody ground just over the horizon, or just this side of it, where we confronted *in their own territory* the original possessors of the continent.

So long as a single untamed Indian inhabits it, any piece of American space can become to the poet's imagination an authentic West, as the small Vermont town of Acton was transformed, even in the twentieth century, by the vision of Robert Frost's extraordinary poem "The Vanishing Red." Beginning with the lines: "He is said to have been the last Red Man in Acton. And the Miller is said to have laughed . . ." it ends by becoming a parable of the war to the death between White Man and Red, though Frost pretends, ironically, to refuse to tell it:

It's too long a story to go into now.
You'd have to have been there and lived it.
Then you wouldn't have looked on it just as a matter
Of who began it between the two races.

It is, however, only a desperate sort of Last Western, a hymn to the end of one more West, that Frost manages to write, as seems appropriate to our time. For, by and large, we have used up the mythological space of the West along with its native inhabitants, and there are no new places for which we can light out ahead of the rest—even Alaska being only a fiftieth state. Can we reestablish the West anywhere at all, then? This is the question that troubles certain of our writers, eager to dream the old American dreams. The earth, it turns out, is mythologically as well as geographically round; the lands across the Pacific will not do, since on the rim of the second ocean, West becomes East, our whole vast land (as Columbus imagined, and Whitman nostalgically remembered at the opening of the Suez Canal) a Passage to India.

Maybe the moon will serve our purposes, or Mars; maybe up and out will turn out to be a true archetypal equivalent to the Way West, as we have already begun to surmise, calling some of the literature of space adventure "space operas," on the model of "horse operas," which is to say, Westerns. But unless "stern and imperturbable" Martians await us, or lovely and complaisant lady Lunatics—as certain makers of science fiction have already tried to assure us—whom we can assimilate to our old myths of the Indian, Outer Space will not seem an extension of our original America, the America which shocked and changed Europe, but a second, a meta-America, which may shock and change us. On our shores, the myth of the West which had teased the European imagination up to the time of Dante—the myth of an unattainable and unpeopled world—was altered into one of a world open to "plantation," but inhabited by hostile aliens: a myth so deeply rooted in us that, in spite of scientific testimony to the contrary, we insist on imagining the New Worlds we now approach inhabited by natives, "savages" benign or threatening.

We have defined the "territory ahead" for too long in terms of the mythologies created out of our meeting with and response to the Indians to abandon them without a struggle. They have proved sufficiently adaptable to describe our relations with Negroes and Polynesians, with all colored peoples, in fact (Twain's Nigger Jim and Melville's Queequeg are mythological blood brothers, after all, to Cooper's Chingachgook); and we dream of taking those same terms with us into a future not quite so terrifying and unfamiliar as it sometimes seems, if only they will work there, too. ●

John C. Ewers, senior ethnologist at the Smithsonian Institution, has written "The Static Images," in which he points out that the "richness and variety of Indian life . . . and the dynamics of Indian history . . ." cannot be appreciated by people who persist in thinking of Indians in terms of "a few static and stereotyped symbols." Unfortunately, that is just what filmmakers have done. Ewers discusses the fact that "elements of such stereotyping are not just the figments of the white imagination. One can find bits and pieces of these elements in the Indian cultures of North America, but it is only on films, in television, and in other popular forms of entertainment that they appear in combination. Tipis, tomahawks, and feathered warbonnets of different tribes have been depicted in films as belonging to one homogenous tribe." Ewers contends that the white culture has accepted the Plains Indian as the symbol of Indianness, and such homogenization of the Indian distorts the variety and richness of Indian culture.

3

THE STATIC IMAGES

JOHN C. EWERS

THE richness and variety of Indian life in North America, and the dynamics of Indian history, cannot be appreciated by people who persist in thinking of Indians in terms of a few static and stereotyped symbols. The popular image of the Indian as a man on horseback, wearing a flowing feather bonnet, breechclout and moccasins, holding an upraised tomahawk in one hand, seems to persist. His wife is envisioned as wearing a beaded browband with an upright feather at the back, a long, beaded buckskin dress and moccasins. Together with their papoose they are thought to live in a painted tipi, while the husband carves totem poles and the wife fashions painted pottery in her spare time.

The elements in these Indian stereotypes are *not* figments of the white man's imagination. All could be found among *some* Indians in *some* areas of North America at *some* time. But they appear in combination only in works of fiction and in such visual forms as comic strips, motion pictures and TV dramas.

From *Look to the Mountaintop*, edited by Robert Iocopi. (San Jose: Gousha Publications, 1972, 107–9). © The H. M. Gousha Company. Reprinted by permission.

FROM THE PLAINS INDIANS

A majority of the traits composing these images appeared among the Plains Indians during the nineteenth century. Certainly the non-Indians of this country and abroad did not. begin to visualize Indians in all of these terms until the Plains Indians became known to them through illustrated books and magazines and the works of such artists as George Catlin, Karl Bodmer and Felix O. C. Darley, America's most popular illustrator of the mid-nineteenth century. The dramatic Plains Indian Wars continued to focus attention on those Indians during the decades of the 1860s and '70s. Buffalo Bill's Wild West show, which toured the major cities of Europe as well as America between 1883 and World War I, further publicized and popularized the Plains Indians. Its success led to the formation of other traveling Indian shows, large and small, in which Indians of other tribes dressed like and acted like Indians of the Plains. The movies did not originate these Indian stereotypes. They merely perpetuated them.

Those colorful, flowing feather bonnets, with or without long trailers of eagle feathers, probably originated among the Crow or the Sioux of the Northern Plains after these tribes obtained horses through Indian intermediaries from the Spanish settlements of the Southwest. A few prominent warriors of these and other tribes of the Plains wore the bonnets in their fights with other Indians as well as with whites, although many outstanding war leaders preferred horned bonnets (with or without feathers); as potent war medicine. During the period of the Wild West shows, the custom of making and wearing feather bonnets spread to tribes of the forested East as well as to ones living in other areas of the West. Indians as separated as Maine, North Carolina, Arizona and the Pacific Coast adopted the feather bonnet as a picturesque symbol of Indianness for wear on dress occasions. Members of Indian delegations to Washington took their feather bonnets along to impress high government officials. In 1921 the aged Crow chief Plenty Coups placed his handsome feather bonnet upon the casket of our first Unknown Soldier in the formal burial ceremonies at Arlington as a tribute from all American Indians. In 1958 a Mattaponi Indian of Virginia, who was wearing one of these feather bonnets he had made himself, told me, "Your women copy their hats from Paris, because they like them. We Indians use the styles of other tribes because we like them too." Among whites the mistaken idea was implanted that an Indian who does not wear a feather bonnet is not a real Indian of importance.

HEADBANDS AND BEADS

Headbands appear in the imaginative illustrations of Indian women created long ago by white artists who may never have seen an Indian. However, it is doubtful if many Indian women wore beaded headbands before movies became popular and intertribal powwows were promoted in Oklahoma and elsewhere during the early decades of this century. Still more elaborate ones have crowned the heads of very attractive Indian "princesses" who have represented their respective tribes in intertribal beauty contests within recent years. It is unlikely that the "princess" concept was known to the Indians before Englishmen bestowed that title upon the famous Pocahontas, daughter of the powerful chief Powhatan in colonial Virginia.

In prehistoric times some Indians wore beads of shell, bone, turquoise or other attractive stones in necklaces or pendants. But glass beads of Venetian manufacture were introduced among the Indian tribes by white fur traders. The larger ones were used for necklaces and pendants, the smaller ones in embroidery. They appeared on garments sparingly at first. But beads gradually replaced dyed porcupine quills in the decoration of costumes among the Indians of the Northern Plains and Woodlands, while other tribes, who had never made quillwork, adopted trade beads to accent or replace painted decorations. The very great majority of the heavily beaded artifacts from the Plains and Woodlands preserved in museum collections in Europe and America are less than a century old.

CLOTHES OF SKIN

The long, short-sleeved buckskin woman's dress also appears to be a nineteenth century development. Earlier references to the skin dresses of women among the tribes of the northern Woodlands and Plains describe them as supported by narrow straps from over the shoulders. For winter wear separate sleeves were added, tied together at the back of the wearer's neck. The most common garment of Southern Plains Indian women was then a short, wrap-around skin skirt. In colder weather a short, sleeveless skin poncho also was worn. During the early historic period women in many parts of North America wore no clothing above their waists; although Pueblo women wore dresses of woven cotton which covered their upper bodies.

As for the men's breechclout, there is evidence to suggest that it was not worn by Indians of the Northern Plains before cloth was obtained from the fur traders. Probably deer or antelope skin leggings with flaps crossing at the waist were worn earlier and concealed the privates. But some early observers noted that exposure was not considered indecent among the tribes of the Upper Missouri.

Moccasins, of course, are of Indian origin. The word, derived from an eastern Algonquian dialect, may have referred to a type of footgear made from a single piece of soft skin which enclosed the foot, with the seam lengthwise of the center of the instep. The term was extended to cover all types of footgear made of skin and worn by Indians, even to the one with a separate sole of tough rawhide sewn to a soft skin upper, which may have been suggested by the white man's shoe, and did not become common among some of the tribes of the Northern Plains until 1875 or later. Of the several types of moccasins, perhaps the most ingenious was a rawhide-soled Apache one with a short, upturned frontal extension to protect the foot from contact with the spines of cacti. Yet many tribes of the Far West generally went barefoot, while those of northern Mexico wore sandals.

TOMAHAWKS AND TIPIS

"Tomahawk" is another Indian word of Algonquian origin. In early colonial times it commonly referred to a wooden war club with a solid, round head, much used by Woodland tribes. The term later was extended to refer to all types of war clubs used by Indians, including iron ones introduced by white traders. The metal tomahawk pipe, combining a sharp axe-like blade with a pipe bowl, fitted to a hollow handle which also served as a pipe stem, became a popular type. Made by white blacksmiths for the Indian trade, many of these also were presented to prominent Indians who prized them as status symbols.

During the second half of the nineteenth century a stone-headed war club was still used by the Sioux and their neighbors of the Plains. Known as a "swinging rock," its head was pointed at both ends and hafted in a crosswise position to a long, thin wooden handle by a binding of wet rawhide. As the rawhide dried it shrank and secured the head to the handle as tightly as if it had been riveted to it.

The tipi bears a name of Siouan origin (*ti* "to dwell," *pi* "used for"). This ingeniously designed dwelling had a cover of soft buffalo cow hides over upright poles tied together near their tops. Although often referred to as conical, the back is steeper than the front to make it stand firmer against prevailing west winds. The doorway on the east was both out of the wind and facing the morning sun. A pair of movable flaps, or ears, at the top could be adjusted to control the emission of smoke from the central, ground-level fire within. The Spanish explorer Coronado saw pedestrian nomadic hunters on the southwestern Plains living in tipis and observed the relative ease with which they dismantled their dwellings and transported them with the aid of strong dogs. Throughout the Plains, tipis were used in buffalo days as year-round homes by the nomadic tribes, and as temporary ones by farming tribes on their extended buffalo hunting excursions away from their more permanent earthlodges, or bark-covered dwellings. After they settled on reservations, Plains Indians reluctantly moved into log or frame houses, but they continued to make tipis of canvas for occupancy during their summer ceremonial encampments.

Many other kinds of dwellings were built by other North American tribes—ranging from the frail, brush-covered wickiups of the Desert and Great Basin tribes, to the larger bark-covered long houses of the Iroquois, to the sturdy, rectangular plank houses of the tribes of the Northwest Coast and the many-storied, large apartment houses of the Pueblos.

TOTEM, POTTERY, PAPOOSE

The totem pole was an invention of the tribes of the North Pacific Coast, made from the trunks of large and rather easily carved cedar trees.

The vertical series of bird and animal forms carved on these posts represented the family crests of their owners. Spanish explorers saw carved wooden posts at the entrances to temples in the villages of Southeastern Indians, and other carved posts of religious significance were erected by the Iroquois, and the Cree Indians of central Canada.

Pottery vessels were widely made and used for cooking and storage among the agricultural and more sedentary tribes of North America, even in prehistoric times. There is evidence that some of the nomadic tribes of the Great Plains made crude pottery during the early historic period. But after they acquired metal kettles, pottery making declined rapidly among the farming tribes of that region as well. The Southwest continues to be the major center for the making of painted pottery. On the Northwest Coast, where no pottery was made, Indians cooked in watertight wooden boxes.

"Papoose" was an Indian word for an infant in one of the dialects spoken by Indians in New England in early colonial times. Whites extended its application to all young Indian children. Indians of many tribes took great pains in making elaborate cradles for their papooses. The heavily beaded ones from the Plains Indians reflected the prestige of the child's parents. Less affluent Indian women carried their infants high on their backs, inside their buffalo robes, shawls or blankets.

INDIAN WAYS WITH WORDS

Moccasin, tomahawk, tipi, papoose—these are but four of the many Indian words that have found their way into the English language. One cannot travel far in the United States or Canada without encountering numerous Indian names for towns, rivers, mountains, states or provinces. Even so, the notion persists that all Indians spoke the same language, which was so limited in vocabulary that they had to supplement it with gestures in order to communicate freely with one another. This is far from true. Nearly a century ago linguists distinguished some 56 distinct language families among the Indians of North America. Although this number has been reduced through further studies, the number of mutually unintelligible dialects—about 2,000—was a factor of greatest importance for practical communication. Neighboring tribes, such as Crow and Sioux, might speak dialects of the same basic language but could not communicate any more easily by word of mouth than can Americans and Frenchmen unless they study each other's language. Furthermore, Indian languages were rich in vocabulary and capable of making many fine distinctions in meanings.

Indians also revealed great ingenuity in coining descriptive names for people and objects they had not seen until they met white men. For example, translations from the Blackfoot language show that those Indians came to call blacks "black-white men," bootleggers "sneaking-drink-givers," lawyers "loud-mouthed-white-men," whiskey "white-man's-water," peaches "looks-like-hairy-ears," and an automobile "skunk-wagon."

The sign or gesture language of the Great Plains was developed to facilitate communication between tribes who spoke different languages. It could also be used effectively by men of the same tribe under conditions when silent communication was desirable—as when approaching wild game or enemy camps. This sign language was rich enough in gestures to permit the telling of stories and silent conversations.

Today English has become the common language employed in the exchange of ideas between members of different Indian tribes.   ●

4

Donald Kaufmann traces the image of the American Indian as it has been "handed down" from early writers to Wild West shows to stage, film, and television. He offers comparisons between Indians and Blacks to focus on the white attitudes toward relations between the races and to show how these attitudes have been manifested in the media. Most important, Kaufmann notes, is that the public must be "made aware of Indians in the present tense." He is professor at the University of South Florida and an author and scholar of American literature and culture.

THE INDIAN AS MEDIA HAND-ME-DOWN

DONALD L. KAUFMANN

THE original Americans, the Indians, were among minorities the first clear-cut victims of media bias. An American newspaper in the 1860s described Irish immigrants as "born savages . . . as brutal a ruffian as an untamed Indian." Of these two groups of "savages," only the Irish made a visible mark on twentieth-century American experience. The Indian vanished with the closing of the frontier, a vanishing act played out in the white mind of the 1960s until Blacks were everywhere, Indians nowhere.

The "Vanishing American" had been given a permanent time-out. American history had played an untimely trick on the Indian, making him the one racial minority with a deprived present. The census made the closing of the frontier official in 1890. Since then, the American Indian became more and more the ward of the government and the guardian of the national urge to dream, forever, about the Wild West. Americans—from the movie-goer to the anthropologist—had remained fixed on the image of the Indian as the semi-nomadic hunter, occasionally squatting in a tepee, or making pottery, picking berries before taking off, pronto, alternating between canoe and horse, wearing feathers, ribbons, beads and of course giving off the masterful grunt of a doomed race. The Indian stereotype had been put in a time freeze. Unlike Blacks, whose stereotyped roles evolved with the times, the Indian found himself typecast as a historical relic, as the American who had vanished with the prairie, whose viable role in American life faded somewhere between the dime novel and the Hollywood Western. In terms of media exposure, the Indian got too much, too soon.

From the colonial beginnings, the Indian entered the white mind as in-

From *The Colorado Quarterly* 23 (Spring 1975): 489–504. Reprinted by permission.

stant drama void of any individualized humanity. Early white settlers on first contact saw the redskin as a stock figure caught between two opposing truths—noble or ignoble? Rousseau and other romantics attacked scientific progress, glorified emotion, and praised the "natural man." The American Indian seemed destined to lose his forked tongue. But zealous Christians, such as Cotton Mather, insisted that Indians were evil incarnate servants of the Devil. Satanism had gone red. Caught between typifying a philosophical ideal and a religious scourge, the Indian both attracted and repelled the first white settlers. Most of what passed for popular literature consisted of what those fascinating red savages were doing, real or otherwise. So-called captivity narratives became white America's first escapist literature. These were sensational accounts of white people abducted by red minions of Satan, intent on capturing white Christian souls. A mixture of fact and fancy, of gut sermon and adventure story, captivity narratives titillated the colonial whites and later generations, well into the nineteenth century. In terms of being redefined as a flashy cipher in the white imagination, the American Indian ironically was the real captive.

This reduction in earlier print media of Indian life into white fantasy could not be countered or undone because there was no authorship (as the white man knew it) among Indians. Instead of relying on complex writings, Indian tribes sometimes transmitted the great events of their past through sign language or picture writings on rocks or skins. Much more often, oral art kept the historical record. Prime events, memorized by favorite tellers, were passed on by word of mouth, retained by the individual and collective memory of the tribe. Once the genocidal whites came, whole tribes were snuffed out without any record of their inner life retained. Indian heritage, as such, went up for grabs to the nearest white consumer of land and people, with the heritage eventually to be ossified in books.

Filling the void of an authentic Indian literature became a white aesthetic pastime. An inferiority complex on the part of early American writers toward European standards for beaux-arts—known as the Colonial Complex—had put most of American experience off limits as high art. But the Indian—he was an exotic something European artists never had. Indians consequently were romanticized, spruced up in white literary and dramatic modes, with the Pocahontas legend leading the way.

The American stage in the early nineteenth century overflowed with Indian stock figures, mourning their lost heritage or rhapsodizing on their kinship with the wilderness. Hackneyed themes echoed in the titles— *Metamora, or, The Last of the Wampanoags* and *The Indian Princess, or, La Belle Sauvage,* both smash successes. Edwin Forrest, the national idol of the American stage, created the early stereotype of the Indian chieftain who could rave and rant with a Shakespeare tongue—all the more grotesque when compared with the stoney-faced, hooded-eyed Sitting Bull who would be later led through Wild West shows. Early Indian drama was strictly a white man's show. Forrest (who also played plantation Negroes) virtually did a one-man minstrel show as tragedy that befitted the doomed redskin.

What did it matter—blackfaces (stomping and singing) or elegaic faces painted as red as the setting sun. Negroes or Indians? All was a racial blur to white audiences. Pocahontas kept rescuing colonists while dusky warriors spoke in either blank verse or monosyllabic baby talk. Dozens of Indian plays kept featuring the doomed chieftain and shadowy princess. Indian reality had turned into a white travesty.

Like the Negro the Indian had found his place, a pawn to the illusion that pioneer life in America would never go away. In an age given over to the visibility of Black slavery, historians hardly noticed the Indian enslavement to a national ideal that would keep white America dream-locked for over two centuries. Red slavery, after all, was more insidious and (as history will show) far more lasting.

Early American novelists and poets, an exclusively Wasp group, complemented the vogue for Indian drama with their version of the Indian as a literary fixture usually unfit for American masterpieces. Earlier writers such as Charles Brockden Brown did use Indian characters in bits and pieces, usually as spooky or barbaric frills. At rare times, there was sympathy for the Indian. For example, Philip Freneau's "The Indian Burying Ground" treated the Indian with the melancholy and curiosity of a poet turned anthropologist. But the three nineteenth-century writers who did the most to deep-freeze the literary Indian were Henry Wadsworth Longfellow, James Fenimore Cooper, and the lesser known Robert Montgomery Bird.

Of these, Longfellow relied most on his Wasp imagination to sugarcoat the Indian enough to make him palatable for the old and young in the parlor or classroom. His enormously popular *The Song of Hiawatha* (1855) converted the Indian into an exotic trinket of Brahman sensibility. In the introductory section, Longfellow spelled out his thesis that

> Every human heart is human
> That in even savage bosoms
> There are longings, yearnings, strivings
> For the good they comprehend not.

Who said a "savage" could not have a "bosom"? Longfellow's red minstrel show kept tune to quaint New England art until the end when Hiawatha (the red-faced epic hero) drops "words of wisdom" to his people, to accept the white man's religion; then, he gets into his magic canoe and sails westward. Walt Disney (had he lived then) would not have changed a word, as the Longfellow Indian merged into the sunniest side of the American heritage.

James Fenimore Cooper, unlike Longfellow, had the reputation of being more fair toward the Indian, fair in that he gave equal time to opposing stereotypes—Indians as either horribly bad or goody good. Among the latter was Chingachgook, the noble comrade of Natty Bumppo; Chingachgook's foil, in *The Last of The Mohicans* (1826), was the villainous Huron renegade, Magua. Or in *The Prairie* (1827), the satanic

Mahtoree, chief of the "dangerous treacherous race" called the Sioux, did battle with the Pawnee Hardheart, a "noble leader of noble savages." Cooper, with little or no direct experience with Indians, romanticized freely for his readers, either prissy Easterners or remote Europeans who could afford to see a prim gap between good and bad Indians, so long as red never proved racially superior to white. And this aesthetic mistake, Cooper never made. But the Negro (with no land or body to call his own) was an ideal vehicle to show off admirable qualities of certain Indians. Cooper's Indians in such works as *Satanstoe* (1845) and *The Redskins* (1846) turn out to be far superior to his Negro characters. In Cooper's time, racial laurels (with white supremacy assumed) had to go to the "first Americans" who, unlike Blacks, still owned much land, and that was language that Cooper's readers, especially Southern slave owners, could well understand.

Although Robert Montgomery Bird could not immediately match Cooper in mass adulation and literary prestige, his blunt conclusion about the Indian was the one that most survived in the pop mainsteam. Nathan Slaughter—the aptly named hero of Bird's *Nick of the Woods, or, The Jib-benainosay* (1837)—made the murder of Indians his life's mission. Such one-man genocide seemed natural in Bird's novel, which zeroed in on Indian uprisings that pinpointed the racist creed that all redskins were bestial and beyond white redemption. Nathan Slaughter has his own "final solution." With his dog Peter, tracking down the smell of savages, "Bloody Nathan" continued his slaughter through twenty-four American editions, a popularity second only to Cooper's. Leather-Stocking could keep his quota of good Indians. The white popular mind began to prefer Bird's new theme: "The only good Indian is a dead Indian."

The attitude was ready-made for the dime novel. The shadow of Nathan Slaughter fell deep on Daring Dick the Apache Killer and other heroes of the dime novels on the psychopathic hunt for Indian blood. Readers of these yellow-backed novels, with minds seeking adolescent thrills, had little use for Cooper's forest philosophy delivered in Biblical tones by gabby Indians. For ten cents, "ugh" was good enough. The rage for the dime novel began in 1860 with the big seller, *Malaeska, The Indian Wife of the White Hunter*. Success followed success, the formula being pioneer life spiced with Indian fighting. Buffalo Bill eventually emerged as the star hero. As backdrop for the pulp adventures of cowboys and Indians, the federal government speeded up its policy of forcing Indians off their prize land and herding them ever westward onto reservations. Live Indians were becoming a rarity, except in the dusty pages of dime novels before the final showdown with white supremacy that sprinkled redskins on the bloody land.

As an aesthetic force, the Indian remained off the American map of high art. Except for Cooper's work, literary masterpieces in the nineteeth century ignored the Indian. America's romance with the "good" Indian was over. The Colonial Complex still geared the Wasp writer to emulate the best of European letters, modes now thought unbecoming to savages as characters. Most of the literati was also smitten with the prevailing opinion that the workings of God or Nature had decreed the end of the Indian in American life. A vanishing race had no business in beaux-arts. The Indians' lot fell to hacks who turned out pulps, where it was always open season on redskins.

After the Civil War, white Americans—their memories of being a frontiersman, backwoodsman, or small farmer fading in the new reality of the industrial city—consumed dime novels and Indian plays until the Indian himself seemed a ghostly ancestor that had somehow never existed.

The Indian's last go-around as live entertainer coincided with the official closing of the frontier. In the 1880s, the Wild West show became the new American mania. It was a potpourri of circus, parade, carnival, and shoot-em-up melodrama. Raw history had provided the cue for America's final craze for things Indian. Like Blacks today, the Indian had the media limelight. Instead of fanfare in the name of Civil Rights or Red Power, the Indian was engaged in a pop rerun of Cooper's *Last of the Mohicans.* Manifest Destiny—in the aftermath of the Custer fiasco at Little Big Horn—put on a white finale of the winning of the West by rooting out the last Indian resistance. This last Indian war whoop made headlines. Indian leaders, such as Sitting Bull, Crazy Horse, Chief Joseph, and Geronimo, vied with national leaders and world statesmen for top billing.

This would be the last time that Indian leadership would have such visibility. Then the public reacted to last-ditch Indians with an ambivalence that most Americans reserve for the underdog—scorn tempered with sympathy. Custer's defeat immediately brought white vengeance as show biz: THE RED RIGHT HAND OR BUFFALO BILL'S FIRST SCALP FOR CUSTER. Other Wild West shows featured Buffalo Bill and Texas Jack knifing and gunning Indians. Yet, the public was fickle. Sympathy for a so-called dying race made Sitting Bull popular enough to parade in Wild West shows, a cross between a dignified warrior and beloved freak. A few years later Geronimo, the last great Apache chieftain, surrendered to federal troops for the second time in 1886, and after taking up farming and Christianity, he became a celebrity, a special added attraction at the Omaha and St. Louis Expositions and at Theodore Roosevelt's inaugural parade. That was, in ironic retrospect, the Indian's finest political hour.

With his cowboy mentality, Teddy Roosevelt naturally preferred to show off with Indians rather than Blacks. Besides, Negroes never had the honor of being dubbed "first Americans." Historians, of course, had neglected to tell about the many Negro cowboys who roamed the prairies and, occasionally, the Wild West shows. In the popular white mind, the Wild West would remain strictly an Indian show.

Sixshooter country that had fostered the Indian as entertainer, dead or alive, would soon turn to the new medium of movies. The vogue for Indian drama ran dry after the last two stage hits—William De Mille's *Strongheart* (1905) and Mary Austin's *The Arrow Maker* (1911). The Wild West show grew seedy before its demise in the early 1900s. Cowboys and Indians in order to keep up with the times threw away their sixshooters and tomahawks and engaged in football games. As the West turned into what Richard Harding Davis called the "Mild West," Hollywood as America's new "Dream Factory" assimilated whatever was usable of the Indian stereotype from the Wild West show and the dime novel, the last of which appeared in 1912. Twelve years earlier, the death of Sitting Bull and the message of the Ghost Dance had led to the massacre of Indians at Wounded Knee, the last major battle of the Indian wars. History had its final say on the Indian as a shaping force in American experience. White paternalism, in league with the new media of the twentieth century, became the red man's burden.

With the red man no longer a threat and with the Indian Question supposedly settled, some minor writers joined the ranks of paternalists with a leftover guilt. Earlier, Helen Hunt Jackson had castigated whites for their unjust treatment of Indians in *A Century of Dishonor* (1881), which had prompted an irate Teddy Roosevelt to reply: "The most vicious cowboy has more moral principle than the average Indian." But the age of the cowboy without the Indian in Western literature was ushered in by Owen Wister's *The Virginian* (1902), dedicated to Teddy Roosevelt, which by 1970 had sold over two million copies. Wister's novel mentioned Indians once or twice. The cowboy, introduced to romantic love and other complications of civilization, took on new psychological dimensions of the more complex modern novel. But the Indian in the new Western novel remained a simplistic throwback to the great romantic legend of the American West.

What grew more complicated was the white response to this figure of the Indian in past tense. Hindsight sweetened with liberalism caused some writers to rediscover the Indian on less racist terms. In *The Book of the American Indians* (1923) and elsewhere, Hamlin Garland exposed a white history of Indian racism and argued that Indians should have been allowed to have the best of both white and red worlds. Oliver La Farge in his Pulitzer Prize winning novel *Laughing Boy* (1929) showed that idyllic love among Indians could never run smoothly unless both parties remained true to their tribal ways. Sympathy for the Indian (and good whites) turned into pure melodrama in Zane Grey's *The Vanishing American* (1925). Despite his gallery of greedy, bigoted missionaries and other white molesters of Indian dignity, Grey (with his enormous popularity) only succeeded in burying the real Indian in sensational fiction. As Grey's title unwittingly indicated, the Indian was ready to "vanish" into the melodramatics of history.

One index of the Indian's entrapment in pseudo-history was the peculiar tolerance whites gave to Indian miscegenation. When it came to interbreeding, Indians clearly outranked Negroes. The best of Wasps, horrified at having one drop of Negro blood, somehow imagined that all went well in the family tree after an illustrious male ancestor stepped off the Mayflower and mated with the first available Indian princess. Such pride in having a select type of Indian blood was only extended to female royalty of an otherwise inferior race. To claim a male Indian, even a chief, as an ancestor was a faux pas. It might suggest that the family bloodline was susceptible to the warrior ways of the savage. But a well-groomed kind of Pocahontas as a great-great-grandmother—that was real Puritan get-up-and-go. Such a family would have greater social clout, since history had cushioned the first shock of white touching red.

The print media had made sure that Indian, not Black, miscegenation would receive special treatment. Though rare in literature about the West, when the theme of miscegenation did occur, it did not focus on what plagued Blacks mixing with whites—social ostracism. What was emphasized, instead, was initiation into a strange culture, usually a white hero taking up Indian ways. This was the message of the interracial marriage in A. B. Guthrie's *The Big Sky* (1947). Unlike Black experience, Indian ways were not inferior to the white man's life-style. In fact, dropping out of white society and going Indian sometimes turned into a glamorous gesture, in line with the neo-primitivists who urged overcivilized man to return to a more simple, natural existence. To feed this new white escapism, American writers worked over a backlog of Indian stereotypes—uncanny woodsmanship, super-coolness, stoic mysticism and so on—and turned them sunnyside up for a readership despairing of city ways. If printed interbreeding of whites and Indians ever smacked of the racial stigma reserved for Blacks, American writers would follow the lead of Helen Hunt Jackson whose once famous *Ramona* (1884) pleaded in straight liberal terms for the acceptance of an individual regardless of . . . and everybody knew what.

But odds said that in white bedrooms Indians would not be confused for Blacks. Redskins, once the scourge of pioneer women, had long since stopped being a sexual threat. Unlike the ubiquitous Negro slave slinking in and out of cotton fields and master bedrooms, the American Indian had to check his sexual energies at the nearest reservation. Both the dime novel and the later Western movie—by keeping the earlier stereotype of the doomed warrior chieftain and by dropping the dusky celestial princess—went along with keeping Indian sex in a deep freeze. White America (if it wished) could vicariously have its Pocahontas without its Sitting Bull.

Visibility was the key to why Indians were exempt from the racial catastrophe of one drop of Negro blood transforming a white into a nigger. The standby racial imbalance of the popular prints of Currier and Ives, of slapstick darkies next to stately redmen, had stuck in white consciousness. And so the movies and other entertainment media had never left the Indian world of Currier and Ives, while Blacks swapped plantations for the streets and were everywhere in the white world in present tense. Blacks had superseded Indians as America's favorite neo-primitives. The Indian, at least, had the consolation of chic miscegenation—an "Indian Love Call" for every red-blooded white itching for a new frontier.

Another white mood that set off Indians from Negroes was guilt. It was rooted in a priority of white wrongdoing. First came a greed for land and a necessity to dislodge the Indian who put the land to communal use.

Instead of a reverence for land, the white man substituted a craze for individual ownership. Once whites had a taste for owned land, the next logical urge was to own human beings. Slave ships docked and Black America was born. The white psyche, after over two centuries of unacknowledged racism, finally succumbed to an overdose of remorse, and the collective Wasp consciousness had little trouble updating *Uncle Tom's Cabin* and making Blacks the most likely source for the release of guilt feelings. And if not guilt, certainly fear. Whites—from the liberal with his guilt feelings toward any ancestor who owned slaves to the bigot with his fear that the "colored" would take job or daughter—had been conditioned by the media overwhelming the public with the visibility of Blacks, while twentieth-century Indians remained out of sight.

With the red man moth-balled in the nineteenth century, white guilt toward the Indian was based on ignorance. It embedded guilt into what might be called America's first "racial memory." If it ever would surface, whites would be forced to remember how an estimated million and a half Indians at the time of the Pilgrims had dwindled to less than a million when the West was won;* or, when blankets (gifts for the tribes) were infected with smallpox; or the four thousand of fourteen thousand Cherokees who died on the "Trail of Tears" from Georgia to Oklahoma. But such memories of the genocidal winning of the West now seemed irrelevant. Land, always the official means of recognizing the Indian as a human being, still remained the key to the Indian's presence. What most haunted a white when first meeting an Indian was a dread reminder of the Original Sin done to the land. This was a mode of guilt ready-made for a nation weaned on a middle-class mania to own house, home, land, anything. White guilt toward the Indian thus dealt with property rights of otherwise nonexistent people. White guilt had nothing to do with Indians as people still surviving in the 1970s as a minority, oppressed at the socioeconomic bottom. That Indian remained invisible. America's first racial memory was limited by the media refusing to let the Indian cross the Great Divide from 1890 to modern times.

Media in the twentieth century greeted Indians with a select popularity to fit a "vanishing race" with much less land and warpaint. Actual anti-Indian racism had ebbed. But the Indian fared no better as entertainment stuff. In fact, the blunting of white racism sometimes boomeranged and worsened the image of the Indian. With less need to be relevant about actual Indians, moviemakers, writers, and pop marketeers converted the Indian into a total cardboard figure, either the good Indian companion like Squanto who welcomed the Pilgrims or (more usually) the bad Indian as villainous as a Nazi or Jap in a World War II propaganda movie. An offshoot of abstracting the Indian showed up in a new array of books (scholarly or otherwise), all purporting to solve the "Indian Problem." Most whites not caught up in slick paternalism still preferred their Indians less esoteric, as vintage grunters with war feathers.

* It should be noted that Kaufmann's estimate of 1½ million is far lower than recent estimates which place the original population at 10–15 million. [Editors' note.]

Still, the so-called modern Indian had his momentary stardom, too much, too soon, as mass exposure of later Negroes will show. In the early twentieth century, when Black superstars were yet unknown, Indian Jim Thorpe became the darling of white America.

Jim Thorpe, probably America's greatest athlete, confirmed for whites some of their prize Indian stereotypes. The mass belief that Indians, inherently and historically, had amazing eye and hand coordination and an overall superior agility came to life every time Thorpe scored a touchdown at Carlisle Indian School or won a medal at the 1912 Stockholm Olympics. One Indian, at least, upgraded his stereotype into (in today's language) red power.

But, the Indians had no counterparts to Flip Wilson, Dick Gregory, and numerous other Black comics. In the popular mind, Indians took on the stoney-faced image of a low-keyed stoic, out of touch with the energy of Blacks on the move. Black super-athletes like Joe Louis and Sugar Ray Robinson and a Black array of show biz personalities would follow Thorpe but would have a much greater and more lasting effect on mainstream America. The Indian as superstar had missed out on television and the full impact of the minority report in McLuhan's "global village."

One Indian caricature, however, continued to vie with Blacks for top honors by white entertainment standards. That was Tonto, the "friendly Indian companion" of the Lone Ranger. "Kemo sabe" and "get-em up Scout" showed white people that Tonto knew his linguistic place. Tonto, with his clipped baby talk had at least advanced the Indian from "ugh" to "kemo sabe." But the Lone Ranger's vocabulary and mellow Waspy voice befitted the white half of the act. Whatever the Lone Ranger was, Tonto was less—less fast, less a sharpshooter, less domineering. Even his horse, Scout, was less white. Only when it came to the old Indian standby, primitive wisdom, could Tonto compare with the "masked man." Otherwise, when the Lone Ranger judged a situation, Tonto played out his role as monosyllabic yea man. The Lone Ranger led his friendly but inferior comrade into the mass popularity of newspapers, comic books, movies, radio, and TV until Tonto became the best of all possible Indians in a West so wild that Wasps had to wear masks. Pseudo-history—so the entertainment media insisted—was the only kind of Indian reservation that would appeal to mass America. Actual reservations with their appalling living conditions were off limits. Lousy family entertainment.

When the Hollywood Westerns became the rage during the twenties and thirties, the cowboy-and-Indian formula of the dime novel and Wild West show merely passed into a new media. Movies abounded with "Me-Chief-Rain-In-The-Face" portrayals, instant fodder for gun-happy but law-abiding cowboy heroes. For those whites who still preferred their Indians in print, newspapers and comic books offered "Way Out West," "Red Ryder," "Little Joe," "Hopalong Cassidy," and of course "The Lone Ranger."

Jay Silverheels, the actor who played Tonto, soon saw his image in movies being duplicated en masse—not quite as friendly and a little less inferior. This new and improved Indian stereotype stemmed from the new Hollywood fad (a product of commercial exploitation and not genuine guilt) to even up the lopsided ratio of bad Injuns and good palefaces. Chic Westerns now admitted that certain whites did speak with a "forked tongue." Showing the new history of savages (if not noble, at least law-abiding) being victimized by a few renegade whites was a leftover of the Hollywood campaign against Hitler and his racism.

World War II movies usually featured a Tonto-like GI who helped save the platoon through his animal sense of sniffing out for miles any Nazi or Jap. As a follow-up of the anti-Nazi mood, postwar Hollywood went on the warpath against ethnic or racial persecution. Jews took advantage by working up a literary and cultural Renaissance. For a while, Blacks were satisfied with their movie line about being "a credit to their race." Unlike Jews and Blacks, whose persecution was portrayed in contemporary settings, the mistreated Indian was still mired in a history showcase. Moviegoers never realized that some Indians once owned Black slaves and that Black Union troops had gunned down Indians. Pseudo-history still reigned. The Wild West now crawled with unscrupulous whites dealing out illegal guns and firewater to Indians who otherwise respected their "Great White Father." But for every tainted white, Hollywood producers made certain that there was a sterling white, superior to the best Indians. Like other minorities caught up in a fad for sympathetic treatment, Indians had fallen into the media trap of becoming stand-ins for roles formerly reserved for whites.

Television for the fictitious Indian was just a new way of doing old things. First, the typecast Indian made a brief stopover in radio, a medium not tuned to the Western which required the visual to put over the adventuresome sense of time and place. Radio did feature an occasional redskin as support for singing cowboys like Roy Rogers and Gene Autry and kiddie shows like Tom Mix and Hopalong Cassidy. But somehow the Western lost too much in translation on radio. TV, combining the film eye with the radio ear, was ideal for keeping up with time-rusted cowboys and Indians. Again, the Indian was hexed by white insistence of his visibility in past time, in a never-never land. This was consumed by TV which whisked the Wild West from movie theaters into living rooms. Once again, the Indian went through the visual motions (the color line between winning and losing the West) for millions of kids and adults who cheered on their eye-catching Mix, Cassidy, and the new Sheriff Matt Dillon. "Gunsmoke" raised the classic Western into adult fare and gave Indian extras (real or otherwise) something to do. "Bonanza," another long-time favorite, introduced many cowboys and a few Indians to the sensibilities of the soap opera. Those rare times when a TV drama or documentary attempted a real and honest portrayal of Indian life past or present were more than offset by constant reruns of old and new Hollywood films that preserved the old Indian stereotypes. As television imitated Hollywood to death, the Indians in the process became a rerun of a rerun.

The postmortem view of the Indian in media pinpointed why racial conflict in the 1960s and 1970s was exclusively a Black and white affair. The contemporary Indian and his problems had been shelved. It was a follow-up of the white man's tampering with his own historical expectations for Indians.

From the beginning, Indians and Negroes were destined to have differing racial roles. Blacks were to be systematically excluded from the political, economic, and social world of whites. But it was the reverse for the Indian. After the federal government legalized him with land treaties and after churches and universities stuffed him with paternalism, the Indian was pressured to emulate and to enter the white world.

As law after law included Indians and excluded Negroes, a racial paradox resulted. With their clear-cut exclusion, Blacks became the racial outsiders to be encountered in every attempt to preserve white supremacy. But the sanctity of Indian treaties disappeared along with the frontier. For every law demanding that Indians conform to white institutions, there were ten movies with Hollywood redskins wearing feathers and "ughing" themselves back to the nineteenth century. The idea that Indians could join the so-called melting pot looked more and more absurd. To blur what-might-have-been in the world of law and what-is in the world of entertainment, white discrimination against Indians turned into a fine art. With no "Jim Crow" laws to keep them in their places, the "first Americans" found themselves either chasing Custer's ghost or being parked in front of cigar stores or (the greatest honor of all) becoming the names of the Cleveland Indians, Washington Redskins—the only ethnic group ever to become mascots of baseball and football teams.

Media had played another trick on Indians that set them off from Negroes—while Blacks (viewed as outside ciphers in the nineteenth century) strive to get into American history, Indians try to escape from American history. This helped to explain the vacuum in Indian leadership during the sixties and seventies when Black leaders stole the media show. Indians had no one to match the likes of Martin Luther King or Reverend Jessie Jackson or, in entertainment, Sidney Poitier and Flip Wilson. Another void created by the media was Indian humor. The stereotyped granite-faced red man had hidden the fact that Indian people laughed and played. While Dick Gregory and other Negro comics were livening up the Black Revolution, white America barely noticed Indian militants with their bumper stickers that read: GOD IS RED or CUSTER DIED FOR YOUR SINS. Whites were too busy laughing along with Blacks to worry about Indians, Custer, or the color of God.

Blacks, with a media boost, had also eclipsed Indians as to the racial life-style to be emulated by white youth. Woodstock Nation was strictly a black and white show, despite Abbie Hoffman's philosophical aside: "It's a nation of alienated young people which we carry around in our minds just as the Sioux Indians carried around the Sioux nation in their minds." Asserting group sovereignty by alluding to Indian tribalism might have seemed appropriate then, when the Woodstock Nation, during its high moment, seemed to have universal overtones. No doubt there was scattered evidence of Indian presence—an overlap in hippie clothing that included moccasins, beads, leather accessories, and headbands. But the overall record that led to Woodstock showed little direct Indian influence. When "alienated young people" yearned for transcendence from Western abstractness, they went directly to the Third World for their mystical messages, not to the American Indian who, at best, remained a Third World refugee stuck on the wrong continent. Some at Woodstock knew their Zen, but few, the religion of the Sioux. Even though an occasional hippie pilgrim visited a reservation to "experience" Indians, ignorance about the Indian was still a white shortcoming among young and old.

Who could blame the Woodstock people? Were they not the first generation trained by television that warmed over such Indian grotesqueries as Chief Thunderthud and Princess Summer-Fall-Winter-Spring on the "Howdy Doody Show"? Musical overtones at Woodstock had also passed over Indians in favor of Blacks. White rock music—when it sought relief from blues, soul music, and other Negro roots—went directly to Ravi Shankar and the sitar and other sounds of Asiatic India, not those of the Sun Dance of the American Sioux. With its museum piece Injuns forever keeping open a closed frontier, the entertainment media had shorn the contemporary Indian of any popular appeal. Even tobacco or the "Indian drug" was misplaced with the marijuana cloud at Woodstock. The Indian also was out of step with the revolutionary passion of white youth. Black power with gut energy came down the center of the street, while mute Indians hugged curbs and ignored demonstrations and confrontations. With the action went the media, creating leaders, drama, fun, and relevancy. Black energy, not red passivity, moved white America, both old and young. The Indian presence at Woodstock was more myth than fact.

Since the mid-1960s, however, there are signs that the media might in the future clean up the image of the Indian. In 1967 the ABC television network canceled, after nine episodes, its series on General Custer, bowing to pressure from Indian protest organizations which labeled Custer the Adolph Eichmann of the nineteenth century. The authentic film documentary also began to appear (usually on Public Broadcasting stations) that did away with stereotypes and focused on Indians, not as savages muttering over beads, or as boobs mired in poverty, but as people with their share of ethnic weaknesses and strengths. TV news cameras would now occasionally veer from Blacks and Chicanos to Indians as newsmakers: for example, the Indian occupation of Alcatraz as a symbolic return to land stolen and misused by whites, or racist violence against Indians in places like South Dakota, sometimes called the "Mississippi of the North." Films outside of TV would now and then depict authentic slices of Indian experience. Indians portrayed in films like *Soldier Blue, A Man Called Horse, Little Big Man,* and *Journey Through Rosebud* came out far more real and alive than the dead Injun rubbish of John Wayne type movies.

In print media, most Indians respected Thomas Berger's *Little Big Man* (the source of the film) for its insight into Indian attitudes toward life—an example for other serious white novelists to follow. Dee Brown, a white scholar, set the historical record straight with his brilliant best-seller *Bury My Heart At Wounded Knee (An Indian History of the American West)* 1970. To read Brown was to enter a time capsule with Indians faced with white greed for land spiced with a genocidal twist. Brown's indictment reached enough white readers to start a mild fad in the early 1970s for Indian things in print.

Indians may be inching toward a future in media when their presence will be as powerful as that of Blacks today. If so, white America must be made aware of Indians in present tense. As long as the media locks the Indian into the American past, racial relevancy will go by default to Blacks. In the nineteenth century when the media spotlight was on the "first Americans," Indian experience may have had a different message for whites if the media then were as sophisticated as the electric coverage that communicates Black experience to white America today. A "global village" look at Pocahontas's wedding, the "Trail of Tears," Little Big Horn, and the massacre at Wounded Knee might have put to sleep America's longest surviving Siamese twins, cowboys and Indians. With that accomplished, the Indian might have become a prime shaper of American experience, past and present. Instead, there is a modern "happy hunting ground" dedicated to keeping America's cowboy mentality in its place—the TV Western as the last frontier in the living room. No other American minority has had to pay such a high price as a caretaker of a national dream, of having a deprived present, of being, not people, but a figment of history always in the making and never coming to an ethnic rest.   ●

The authors trace the development of the stereotype of the Native American in the popular media as an object of entertainment. The essay broadens the notion of media stereotyping to include other than the film and suggests just how pervasive such distortions became. They suggest that the emergence of the Indian entertainer over the last few years is beginning to change such treatment, as these Native Americans interpret their culture in a much different way from the white perspective that has dominated the entertainment industry. The authors are scholars and educators who teach at the University of Colorado.

5

EXAMINATION OF STEREOTYPING:
AN ANALYTICAL SURVEY OF
TWENTIETH-CENTURY INDIAN ENTERTAINERS

WARD CHURCHILL, MARY ANNE HILL, and NORBERT S. HILL, JR.

Durifying URING the 1960s and throughout the 1970s, Indians have begun to achieve autonomy and popular recognition as entertainers in the contemporary sense. However, the historical treatment of these poeple, particularly in this field, has left a lingering effect which tends to force even the most independent and talented professionals to seek directions of performance that might otherwise not have been sought. They are left with the unpleasant option of either ignoring their heritage or assuming a stance of militant advocacy. There is no middle ground. But before a discussion of contemporary entertainers' lives and work can be made relevant, it is perhaps necessary to review the historical (oft hysterical) treatment of Native Americans over the years.

During the 1880s the United States was undergoing the first period of its national history relatively free from territorial expansion involving armed conflict with the Native population. True, occasional flashes still appeared such as the Modoc "war" and the endless police actions against the Apaches along the border of Mexico, but gone forever were military episodes carrying the psychic weight of Sand Creek, the Washita, Ft. Mimms, and the Little Big Horn. The eyes of empire had already turned outward to the Spanish Caribbean, the Philippines, and the Orient beyond.

It was during the 1880s that the last of the great free leaders of in-

Reprinted by permission of Ward Churchill, Mary Anne Hill, and Norbert S. Hill, Jr.

digenous people became seen as standard objects of entertainment. The most obvious example of this tendency is, of course, the attachment of Sitting Bull (Tatanka Yatanka) to the Buffalo Bill Cody Wild West Show. Here, in a single individual, was the embodiment—to the white mind at least—of all that was Indian. He was the leader and holy man of the last group of free Sioux, reputedly the mastermind behind Custer's defeat, the subject of distortion in literally dozens of dime novels and journalistic misadventures. And now, here he was, being put though his paces for the edification of the fantasies of white eastern audiences at a rate of $25 per month (as opposed to the thousands grossed by his white ''managers'').

Sitting Bull and the other plainsmen who participated in spectacles such as Cody's and those of Pawnee Bill and Colonel Frederick T. Cummins had their reasons. There was a pressing need for revenue for their impoverished peoples, an ingrained desire for mobility, perhaps a hope of communicating some sense of their cultural identity to an ignorant and overbearing race of conquerors. But surely if the latter is the case, they failed. And they were not alone in their failure.

It had long been a policy of the whites to bring ''wild'' Indians East to dress up ceremonial occasions. There were Red Cloud and Spotted Tail of the Sioux, Black Kettle of the Cheyenne, Little Raven of the Arapaho, even Quanah of the Comanche, to list but a few. Always they were displayed in regalia and feather heraldry, always they attempted to represent their peoples and cultures, and always they failed before the prejudgmental myopia of their land- and mineral-hungry hosts.

Native people were broken upon the wheel of an alien culture superior in terms of numerical population, weapons technology, and mental aptitude for total war. Of the last, the abilities to reduce one's opponents to nonhuman terms and to miscategorize diverse opposing groups into homogeneous lumps are paramount. Such stereotypical perceptions on the part of whites begins to explain much that is otherwise unexplainable about Native/white relations. It is thus that scalp bounties could be offered by both British and colonists for Indian flesh, that whole tribes could be relocated from East to West in the name of humanity (after all, if the Pawnee and Osage could prosper out there, so should the Iroquois and Cherokee), that peaceful villages could be sacked as examples to warring members of completely separate tribes, or that Geronimo (Golthlay) of the Chiricahua Apache might be expected to publicly appear in Comanche attire.

It is somehow fitting that the image selected by white America for its stereotype of the Native American was a superficial visual likeness of the Plains Sioux, the last indigenous group capable of offering serious military resistance. It was the defeat of this people that most dramatically symbolized the final conquest of North America by the United States. Then, there is the fact that plains tribal feather heraldry (which the Sioux epitomized) offered a most striking contrast to the European norm of appearance. Finally, there was the sheer availability of reservation ''tamed'' leaders such as Sitting Bull, Hollow Horn Bear, and Quanah to carry the visual symbolism directly to relatively mass audiences via the entertainers' instincts of the likes of Bill Cody and various administrations of the U.S. government.

At first, the stereotype was tactical—bent toward specific land acquisitions on the part of whites (Indian campaigns, treaty manipulations, later land booms, Dawes Act allotment procedures, etc.)—and was probably more subliminally dictated by situational gravity than by the propagandist's intellectual articulation. But gradually, as the empire began to stretch its legs for the long haul of consolidation and exploitation of its gains, the need for a solidified and reasonably articulated mythology became a matter of strategic necessity.[1] The history of conquest needed popular revision if it were to be utilized as a matter of national pride; the Native had to be universally and negatively dealt with if such a pattern were to be actualized, and consistent stereotyping was the most effective means to this end.[2]

Today, after at least three-quarters of a century of systematic stereotyping has transpired, the results may be categorized into three major themes which tend to interrelate to a high degree. These may be elucidated briefly as follows:[3]

1) *The Native as a creature of a particular time:* Under the conditions of this theme, the Indian is trapped within the temporal context of the plains cultures (primarily Sioux) between the approximate dates of 1800 and 1880. While there have been occasional excursions beyond these confines by filmmakers and other distributors of popular history, these remain a comparative handful and deal essentially with other geographic/temporal aspects of white-Native conflict. The time line is invariably pushed back a few years, but never beyond the period of European invasion. It is virtually unheard of to push the time line forward into the twentieth century. Thus a 15,000–25,000-year history of race is compressed into a period spanning four centuries at best and, more usually, less than a single century. The Native equivalent of *Ben Hur* or *Cleopatra* has yet to be made. The most effective film concerning Native realities to date, *Journey Through Rosebud,* was withdrawn from circulation almost before it was released.

2) *Native cultures interpreted through white values:* Here we find the motivations and beliefs of literally all Native cultures voided and new contents assigned which correspond to white cultural biases and historical views. Two factors are accomplished therein: a) The real Native identity is destroyed in favor of a more palatable (to whites) fictitious one, and b) the fictitious identity (white in nature) is the same regardless of the tribe or culture theoretically portrayed. Thus the grossest motivations of white duplicity and greed-oriented brutality are ascribed to the Indian, neatly converting the victimizer. There has yet to be a commercial film or video release made that relies upon an actual Native cultural perspective to provide its orientation.

3) *Seen one Indian, seen 'em all:* In a way, this theme tends to be an overview of the preceding two. However, it has assumed a continuity and dimension that provides it a life of its own. Herein, even the visual cultural characteristics that tend to individuate tribal groupings begin to blend into

an all-encompassing haze (although publicity claims usually run entirely to the contrary). Take, for example, the film *A Man Called Horse,* touted by its makers as "the most authentic depiction on North American Indian life ever filmed." In this epic of "Western" genre, not only have cultural values and motivation been demolished and reconstructed to white specifications—resulting in the necessity of the single white captive (Richard Harris) to educate the Sioux in the use of the longbow, a rather traditional Native weapon—but the entire visual panorama proves equally misleading. Here, the people were ostensibly Lakota (due to geographic location), the style of the village leader's hair was Assiniboine, the ceremonial events depicted were Mandan (with their purposes utterly misrepresented even then), and the method of burial seemingly Piegan. One could go on, but the point should be made, summed up as, "All Indians wear feathers and ride horses."

The net effect of all this has been to create a situation where Native individuals and cultures have been reduced to a degrading parody of themselves within the public consciousness. Worse, the lampooned peoples have been systematically credited with no contemporary significance whatsoever; they are creatures of a false nostalgia, feathered cousins to the bygone buffalo. Yet, if all this began in earnest with the involvement of Sitting Bull in the Wild West show, what of other Indians who have since sought personal participation as entertainers in the arena of popular American media?

The legacy of Wild West shows to the status of Indians as objects—as entertainment rather than entertainers—crystalized in the notion that anyone who looked like an Indian could portray an Indian. There was no cultural content within the stereotype. However, the movie Indian required time to develop due to limitations of the medium. The lack of sound in early films such as D. W. Griffith's *Massacre* (1912) decreed that the Native must be merely picturesque (the origin of the stoic Indian?); hooves could not thunder, heathens could not whoop, their victims could not shriek with horror or groan under the scalping knife. But, despite these obvious handicaps, the public wanted Indians—and it got what it wanted.

The sound era began in 1927, and almost immediately screaming savages were everywhere burning, pillaging, abducting, raping, scalping, and generally just being "Indian." They were as necessary to Western action films as horses, wagons, forts, and guns. In short, they were props, and their function was to look vicious before expiring under a hail of lead thrown by soldiers, cowboys, settlers, ranchers, miners, hunters, preachers, or whatever whites happened to be hanging about the set that day. The Indian was scripted as a mobile target, not a dramatic character.

Perhaps the clearest example of the tendency to diminish the humanity, not only of the objects of film, but of the Indians cast in such roles is Paramount's *Geronimo* (1939), directed by Paul Sloan. The title role went to a Cherokee actor, Victor Daniels, who went by the stage name of Chief Thundercloud. He received no credit under either name, however, as star billing went to Andy Devine, Preston Foster, and Ellen Drew—all white. Daniels was a main prop in this film about Indians and his face was cosmetically altered to enhance whatever he could achieve in the miming of evil expressions. The idea was to exploit stereotyping, and promotional suggestions distributed by Paramount to theater owners leaves no doubt as to the studio's intentions.

And then there was Delmar Daves's *Broken Arrow,* generally acknowledged by sophisticated white reviewers as the first modern film to deal sympathetically with the Native. The role of Cochise, the reasonable Apache, went to Jeff Chandler, a rather white actor; that of the "evil" Geronimo went to an Indian, Jay Silverheels (later cast as Tonto in TV's "Lone Ranger" series). One is tempted to say that Hollywood's idea of "sympathy" boils down to a rule-of-thumb: "The only bad Indian is a real Indian."[4] The pattern held true, with only minor variations, right on through the mid-century mark. Between 1951 and 1970 alone at least 86 Indian vs. Army films appeared, all of them constructed along standard stereotypical themes.

Nor was treatment of Indians better in other forms of media. From comic books through broadcast radio Natives were ridiculed and parodied, rendered stoic, and portrayed as the heavy in virtually the same sense that the shark was the villain in the recent film *Jaws* (1975). An excellent example of radio stereotyping may be found in the portrayal of Tonto in "The Lone Ranger." The voice in question belonged to John Todd, an elderly Shakespearean actor who slept through most live performances, awaking only to emit timely "ugh's" and other gutteral interjections.

Actually, in relation to the quantity of media exposure devoted to stereotyping Indians between 1900 and 1960, very few members of that race were able to develop a livelihood based on acting. Among those who did were the aforementioned Victor Daniels and Jay Silverheels, as well as X-Brands, Eddie Little Sky, Chief Yowalchie, Roy Rogers (who made it as a cowboy), Chief Nipo Strong Heart, and Dark Cloud, a former model for Frederick Remington, possibly the son of a Little Big Horn combatant and, along with Eagle Eye, a protege of D. W. Griffith. Each of these individuals found himself in the paradoxical position of commiting psychic suicide professionally in order to attain more or less consistent employment in the media. Most found a means in their private lives to counteract the personal costs of acting out their stage roles. Some did not and, like the great Indian athlete-cum-actor, Jim Thorpe, ended amidst the squalor of alcoholism and suicide.[5]

Perhaps the only Native American to achieve the true status as an entertainer prior to 1960 was Will Rogers, the noted Cherokee actor, humorist, and news commentator. Beginning his career as a rope artist and rough rider (under billing as the "Cherokee Kid") with Texas Jack's Wildwest Circus in 1902, Rogers kicked about the edges of the entertainment world for a number of years. By 1922 he had gravitated to writing and produced a series of weekly articles for the *New York Times.* Eventually, the series was syndicated to more than 350 newspapers and demand began to build for his services as a lecturer and broadcaster.

The media were far less compartmentalized during their early years than they are today. Talent became cross-indexed rather rapidly. Thus Rogers's talents were being fully employed by the movies after 1929 in such box office hits as *State Fair, A Connecticut Yankee,* and *Judge Priest.* At the time of his death in 1935, the Indian kid from Oklahoma was earning $200,000 per film with a combined annual income of $600,000—the highest rates paid to any performer of his day.

Possibly more instrumental to this man's phenomenal success than sheer ability was the reputation he acquired as an inordinately generous and hard-working humanitarian. He was popularly known as a warm-hearted cowboy philosopher (who simply happened to have a little Indian blood) and a great *American.*[6] This is as it should have been for, as Rogers put it in one of his spontaneous movie lines, "I had no ancestors on the Mayflower, mine met those folks at the boat."

As great as Will Rogers's success was he remained an essentially isolated example, a solitary voice in a wilderness of misportraiture and gross distortion of culture reality. Nothing underscores this point so well as a glance at the non-Indians who were cast in Native roles (usually the speaking parts) during the period in question. Since the stereotypical appearance of Indians was necessarily evil and brutal, it was natural that the stars of horror films and stock heavies such as Bella Lugosi, Lon Chaney, Bruce Cabot, Claude Akins, and Charles Bronson should be employed in portraying them. When drunken Indians were needed for comic relief, there were the likes of Buddy Hackett and Joey Bishop to fill the bill. Indians always rode horses, so sometimes cowboy stars like Audie Murphy, Guy Madison, and Chuck Connors were used. Indians were a very physical (as opposed to cerebral) people, so former Tarzan film types Buster Crabbe and Lex Barker were perfect, as were Rock Hudson and Elvis Presley. Black actor Woody Strode struck a blow for minority participation by helping to misconstrue another minority. Native women were silently and seductively depicted by Loretta Young, Donna Reed, Katharine Ross, and Audrey Hepburn, among many others. Indian look-alikes could even be found in actors such as Anthony Quinn and Michael Ansara.

What all these people had in common in relation to their deployment conveying impressions of Native people and cultures was an almost perfect ignorance of Native people and cultures. Far be it from any of them to resist a stereotypical portrayal of people and events they knew nothing about—and did not care to learn about. After all, they were merely doing their jobs according to the script. Yet, they were the name brand talent against which the aspirations of Indian entertainers were gaged and through which Indian cultures and personalities were popularly perceived. Small wonder that it was hardly uncommon by the 1950s for Indian children to cheer the cavalry when watching television or the movies. Who wants to identify with the natural loser in everything?

Although the scales of history cannot be truly brought to bear on events so recent, it seems safe to say that the 1960s marked something of a crossroads for the United States. At the onset of the decade, forces began to congeal around issues involving interracial relationships. Initially, the focus was on relatively small numbers of Blacks and white supporters led by Dr. Martin Luther King, while later developments saw the evolution of mass movements such as SNCC (Student Nonviolent Coordinating Committee)[7] and its offshoot, CORE (Congress Of Racial Equality). Certain whites—students, for the most part—participated by first joining the Black organizations, then establishing their own parallel groups.[8] Altogether, these social activities represented a systematic and coherent demand for change in the status of American nonwhites.

It was perhaps inevitable that within the context of any widespread adjustment of relative racial power in the United States—even superficial readjustment—Native Americans must become involved. But, at first, the nature of such involvement remained an open question. The Black model of social activism was obviously not well adapted to Indian needs insofar as the Black population exceeded that of the Natives by over 1000%.[9] Blacks also maintained a certain leverage stemming from their heavy participation in the urban labor force while the Native population was widely scattered in areas remote from the nation's industrial centers. The response of a race that had experienced outright physical genocide at the hands of the national majority within the past century, as well as the overt cultural genocide of termination as recently as 1953, was necessarily cautious.

One thing readily observable about the various groups that came to be known as the "New Left" was their general and consistent employment of media for debunking the white-created mythology about nonwhite racial groups. Blacks and their supporters were utilizing, for their own purposes, a major tool of white power and social control. It was also obvious that, radio, TV, and print media notwithstanding, music—folk music, specifically—was the preferred medium of "the movement." It was *the* expressive vehicle because of its capabilities for transmitting social messages and because it harkened back to the battles of radical union organizing and a time before the present *status quo.*

Here was a means of participation in the flow of more or less portentious social events which, for the nation's Native population, did not hold an immediate threat. All things being equal, this medium seemed a weapon. But a lever was needed to open the door of this medium, if even a crack, and—given the historical treatment of Indians within the media—such an opportunity was sadly lacking. For a while.

Among the luminaries of the radical-based folk music world in 1963 were Odetta (Black), Joan Baez (Chicana), Bob Dylan, and Pete Seeger (both white). And then, almost miraculously, there was Beverly Sainte-Marie, also known as Buffy.

Born of Cree parents in Canada, then orphaned, Buffy Sainte-Marie was adopted at an early age by a Micmac family living in Maine. She showed an early interest in music, first as a pianist, and in her teen years as a singer who played the guitar. By that time she was already composing. At 18 she enrolled at the University of Massachusetts to undertake the study of Oriental philosophy. She experienced identity problems, traveled to Mexico, fell in and out of love, sampled codeine addiction, and began to realize herself as a Native American. The pivot to her career occurred when she received an invitation to sing at a Greenwich Village coffeehouse. The result of her performance was a battery of offers to record, appear on television, and to begin a concert tour.

It is entirely possible that the white talent scouts who first discovered Buffy were looking, above all, for an Indian to round out their ethnic "stable." But regardless of the mercenary motivations of the agents, talent comes to the fore. By 1963, at the age of 21, Buffy Sainte-Marie had achieved a solid status as a professional singer/guitarist behind her own compositions such as "Universal Soldier" and "Until It's Time For You To Go." (To date, she has written and published over 200 songs.) For the most part, the early music that brought her to the top dealt with themes and musical forms that were within the purview of the mainstream.

Given that Buffy could have succeeded as a major folk star on the basis of relatively neutral lyrical/musical content, what could possibly have caused her to risk the security of such a life? Due to the course her career has taken since its fledgling days, the only answer would seem to be her heritage. The status of Native people was intolerable to her as a matter of principle. Forged by personal experience, and as a media figure of acknowledged stature, she set out to provide a Native counterpoint to white stereotyping. She first learned the tricks of her trade, and then began to turn her position, knowledge, and artistic ability against those who would caricature and oppress her people.

The most immediate result of Buffy's determination to bring Native realities into her music was the recording and general distribution of songs such as "My Country 'Tis of Thy People You're Dying," "Now That the Buffalo's Gone," and "Native North American Child." The music was well received by Indians, young and old; but it initially left most others, including the New Left, somewhat flabbergasted. Contemporary Native America was something no other group in the country seemed prepared, either culturally or ideologically, to cope with. The "progressives" were as locked into the stock media stereotype of Indians as the "conservatives." Buffy, consequently, began to find herself being cheered at concerts by white audiences after songs that should have left them in stunned silence, or at least pensiveness. Frustrated, but undaunted, she escalated by providing explanations of the realities behind her lyrics and ending with the statement, "I hope you're offended."

The buildup of the Vietnam War rapidly clarified the issues addressed in Buffy's music. The parallels between U.S. military operations directed against an entire Asian population and historical cavalry campaigns were simply too glaring to be ignored. Black leader Stokely Carmichael (of

SNCC) publicly adopted a position supporting Native land rights and condemning the American intervention in Southeast Asia as being similar to "policies directed by this government against Blacks and Indians."[10] White radicals such as Tom Hayden concurred. Thus, by 1967, in the eyes of the rebels at least, Native Americans had become an integral (if superficial) part of contemporary reality.

Had Buffy Sainte-Marie's contribution as a Native American entertainer ended here, it would stand as unique. It was as if Will Rogers had returned to predicate his stature upon a specifically Indian, rather than generally humanitarian, basis; or that Roy Rogers had turned his cowboy stardom into an uncompromisingly militant advocacy of Indian rights and heritage. She has consistently devoted herself to revising both the public perception and real situation of her people on all levels—whether in performing benefit concerts for Nativist causes or groups, funding the transportation of water to Indians who occupied Alcatraz Island during the land rights confrontation there in 1969–70, utilizing Public Service Television via a children's program ("Sesame Street") in order to sing and teach of Indian culture before a wide and impressionable audience, or recording her music free from commercial censorship. Her latest album, "Sweet America" (1976), comprised almost entirely Indian musical themes and emphatically Indian lyrics.

Given her success and heritage-proud posture over nearly a decade and a half, Buffy has had an incalculable impact on the bulk of a generation of Indian youth. Her demonstration of the viability of becoming a self-respecting Indian entertainer rather than an object of racial/sexual entertainment has spawned a number of emulators (in goals, if not in style). Among these are Xit, an Albuquerque-based all-Indian rock band featuring Native social consciousness lyrics; and Redbone, a San Francisco group operating within a very similar format. There is Buddy Redbow, a Lakota from the Standing Rock Reservation who specializes in converting popular songs into his native language as well as producing blues and country-style songs of his own composition. A Yankton from the Sisseton Reservation, Vic Runnels, works in the same vein. Small-scale formation of bands has become a common occurence within many Native communities to a degree unimaginable only ten years ago. Many are attempts to make direct personal statements of concern for and pride in indigenous cultures through media historically utilized by white society to stereotype and repress them. Although some Indian entertainers are still demonstrably attracted to the glitter of mainstream American media, a large number seem to be motivated by the priority stated in the title of a song written by the Canadian Micmac/Metis country-style singer, Willie Dunn; they are "Workin' for the People."[11]

Buffy's impact has hardly been restricted to influencing younger people who would follow in her footsteps. The apparently spontaneous interface she achieved with other social elements was instrumental in establishing the environment that allowed (as opposed to caused) the emergence of overtly political Native organizations such as the American Indian Movement (AIM) during the late sixties. Indian activists such as Russell Means have utilized a recently acquired confidence in their abilities as Indians to play upon the media while pressing for radical change in the social status of their people. By and large, these individuals are of Buffy's age group, or older, and employ a different methodology within a forum she was instrumental in creating. They, in turn, have assisted in developing a substantial and receptive audience for autonomous Native entertainers. And, they would seem to have her blessing.[12]

While music has been the primary vehicle of media involvement by Native Americans, as well as that of the bulk of the nation's youth, it has been by no means the only format. Indian participation in film and television has been steady, though much more understated than in the auditory counterpart. Native actors have continued to be much less publicly vocal and inclined to radical communications than their musician peers, possibly because a major portion got their start before the onset of the period of major social activism.

Of these, John War Eagle, a Yankton Sioux, is a leading example. Born John St. Pierre in 1902, War Eagle early evidenced an overriding commitment to his people. This led to a heavy involvement in tribal politics (both internal and external) for a period of several years. Eventually, completely frustrated with the molasseslike consistency of American political fluids and the sheer wall of ignorance that faced him with each foray beyond the limits of the reservation, he became one of the first to adopt a fully developed argument for a Native media response to white racial misrepresentation. A move to Hollywood was necessary to the actualization of such beliefs, and this happened to coincide with filmdom's sadly tardy realization that Indians who say more than "ugh" were sometimes useful accoutrements. It was discovered that War Eagle possessed both raw acting ability and a firm dedication to the craft. Bit parts in a number of films followed, and he more recently appeared in such television series as "Kung Fu" and "Grizzly Adams."

In some ways, it is obvious that John War Eagle prefigured many of the attitudes elaborated by the most outspoken Native entertainers of the sixties and seventies. However, by the time his career had assumed an actual national visibility, others had carried his principles into reaches beyond his grasp. Thus he is caught in a strange limbo; at once a pioneer of native challenges to white stereotyping, and a by-product of the bad old days of rampant caricature. Though dead, he is still to be seen today portraying the feathered spectre of "romantic" fiction, but doing so with a dignity that softens the image and renders it human.

Another, more marginal, member of this group of actors is Chief Dan George. Born in 1899, a descendant of six generations of Tse-lal-watt chiefs, he spent an early life often depicted in the movies. He traveled by canoe from his British Columbia home to Vancouver and learned the logging trade from both his father and grandfather. Married at 19 and the father of six children, he spent twenty-six years as a longshoreman until an accident left him with crushed muscles in his arms and back in 1947. After that he spent the next twelve years as the elected chief of his tribe.

He began acting at middle age with a part in the Canadian Broadcasting Company series, "Caribou Country." His first film role was to deliver Chief Joseph's surrender speech to Glenn Ford in the Walt Disney potboiler, *Smith!* (1959); this was followed by an extended absence from media. Finally, in 1969, producer Gene Lasko was searching for an elderly Indian to cast as Old Lodge Skins in his upcoming movie, *Little Big Man* (1970). Lasko saw a photograph of George, contacted him with an offer of the job, and the chief accepted but with qualms because this was probably the most extensive speaking role ever offered to an Indian. Finally, he took the part for several reasons. "I don't like the cowboy and Indian movies one bit," he said. "They always looked phony to me. An Indian can always play an Indian better than a white, simply because he is playing his own nationality."[13]

Little Big Man itself represents a rather transparent attempt by Hollywood to buy off dissident criticism via a "sympathetic" approach to the standard stereotypical themes. The time structure is fully within the vastly overabused period of the 1860s and 1870s. The Indians are the perfect plains type so loved by filmmakers, and, of course, the lead character just happens to be a young white captured by wild Indians, and who, incidentally, just happens to carry the rather unique name (same as the film title) of an actual Oglala of historical note.

But, bad as the film may have been, Chief Dan George achieved a touchstone performance in his sensitive and human portrayal of an old Indian man observing the destruction of his people at the hands of a brutal and mindless horde of aliens. Although cast as a stereotype, George avoided the trap through his ability to expose the realities behind the myths. The sheer acting finesse required to accomplish this was publicly recognized in his being awarded the Best Supporting Actor award by the National Society of Film Critics, as well as the New York Critics Award in 1970.

Dan George became an Indian symbol of opposition to the white man's world. His flowing silver hair, seamed face, straight back, and direct gaze seemed to reflect the hardships, pride, and dignity of a race. His personal philosophy can be summarized by his answer to the question, What would you suggest to young Indian actors who want to get into movies? His answer, "Work hard."[14]

Of young actors, probably the best known is Will Sampson, an Oklahoma Creek. At 6'5", a high school dropout and former rodeo rider, logger, and telephone lineman, Sampson would seem an utterly unlikely candidate as a movie star. However, the physical requirements for an actor to portray "Chief" in the film adaptation of Ken Kesey's *One Flew Over the Cuckoo's Nest* (1975) made him a natural selection. Will was everybody's vision of the towering mute Indian. As a result of his excellent performance in this role, many felt that he would be the man to bring the media Native into contemporary life.

To date, he has failed to fulfill such high expectations, following through instead with a four-film contract to produce low-grade epics such as *Orca, the Killer Whale* (1977) and *The White Buffalo* (1977), the latter seeing him depicting Crazy Horse in alliance with Wild Bill Hickok to slaughter the sacred white buffalo of the Sioux.

While these convolutions tend to highlight Sampson's strong links to earlier rather than contemporary models of Native involvement in entertainment, both his demonstrable achievement in *Cuckoo's Nest* and the potential of a projected television series, *Indians* (in which he plays the lead role as "Painted Bear"), indicate that the original anticipation of his impact may not have been entirely misplaced.

There have been few attempts within the celluloid medium to directly rival the message and impact of Native musicians, although a number of big-name producers have claimed to have geared projects along such lines. Perhaps the only person to actually grapple with the matter in a positive manner has been the young mixed-blood producer/director/actor, Tom Laughlin. Operating on a shoestring budget, Laughlin brought out a feature film, *Born Losers* (1969), involving an Indian ex-Green Beret who attempts to return to traditional ways, becomes enmeshed in a running confrontation with a white motorcycle gang, and ends up saving an entire white community from the thugs. The movie must be viewed as a poor rendition of the "superfly" genre, but it does resoundingly dismantle most conventional stereotypes of the Indian.

Encouraged by the original film, Laughlin almost immediately launched a more ambitious project in reassembling his basic plot into a formulation casting white police and assorted business interests as the heavies. He then cast himself into the title role of *Billy Jack* (1971) to act as the here again Indian-trooper-traditionalist-karate expert, and figuratively defend Native land rights and culture. It succeeded in rearranging Indian identity in the media like nothing else before or since. The film was proof that stereotyping could be effectively eliminated as profits spiraled and viewers cheered the Indian.

This success tragically seems to have destroyed Laughlin as a viable, if technically shoddy, film champion of the Indian. His next film, *The Trial of Billy Jack* (1974), was a disaster. Every conceivable social cause was addressed under the umbrella of a circuslike interpretation of Native spiritualism and warrior impulses. The filmmaker's credibility was reduced to nil, and worse, *Billy Jack,* the first unstereotyped movie Indian, became "Silly Jack" to many people.

Stereotypical misrepresentation in media of Native American peoples and cultures has been comprehensive and systematic since the 1880s. The methods of such stereotyping are known and the intent of their employment has been the effective dehumanization of the peoples depicted. This has been a fundamental aspect of the white dominant culture's genocidal expropriation of Native land and resource bases well into the twentieth century.

The Native response to this pattern has been uneven historically. Initial

Indian participants, such as Sitting Bull, probably maintained hopes of somehow explaining their cultures through media participation. They were not equipped to deal with white intentions in this area and were thus co-opted into becoming the very models of stereotyping. Later developments saw Indians extensively employed as stage props in Hollywood films that reserved for the Native an absurdly disgusting and inhuman status. During the 1930s and 1940s, Will Rogers seems to have served as an exception to the rule of stereotyping, but he never really brought the weight of his position to bear on Indian issues.

Finally, in the early 1960s, social circumstances conspired with the emergence of Civil Rights and New Left activists to create a forum for nonstereotypical Native entertainers. Great strides were made in the medium of popular music, particularly through the efforts of singer composers such as Buffy Sainte-Marie and Floyd Westerman.[15] While evolution of Native performance in film and television has not kept pace with that of music, it has the potential to catch up through the work of Charlie Hill and, possibly, Will Sampson. A problem shared by all, and unlikely to be alleviated in the near future, is that the legacy of media stereotyping forces Native entertainers to always respond. Either they must conscientiously avoid reference to their Indianness, or devote their careers to serving as artistic debunkers of white-imposed myths. The greater danger, a possible retardation of any lasting solution to the problem, is that the gains achieved between 1960 and 1975 were intimately connected with the social climate created by various dissident groups of that period. By and large, these groups disappeared from the scene before the second half of the seventies and the results of their loss have yet to be assessed. ●

NOTES

1. To quote the father of media stereotyping, Josef Goebbles (Nazi Propaganda Minister), "The greater the lie, the greater the likelihood of its being believed." Goebbles created a mythology of race which greatly aided Nazi extermination, expropriation, and exploitation programs.

2. A variant of "conspiracy theory" is not at issue here. Rather, the authors refer to the *cultural* imperatives such as "manifest destiny." Hearst Syndicate handling of the *Maine* disaster prior to the Spanish-American War is a good example of the principle applied to groups other than Indians.

3. The descriptions listed are the result of an unpublished research project entitled *Sexism and Racism in Contemporary Media,* Kimmel, Kimmel, and Churchill, Sangamon State University, 1974–75.

4. Quotation comes from *The Only Good Indian . . . .: The Hollywood Gospel,* Ralph and Natasha Friar, New York, 1972.

5. Thorpe appeared in such epics as *Treachery Rides the Range* (1936), *Arizona Frontier* (1940), and *Black Arrow* (1944).

6. In a eulogy, Damon Runyon, the great New York writer, described Rogers: ". . . American's most complete human document. He reflected the heartbeat of America . . . [he] was probably our most typical Native Born, the closest to what we like to call the true American."

7. The SNCC was retained, but the full name of this organization changed to Student National Coordinating Committee.

8. Of the white groups, SDS (Students for a Democratic Society) was probably the most visible and influential.

9. By way of comparison, the U.S. Black population exceeded 22,000,000 in 1972 while Native Americans numbered approximately 800,000 (U.S. Census, 1972).

10. Quote is from a speech by Stokely Carmichael delivered to members of the Third World Coalition and SDS during the 1968 student takeover of Columbia University.

11. Quote is from the song of the same title written by Dunn and released on the LP *Willie Dunn* (1972), White Roots of Peace production, Akwesasne, N.Y.

12. The most objective evidence of this may be Buffy's 1976 dedication of the song "Starwalker" (from the "Sweet America" LP) to ". . . the members of the American Indian Movement."

13. "Chief," *Newsweek* 77 (January 25, 1971): 80.

14. Jeanette Henry, "A Dan George Reception for *My Heart Soars,*" *Wassaja,* October 1975, p. 15.

15. For a fuller treatment of Westerman's career, see Ward Churchill, "Floyd Westerman: A Giant in Lower Case," *Rocky Mountain Musical Express,* July 1977.

Vine Deloria, lawyer, author, and one of the most prominent Indian spokesmen of the twentieth century, elaborates on the Indian stereotype as seen by the whites and offers an Indian perspective on the problems such stereotyping creates. The Indian, Deloria writes, "sees himself as an incompetent and childish figure who must have his mistakes forgiven because he is an Indian who does not really understand." This self-concept complements nicely the white stereotype of the Indian as a savage, untamed child of nature. Only after the Indian can develop a self-image that incorporates both past disasters and a positive direction for the future will Indians free themselves from destructive white images of them.

6

THE AMERICAN INDIAN IMAGE
IN NORTH AMERICA

VINE DELORIA

1. THE NORTH AMERICAN INDIAN
AS SEEN BY THE WHITE MAN

THE American Indian haunts other Americans. He is a shadowy figure who comes and goes in the night, that elusive presence that defies proper and comfortable definition. The first testimony by western Europeans visiting the American continents saw the inhabitants as happy, gentle people, living as in a Garden of Eden, and as uncomplicated as man might have been before the dawn of history. It was only when the acquisitiveness of the European disrupted the continent's tranquility that the whites began to see the Indians in a new light.

John Smith, describing the Powhatan Indians of what was to become Virginia, remarked that "they traded kindly with me and my men," but twenty years later, when the colonists had pushed the Indians into war, Smith described them as "beasts," "a viperous brood," "hell-hounds," and "miscreants." Thus it was that the white men perceived the Indians as savages. Savages they were only in their resistance to exploitation, but the image stuck and was reinforced whenever and wherever the two races met. The Pilgrims fawned over the Indians during the first harsh winter when the settlers had no food and were forced to rely on the Indians for subsistence. But as they gained military prowess the Pilgrims, like the Viginia settlers, turned on their hosts.

William Bradford, a Pilgrim father, in 1620 provided the first rationale for conceiving the Indians as savages, maintaining that America was an

From the *Encyclopedia of Indians of the Americas,* vol. I (St. Clair Shores, Michigan: Scholarly Press, 1974), pp. 40–44. Reprinted by permission.

"unpeopled" country, "being devoyd of all civil inhabitants, where there are only savage and brutish men, which range up and downe, little otherwise than the wild beasts of the same." The importance of Bradford's conception of the Indian went far beyond racial stereotyping. If the Indians were indeed denied the status of people then dispossession and extermination of them could not fall into either legal or moral categories of restraint. And that has been the story of the white man's image of the Indian. It has pervaded the language and colored man's sense of responsibility and brotherhood ever since.

From this conception of the Indian as savage has come the deviation in federal policy from a system of laws to a system of political expediency which purports to govern Indian relationships with the United States government. In 1871 the United States Congress forbade further treaties with the Indian tribes on the theory that it was degrading for Congress to give equal status to nations of *wandering bands of savages:* That the action called into question one of the powers of the Senate as defined in the Constitution appeared to be not quite as important to the people in Congress as the re-affirmation of their exalted status in comparison with the aboriginal inhabitants.

The blindness continued, and the characterization of Indians as savages caused whites to overlook even the most positive aspects of Indian social existence. United States Senator Henry Dawes, for example, visited the Five Civilized Tribes in the 1890s in an effort to determine whether or not the General Allotment Act should be applied to their tribal lands. After noting that "there was not a pauper in that Nation, and the Nation did not owe a dollar. It built its own capitol . . . and it built its own schools and its hospitals," Dawes concluded that "the defect of the system was apparent. They have got as far as they can go, because they own their land in common."

Dawes's solution, a typical response for a "civilized" man, was that "there is no selfishness, which is at the bottom of civilization." That the Five Civilized Tribes possessed a better working society than did Senator Dawes failed to register on him because the Indians were by definition savages and lacked those gentle graces which marked "civilized" man, particularly selfishness. This image has transformed itself many times in each generation as whites and Indians have confronted each other socially, politically, and economically, and generally with the same results. The Indians have lost the battle because they are different, and that difference is seen as cultural and religious inferiority by whites who have failed to question the validity of their own beliefs and values.

We see the image today in the general language which whites use in describing Indian affairs. Even among the most sensitive of liberal whites the word "plight" is used to describe Indian problems. "Plight," of course, describes a condition, state, or situation. It is a word denoting status and not inadequacy or temporary handicap. To thus describe the Indian's "plight" is to say that so long as there are Indians it will be the white man's burden to direct them into avenues of cultural and religious civilization until they finally achieve equality, which, in this context, can only mean the extinction of all those characteristics which make an Indian an Indian.

From the basic premise of the existence of the Indian as savage come the other stereotypes cherished by the white man. The Indian is regarded as un-religious because he is not a Christian. But even with five generations of Christians in some Indian families the status of Christian is not attained, because by definition the person in question is an Indian and therefore a heathen.

It is no accident that one of the most popular and cherished books of recent years, the thrilling adventures of Chief Red Fox, appealed to the American public precisely because the old man who posed as the chief represented that tinge of savagery which Americans desperately wanted to believe in. People cared little that the entire account was fraudulent; they continued to believe in Indian "savagery" because it was unthinkable to believe otherwise. The way, Indian activists concluded, to affect the American public was to parade as warriors of old, and, at Wounded Knee, South Dakota, in the winter of 1972, they provided the television-viewing public with a seventy-two–day Indian war. The relevant social issues of the revolt were buried by the spectacle of Indians on horseback racing around before the cameras. If the activists had understood the history of American-Indian relationship they would have seen themselves as the final clowns of the drama, for they served primarily to reinforce the worst suspicions of whites at a time when the ancient and derogatory image could have been buried once and for all.

After nearly four centuries of contact and confrontation, Indians and whites have remaining only the memories of western spectaculars to comfort them. The history and the events which spawned the turbulence of the past remain hidden beneath the symbols of conflict. Until a clearer definition of the meaning of civilized existence can be gained by all, we will be saddled with—and plagued by—the image of the noble savage riding into the sunset, accompanied by his darker brother, the savage who lurked at the edge of the clearing.

2.   THE NORTH AMERICAN INDIAN AS SEEN BY HIMSELF

At least partially coinciding with the image of the Indian as held by the white man is the image that the Indian holds of himself. Whereas the white man sees the Indian as a savage, the Indian too often sees himself as an incompetent and childish figure who must have his mistakes forgiven because he is an Indian who does not really understand. The two images complement each other in a great many respects and perhaps the most devastating aspect of their complementarity is that the Indian has convinced himself that the white man is naturally more intelligent than the Indian and therefore must receive deferential treatment on policy matters.

The image arose in those unknown decades of the last century when the tribes were attempting to adjust to the reservations. They had fully understood their treaties and expected the government to keep its word. But they had not reckoned with what bureaucrats and lawyers can do with the written word. Suddenly it seemed as if the treaties meant something else, as if a clearly defined reservation boundary was really something else, and as if the world that they had known had transformed itself according to a pattern in which things clearly did not mean what they clearly meant.

The alleged incompetence of the Indian was in fact the reinterpretation of commitments by the federal government so that it might avoid its legal responsibilities to the Indians. But, as might overcame obvious right, the only logical explanation Indians could conceive was that they were very stupid not to see the obvious meaning—and that meaning was the one which the whites, by some magic known only to them, gave to things. Even at the present time the most devastating aspect of the Indian movement is the assumption by many Indians that the whites are always right, or that they have always known what they are doing. Even in the face of the most incompetent and inept behavior by whites, Indians will still assume that there is meaning and purpose in the minds of the whites—meaning and purpose which is so sophisticated that it cannot be immediately perceived by the Indians.

The "I'm just a poor Indian" image which Indians hold of themselves belies the power and impact of Indian community life, life which is far from simple and more sophisticated in its operations than white society. But from the holding of this general attitude has come, at least in part, the recognition of "Indian" as a category of existence. Prior to the coming of the white man, it is doubtful if any of the tribes held a conception of that racial character which today we categorize as "Indian." People recognized their neighbors as co-owners of the lands given to them by the Great Spirit and saw themselves sharing a basic status within creation as a life form. It was not a status markedly different from that of the animals since the relationship between man and animals as experienced in religious activity was not regarded as qualitatively different. If anything the people saw themselves simply as "men," the two-leggeds, in contradistinction to the four-leggeds.

With the advent of the white man and his insistence on seeing all red men as "Indians" came the gradual recognition that the tribes had more in common than they had separating them. Yet this feeling did not transform itself into an identifiable image until modern times, when the helplessness resulting from political and economic status and the acceptance of the innate incompetence of the "Indian" was seen to represent an experience so universal among the tribes as to constitute a new species called "Indian."

It is from this general feeling of helplessness that the new "Indian Movement" has been spawned. While most tribes felt they shared a common denominator, the general idea of Indians working together has always been blocked by tribal distinctions. Thus even if a federal policy applied to all tribes indiscriminately, individual tribal delegations would find that it did not serve the best purposes of their tribe because, even within the category of "Indian," different tribes have different problems. The ambivalence of the present image Indians hold of themselves is such that it vanishes at the first glimmer of specific action. That is to say that Indian leaders will discuss "Indian problems" all day, but let someone propose a solution and "Indian" will vanish to be replaced by specific proposals for specific tribes.

At least a part of the Indian's image of himself is dependent upon a vague oral tradition which has replaced the older and more accurate recounting of tribal history. Thus tribes having no treaty with the United States will complain as loudly about the violation of treaty rights as the tribes holding treaty rights. Specific knowledge of treaty articles has been replaced with vague and undocumented references to "solemn promises" by the United States. Exactly where these promises originated remains a mystery. That they are considered important and sacred goes without saying.

With the destruction of the tribal governing processes of the past and the attempted re-creation of tribal governments in recent decades, the oral traditions which held great religious meaning have been replaced by the oral tradition of discontent. Indians know they have been tricked. Few can give specific instances of how this situation has come about or of the part which their fathers or grandfathers might have played in the disaster. The process of political change, of revolution against present conditions, or of advocacy of constructive change is held back by the inability of the Indian leadership to pin down the United States on its particular acts of aggression. Instead, at least a partial meaning of being Indian is to have been so overwhelmed with betrayals that it is no longer necessary to be specific concerning the events of betrayal themselves.

The final aspect of the Indians' image of themselves is a mystical and ill-defined belief that has emerged in recent decades that somehow Indians will survive the existence of the white man and once again reign supreme on the continent. The feeling has been growing in the last decade and is felt particularly by younger people. It is one of those intuitions that remains unverified by any external events, that is documented by "prophecies" of doubtful origin, and that only gains in strength when debunked. While mired down in the most profound acknowledgements of incompetency, Indians still see themselves as the eventual winners in the long-distance race of history, outlasting the present government, the remnants of the white man, and the state of mankind as we know it.

Whether all these factors tell us what is the real Indian self-image, the fact remains that the motivations that trigger developments in Indian country and the spectacular failures in projects and efforts at political organization clearly tell us that, of the various images groups hold of themselves today, none is more complicated than that held by Indians of themselves, and none holds promise for more mischief and more success than does that of the American Indian.

It may be yet another generation before Indians can create for themselves an ideal image which not only incorporates past disasters but which also inherently indicates within the communities a positive direction for the future. But it seems that today, in the mid-1970s, few Indian groups in America do share such an image of themselves, so that the present confusion of Indians as to what constitutes suitable behavior and beliefs to distinguish Indians from others may not be improper at this state of history. It is as ideas and beliefs struggle for adherents among men that societies rise and fall, and if there is one thing which characterizes the present Indian image it is the determination to survive and the belief that eventually on some greater stage of man's experience the Indian will stand justified and re-deemed. ●

2

THE INDIAN IN THE FILM: EARLY VIEWS

FROM THE EARLIEST DAYS of twentieth-century journalism the Indian in the film has been the subject of a variety of articles. These early reviews were often concerned about the portrayal of the American Indian on the screen, some lamenting the inaccuracies and others justifying the views as accurate. We include in this section a limited selection of the earliest examples of concern about such stereotypical misrepresentation, articles that are significant because of the critics' early realization that Indian people were not in reality as they were portrayed visually and also because of the awareness on the part of the critics that Indian people were upset about the misrepresentation.

Unlike the pattern that developed later, American Indian people were often included as actors in the early films. This led to such reactions as Ernest Alfred Dench's piece, "The Dangers of Employing Redskins as Movie Actors." Because American Indians were forced to act out the image the white director had of them, they played the roles of "savages" or "stoics," many unwittingly perpetuating the inaccuracies.

In the developing years of the movies Indian material provided exciting drama on the screen. The Indian conflicts of the nineteenth century had been settled to the advantage of the United States, and Native Americans had been condemned to reservations. The subjects and perspectives of the first movies were borrowed from the Wild West shows and dime novels which had been the mass media of the earlier era. This first use of the Indian as the subject for films was successful and even as film audiences grew and changed, the popularity of the subject continued. The Western came to be a metaphor for American life—triumph over the land and the people who had once inhabited it, success of the immigrant who had sought and gained new economic and social status, and a visual representation of a colorful past of what was now perceived to be a growing nation. From the beginning the Indian in the film was a political subject, although it is probably true that he was not seen as such until much later by critics who saw the allusions to Communism and the cold war or Vietnam atrocities in films made after mid-century.

There was, however, concern about the misrepresentation throughout the century, concern evidenced by Stanley Vestal's article in the thirties about the caricatures presented by Hollywood producers. He recognized the attraction of the Indian because of links with the past, but he is concerned lest we lose sight of the reality of that past in the romanticism of outdoor life and the wilderness. He is concerned about the careless attitude of producers who seem not to know how to construct an Indian village and actors who do not even look comfortable in their blankets and paint.

Vestal's view, however, was less representative than such views as James Denton's. A decade after Vestal's plea Denton found a great deal of humor in Hollywood's use of Indian actors who had to be "taught" how to act Indian; that is, they were represented as "Indian" according to the vision of the producer.

These earliest critical views of the Indian on the screen suggest some of the ambivalence that existed from the very beginning toward the portrayal of Indian people by Hollywood producers. Although there was a recognition of the lack of accuracy, critics were noncommittal about solutions to the problem. Indians had become a staple in Saturday afternoon serials and necessary to the myth of the West and its portrayal on the screen. Audiences did not generally know the difference between a Navajo and a Cheyenne, so they certainly would not know the variations in tribal traditions or clothing. Producers knew this and knew also that the films would be popular despite the lack of accuracy. Because the Indian's voice has always been an isolated one, his pleas were unheeded. The few critics who spoke out against the misrepresentation during the first half of the century were equally isolated voices. ■

7

Published in 1911, "The 'Make-Believe' Indian" notes that movies do not accurately portray Indians as a "noble race of people, with their splendid physique and physical prowess." The article mentions that a number of Indians resented the "untrue, unreal, and unfair representations of themselves and their habits" and concludes with the hope that a series of films of "real" Indian life will be forthcoming. Brief reviews such as this appeared frequently in *Moving Picture World*, the first journal to deal with the new media of the twentieth century.

THE "MAKE-BELIEVE" INDIAN

CHILDREN revel in the "make-believe," but only when the real is impossible. In generations to come, long ages after the real American Indian has passed into history, pictures of this most interesting race of people will be enjoyed. It will be as easy in the distant future as it is today to produce the "make-believe" Indian. But the question arises, should not the Indians of today be real? A company of Indians who recently saw some of these reproductions most justly resented the untrue, unreal, and unfair representations of themselves and their habits. Truthfulness in picture has previously been advocated in these columns, and it is well that this timely and authoritative protest should come. While we still have the real Indians with us, why cannot thoroughly representative films be produced, making them at once illustrative and historic recorders of this noble race of people, with their splendid physique and physical prowess? It is to be hoped that some of our Western manufacturers will yet produce a series of films of REAL Indian life, doing so with the distinct object in view that they are to be of educational value, both for present and future use. Such a certified series will be of great value.   ●

From *Moving Picture World* 8 (March 4, 1911): 473.

8

Some early movie critics were genuinely disturbed by the misrepresentation of the Indian on the screen. W. Stephen Bush, in "Motion Picture Absurdities," laments the stereotyping American Indians have undergone: always squinting as though they needed glasses, either totally evil or totally subservient as the white man's friend.

MOVING PICTURE ABSURDITIES

W. STEPHEN BUSH

THE greatest of them all is the Indian. We have him in every variety but one. We have Indians à la Français, "red" men, recruited from the Bowery and upper West End Avenue. We have Licensed Indians and Independent Indians—the only kind we lack are the real Indians. Tradition credits the Indian with uncommonly keen sight, which he seems to lose when transferred to celluloid, for on an average every Indian in the picture shades his eyes, as if it hurt him to look, on an average about eight times during a scene. The Independent Indians, especially, seem to be in need of an oculist's services. General Sherman said that there were no good Indians except the dead ones. He had never seen the moving picture Indian. There is no medium of morality about him. He is either wholly good, seemingly transplanted from the skies, or else a fiend and an expert scalper in constant practice. Those who know him best describe the Indian as stoic and unemotional, but what a change when the red brother poses before the moving picture camera. He is as busy and talkative as the "villain" in the first two acts of the old-fashioned melodrama. You cannot escape the moving picture Indian. Recently I visited five moving picture houses in a Southern tour and five in a city in New England. The Indian was everywhere. The filmmakers tell us that the demand for this sort of thing is overwhelming. I studied the audiences in the theatres visited, while the Indians were doing their worst on the screen, and noticed no feverish enthusiasm denoting approval. I sincerely believe they were tired of them, especially as the music with these pictures is always the same. Enter "The Wicked Half-Breed." He is dear to the heart of the filmmaker dealing in Western stuff. The W. H. may be divided into two grand classes, the Canadian and the Mexican. Of the two the Mexican is the more common species. When you see a Mexican in the full dress of a bullfighter and smoking a cigarette and rolling his eyes you are face to face with the W. H. He rarely survives the middle of the reel and is either killed by the hero or lynched by the dear cowboys. The Mexican half-breed is invariably impolite to the heroine, and most of his troubles may be traced to that source.

From *Moving Picture World* 9 (September 16, 1911): 733.

9

Misconceptions about Native Americans were dangerous not only because of their wrongheadedness but because they often led to distortions like the ones revealed in Ernest Alfred Dench's chapter, "The Dangers of Employing Redskins as Movie Actors," in his book *Making the Movies* (1915). Dench tells how employment in films allows Indians to revert to their "savage days" and discusses several incidents where Indians have been carried away by their emotions and actually have committed violence to white actors. Dench concludes by noting that "to act as an Indian is the easiest thing possible, for the Redskin is practically motionless."

THE DANGERS OF EMPLOYING REDSKINS AS MOVIE ACTORS

ERNEST ALFRED DENCH

IT is only within the last two or three years that genuine Redskins have been employed in pictures. Before then these parts were taken by white actors made up for the occasion. But this method was not realistic enough to satisfy the progressive spirit of the producer.

The Red Indians who have been fortunate enough to secure permanent engagements with the several Western film companies are paid a salary that keeps them well provided with tobacco and their worshiped "firewater."

It might be thought that this would civilize them completely, but it has had a quite reverse effect, for the work affords them an opportunity to live their savage days over again, and they are not slow to take advantage of it.

They put their heart and soul in the work, especially in battles with the whites, and it is necessary to have armed guards watch over their movements for the least sign of treachery. They naturally object to acting in pictures where they are defeated, and it requires a good deal of coaxing to induce them to take on such objectionable parts.

Once a white player was seriously wounded when the Indians indulged in a bit too much realism with their clubs and tomahawks. After this activity they had their weapons padded in order to prevent further injurious use of them.

With all the precautions that are taken, the Redskins occasionally manage to smuggle real bullets into action; but happily they have always been detected in the nick of time, though on one occasion some cowboys had a narrow escape during the producing of a Bison film.

Even today a few white players specialize in Indian parts. They are past masters in such roles, for they have made a complete study of Indian life,

From *Making the Movies* (New York: Macmillan, 1915, pp. 92-94).

and by clever makeup they are hard to tell from real Redskins. They take leading parts, for which Indians are seldom adaptable.

To act as an Indian is the easiest thing possible, for the Redskin is practically motionless.   ●

In 1936 Stanley Vestal's article, "The Hollywooden Indian," alerted readers that ". . . in the representation of the American Indian, Hollywood has made little progress; . . . for misrepresentation, sensationalism, and all-around falsity, Indian pictures are in a class by themselves." Although Vestal has a few negative Indian stereotypes of his own—an Indian is "a born mimic," "touchy and quick-tempered," and "a great gossip"—his lament was admirable for the times: "It seems stupid of producers to offer them nothing but caricatures of their race. . . . Let us hope that the Hollywooden Indian may soon go the way of his cigar-store prototype." Vestal's was an isolated voice, however, for his pleas seemed not to affect either the producers or the viewers. Stanley Vestal was the pseudonym of Walter Campbell, a Western historian from Oklahoma.

10

THE HOLLYWOODEN INDIAN

STANLEY VESTAL

A GENERATION ago, every cigar store worthy of the name had standing before its door a life-size wooden image of an Indian offering tobacco to the passersby. Those solemn images, with all their wooden paint and feathers, have become great rarities, collector's items seldom found outside the antique shops. But now a new caricature of the Red man offends our eyes, a figure equally wooden, equally grotesque—the Hollywooden Indian of the screen.

Everyone not born yesterday is aware of the great technical and artistic gains made by the moving-picture industry within recent years. Almost every department of that industry has shown marked improvement. But in the representation of the American Indian, Hollywood has made little progress; the methods used bear almost no relation to those employed in dealing with other varieties of the human species. Of course, everyone who has lived in and knows the West is likely to be critical of Western pictures; we know they are false and sensational, and have to excuse our attendance by saying we like the fine horses and the mountain scenery. But for misrepresentation, sensationalism, and all-around falsity, Indian pictures are in a class by themselves. All Westerners gag at them, finding the celluloid Indian completely indigestible. Nine times out of ten, we leave the theater muttering, wishing we had our money back.

Not that our dissatisfaction helps. The Indian is a fixture in American history and literature, and therefore can never be long neglected by those

From *Southwest Review* 21 (1936): 418–23. Reprinted by permission.

who provide our popular entertainment. For nearly three centuries, the main business of the American people was the conquest of the Red man and the occupation of his lands. If one leaves the Civil War out of account, more people were killed during those centuries in Indian fights than in all our other wars combined. Our history and our literature are full of the Red men. Moreover, every boy—and not a few grown men—believes in his secret heart that the life of the wild Indian was the ideal life for a red-blooded male. Thus, however much we may resent the caricature which Hollywood offers us when we ask for a Redskin, Indians of some kind will continue to appear on the screen as long as Americans care a hoot for their past, for outdoor life, for the romance and heroism of the wilderness. Therefore, in self-defense, it is high time we laid our complaints before the picture-makers, in the hope that they may mend their ways in this department as they have in others.

To begin with, the Indians in many films are not Indians, but hams masquerading in what they fondly imagine are Indian costumes—as unreal and unsatisfactory as the fake Injun of the old-time medicine show. It is, in fact, almost impossible for a white man to impersonate a full-blood Indian. The skeleton of the full-blood differs in certain respects from that of the Caucasian, with the result that he carries himself in a different manner. He moves, he sits, he stands in a way instantly recognizable. These characteristic poses have been caught in the paintings of Charley Russell and Frederick Remington—artists who saw and portrayed the strange and almost oriental stamp of the Indian physique. When an Indian sits, he sits; when he stands, he stands. His movements are purposeful, and he has the poise and muscular control of the outdoor man and the athlete. All this is lost when a house-bred ham pretends to be a noble savage on the screen, even though the ham be muffled up in a blanket. When he is half-naked, his inability to act the Indian becomes pitifully apparent. Indians are not muscled like white men; their limbs are smooth and boyish. They are ephebic. The American painter, Benjamin West, on coming face to face with the Apollo Belvedere, exclaimed, "By God! A Mohawk!"

The man who cast Ramon Navarro as Laughing Boy should do penance before that statue. Navarro has his charms, but they are not Navajo charms. This fact was made all the more obvious by the horde of real Indians continually surrounding Navarro on the screen. He looked more like the Venus de Milo than the Apollo Belvedere. And Lupe Velez, brilliant as she is, was nothing like a Navajo girl—not even a Navajo corrupted by contact with white settlers. I am credibly informed that the author of the book could not be induced to go to see the picture. All this, of course, was not the fault of the actors; it is simply the way Hollywood does Indians.

The costumes in Indian pictures, too, are generally unsatisfactory. It is no doubt inevitable that the Red man should be typed along with everything else in Hollywood; and for that matter, Buffalo Bill established the Plains Indian as the show type long before the screen existed. The Plains Indians include such tribes as the Sioux, Cheyenne, and Crows, who lived in tipis, hunted buffalo, counted *coups,* danced the Sun Dance, and lived—and often died—on horseback. The Plains Indian was the most dashing figure among American Indians because the Plains made him a horseman. Moreover, he was a fighter and is bound up with the conquest of the country, to say nothing of his connection with the Custer Massacre. As the Plains were the last region to be occupied by white men, the Indians of that region are still fresh in the public mind, and many old bucks still live who fought Custer and hunted buffalo. But Hollywood apparently does not even try to keep to this type.

The buckskins used in moving pictures are often obviously cloth, with straight seams sewed on a machine. The feathers are turkey, not eagle; the weapons are not of the right period. Strangely enough, even the costumes of the white men are often wrong. When soldiers of the Indian wars appear on the screen, they are all in neat blue uniforms, their officers carry sabres, and their rifles are not the carbines of the Seventh Cavalry. As any veteran of the Indian wars can tell you, the soldiers wore anything that would keep them warm and dry—cardigan jackets, buckskin shirts, buffalo overcoats. On some of those campaigns, uniforms were the exception in the field.

Even when real Indians are used on the screen, the director commonly makes a frightful hash of their manners and customs. He sends the pipe the wrong way around the circle at council; his warriors mount their ponies from the left side; young men leap to their feet and dash away at the command of a chief, as though the chief were a general; chiefs themselves sit on hilltops directing operations during a battle, though as a matter of fact, Indian chiefs generally led the charge, and very often had no followers until they had themselves killed an enemy. Moreover, in Indian fights, Redskins are made to bite the dust by hundreds, though a loss of two percent was usually enough to make any Indian force give over for the day. Hollywood directors, in short, show an almost complete ignorance of Indian strategy and tactics in warfare.

Indian scouts did not, as they usually do in the movies, stand on a hilltop and peer at wagon trains from under the flat of their hands. In war or hunting, scouts covered their black heads with a white wolfskin, or tied a white handkerchief over their hair, so as not to be seen against the sky when peering over the hilltop. Indeed, they often covered their whole bodies with white robes, knowing that a gray wolf can scarcely be noticed at a little distance, and that moonlight blurs out a white figure even close by. Hence scouts were called "wolves." References to this custom of "making oneself a wolf" abound in books on Indians. But did anyone ever see a scout so dressed on the screen? The scouts who appear on the screen couldn't find eggs in a hen's nest, and would never live out the day. If the enemy didn't kill them, their own comrades would!

The representation of Indian camps is generally ridiculous also. The tipis do not tilt to the rear, as all tents with a smoke hole in front must do. The canvas is not taut over the poles, as all canvas intended to shed wind and water must be. The designs painted on the tents are seldom convincingly Indian. And even when the tipis are real Indian tents put up by Indians, it is obvious that they are not inhabited. They are not pegged down, they contain no duffle. No fly-blown meat hangs on the rack to dry. No mangey dog skulks in or out. Smoke—obviously not wood smoke—pours from the smoke hole as from the stack of a locomotive, in a manner that would make any self-respecting Indian give his wife a lodge-poling. And the ponies grazing about have obviously just had their harness taken off. In view of the fact that, in all likelihood, no primitive people were ever so much photographed as were the Plains Indians, this sort of thing seems inexcusable.

Occasionally one sees a picture where real Indians are employed as actors, and where pains have been taken to get everything right, so far as makeup, costumes, and sets are concerned. As a rule, however, all this effort is wasted because the director, working under pressure as he must, cannot take the time or does not have the patience to put his Indians at their ease and bring out in them their own natural talents as actors. This is the greatest pity of all, for the Indian is a born mimic with a keen sense of the theater, as his sign talk and his fame as an orator demonstrate. Left to himself he can do splendid things. Witness the Kiowa dancers, who take the annual prize at the Gallup Ceremonial every year. Witness too the all-Indian programs put on by the students of Bacone College, in Oklahoma. But an Indian cannot be hurried into a sound artistic performance. Moreover, he is not prone to make suggestions unless they are asked for. He is shy. As a result, an Indian will stand by and let the director make one error after another, errors which could be avoided if the director knew how to draw the Indian out. But that could be done only by a man acquainted with Indians, one who had their confidence. And so, nine times in ten, the dramatic talent of the Indian is wasted, hurried into nothing, and the final effect is bad. The director finds that his Red men have somehow turned into calendar Indians: Red Devils, Noble Savages, Sentimental Hiawathas. There is not a human being in a carload.

Yet the Indian is actually a very human person—humorous, sexy, sensitive, touchy and quick-tempered, a great gossip and practical joker, a born mimic, a politician from infancy, and an incorrigible lover of human society. He even loves his relatives. Besides, he has a genius for formal behavior, for ritual and manners. Add to this the moods which govern his entire life, and you get a pretty good outline of an accomplished actor. Yet it is a rare thing for Hollywood to make the least use of the Indian's talents. To Hollywood, the Indian actor is just a ham, and the Indian has his revenge by living up to expectations. All his rich humanity, all the little human touches which might bring him and the picture to life are killed by high-pressure directing. The Indian actors become confused. The rhythm of their minds, as well as that of their bodies, is wrenched and falsified.

This, it seems to me, is bad business for an industry just now pulling itself out of bankruptcy and multiplied receiverships. There is a vast potential audience for good Indian pictures, if Hollywood would take the pains to produce them. In addition to the great public which likes Westerns, there are in the United States hundreds of thousands of people who are Indians or have some Indian blood, and they are proud of their ancestry. It seems stupid of producers to offer them nothing but caricatures of their race.

Recently the United States Commissioner of Indian Affairs secured the passage of a law making it a crime to offer for sale as genuine Indian work fake Indian baskets, pottery, jewelry, and handicrafts. It seems time for similar legislation designed to prevent the sale of fake Indian drama. It is really too bad that the moving pictures have wasted and ruined such splendid screen material as the American Indian. Let us hope that the Hollywooden Indian may soon go the way of his cigar-store prototype.   ●

James F. Denton's article, "The Red Man Plays Indian," appeared in *Colliers* in 1944. The essay reveals a lack of historical perspective in portraying Indians on the screen as well as echoing the uncritical acceptance of traditional Indian stereotyping. The fact that the piece appeared in a highly successful, mass-circulation magazine reinforces once again the popular biases against American Indians. Its very existence speaks to the virulence of cultural and racial stereotyping.

11

THE RED MAN PLAYS INDIAN

JAMES F. DENTON

THE Sioux and Cheyennes you'll see in the new movie about Buffalo Bill are really Navahos. They got a lot of fun and some cash money for letting the white man teach them how to act like Indians. But they still think the movie people are a little off the beam.

Buffalo Bill might be a legend to the youth of America, but to the red man, as exemplified by the Navaho tribe in southern Utah and northern Arizona, he is worth $6.50 a day and a good laugh.

William F. Cody, known to millions as Buffalo Bill, the last of the great scouts, had a record bag of 4,862 buffalo in one season, but this didn't mean a thing to the Navaho who is a great eater of sheep and goats.

Nevertheless, 251 men, women, and children of the Navaho tribe were busily engaged last summer in learning all about Buffalo Bill at a wage of $6.50 a day each. Their interest, in truth, didn't run exactly at fever heat, but they did seem to have a lot of fun playing Indians in the Technicolor film about the great plainsman's life which 20th Century-Fox filmed in the Utah mountains near Kanab. "Playing" is the proper word because the Navahos didn't appear in the film as Navahos, but as Cheyennes and Sioux.

They had things at hand that were new to them. They had to learn to fire old-fashioned rifles and to shoot bows and arrows, a very difficult feat, even for an Indian. They had to learn to live in tepees instead of hogans, to wear strange and cumbersome clothing and to fight with knives and tomahawks.

One of their more difficult tasks was to learn to run without jouncing the arrows out of the quivers on their backs. Howard Hill, probably the greatest bow-and-arrow expert in the United States, who has appeared in numerous Hollywood films, was brought up from Hollywood to add the finishing touches to the Indians' education in this ancient art of their ancestors.

For the purposes of this film, the Navahos came up from Tuba City,

From *Colliers* 113 (March 18, 1944): 18–19.

Arizona, by the truckload and pitched their camps in small groups near the film site for the historic fight at War Bonnet Gorge led by Buffalo Bill. It is in this great battle that Buffalo Bill, played by Joel McCrea, kills Yellow Hand, portrayed by Anthony Quinn, and keeps the Cheyennes from joining the Sioux in a great war against the white man.

NO TASTE FOR HISTORY

The Navahos didn't know about all this history and didn't seem to care; their only interest lay in the fact that this furnished them a pleasant interlude in their summer wanderings over the reservation.

If the white man wanted to make a motion picture and dress the Navaho up in outlandish garb he had never seen before, it was all right with him, and he would laugh with the white man over the problems of filming such a picture, provided, of course, he got his $6.50 a day. He was a stickler on this point, and not in the least naive. These particular Navahos were selected because they were pretty good horseback riders. It's one thing their ancestors did that they still do, and bareback too. No Indian had to bite the dust, either. Hollywood brought its own stunt men along to do this.

William A. Wellman, noted film director, proved that he was a very smart manager of the Navaho from the very start. He sent each group a goat with his compliments. That was right down their alley. They understood such sign language and they enjoyed the goats. From that understanding start, Wellman became the hero of this film. The Navahos were perfectly willing to let history take care of Buffalo Bill.

Chief Thundercloud, a Cherokee who has been Hollywood's mainstay on Indian lore for many years, was taken to Kanab to advise on technical matters of the Buffalo Bill period, such as the technique of wielding a scalping knife, how the Cheyennes wore their warbonnets, how they looked in their war paint, and such other details.

The Navahos were very philosophical and took all these things in a good-natured way. They did seem to think it was a confounded nuisance, however, to carry a heavy rifle around all the time. When Chief Thundercloud and other technicians were busy with other problems, the Navaho would lean his rifle against the far side of a tree and relax. Director Wellman, their great and good friend, finally devised a simple way of overcoming this difficulty. He discovered that the Navaho kept up his interest in carrying the rifle if he was allowed to shoot a blank cartridge every now and then.

Linda Darnell, Maureen O'Hara, Joel McCrea, Anthony Quinn, and others of the film cast mingled freely with the Indians and were welcomed into their camps. Miss Darnell, who is one-eighth Cherokee Indian, interested the Navahos very much. When asked what they thought of her as an Indian (she plays the role of Yellow Hand's sister), one of the Navaho leaders looked at her hands, smiled, and remarked:

"Hands no work. No good squaw."

The Navahos taught Hollywood a few new things about work. Every morning, the Indians wanted their pay before they would work, instead of waiting until the end of the day or the week. Consequently, they lined up before breakfast in their camp every morning, and each received his pay of $6.50 and his food allowance of $1.50.

The Indians didn't want to be fed. They didn't like the white man's cooking, preferring their own, which consisted mainly of sheep and goats, beans, and a bread made from cornmeal. The Navahos were divided into small groups. Each did its own cooking over small outdoor fires and each was represented by a group leader who negotiated directly with Director Wellman and his staff.

The daily paychecks were the occasion of a difficult problem at first. The Navaho didn't like all the various deductions for social security, unemployment insurance, income tax, and so on. The problem was solved by the studio paying him a flat day rate of $6.50 and assuming all the other costs.

The first day of work was the most difficult. The Indians lined up before the wardrobe tent, and costumes were handed out. They had to be shown how to wear the feathered headdress, leather breeches, and fringed leather shirts. They didn't think this was the kind of thing to wear in that summer heat, but they put their costumes on uncomplainingly.

When it came time to have the war paint smeared on their faces by the makeup experts from Hollywood, the Navahos objected at first. They thought this was a bit thick and that Hollywood was overdoing the thing. Chief Thundercloud finally persuaded them that the Indians of old really dressed and painted this way. The Navahos were self-conscious at first but apparently overcame this when they were given a fine horse each to ride bareback. They laughed and joked over their costumes.

GIVING THEMSELVES A LAUGH

As soon as he was issued his costume in the wardrobe tent, the Navaho would yell to his friends in his language, "Look what I'm wearing!" They all would break out into laughter.

When Chief Thundercloud explained a torture scene in the picture, wherein the Cheyenne proved his bravery by having his back cut, the Navahos laughed uproariously; they thought such action was downright nonsense. There is nothing stoic about the Navahos. They do not bear pain with fortitude nor do they practice self-torture as a sign of bravery.

Among themselves, the Navahos are merry and jovial. Their sense of humor is quick and ready and evident. They admitted that they had a very good time making *Buffalo Bill* and would be interested in seeing the finished picture in one of their two motion picture theaters on the reservation, where films, mostly action ones, were shown every Friday night.

They seemed interested in seeing just what kind of fellow Buffalo Bill really was, now that they had heard so much about him for the first time. They also admitted that they were tired of staying in one spot. They had been on the film location for three weeks and they were anxious to be on the move again. Their sheep would look good to them again after all this talk about buffalos.   ●

3

THE INDIAN IN THE FILM: LATER VIEWS

V ERY LITTLE about the Indian appears in film journals during the 1960s. Perhaps, as Donald L. Kaufmann suggests, the emphasis on Black America during this decade of civil rights obscured concern about other minorities. In the 1970s we have again been made aware of the first Americans in film.

In the first piece of this section John Price provides an academic view of the American Indian in film. His was one of the first articles that combined discussion of popular film with documentary films, recognizing that it is possible to present accurate portrayals of American Indian life. Because of Price's ethnological approach, he finds more merit in *Cheyenne Autumn, Tell Them Willie Boy Is Here, Little Big Man,* and *A Man Called Horse* than have some other critics.

Other essays in this section point out the political implications of some of the recent films with American Indian subject matter. Certainly the mood of the country during the 1960s and 1970s was undergoing significant changes. At the same time American Indian people were visible in the news media with the takeover at Wounded Knee, the Trail of Broken Treaties, and The Longest Walk. Perhaps producers realized that they could no longer portray the old images, that the public was becoming aware of what Stan Steiner called "the new Indians." At a time when "flower children" were searching with Don Juan and Carlos Castaneda for spiritual awakening and protesters were decrying the genocide of Vietnam, new aspects of Indian existence became significant.

Philip French, even more than others, saw the McCarthy era as forcing producers to use allegory to handle sensitive issues. *Arrowhead*, for example, is described by French as an "ultra-right-wing allegory of the McCarthy period in which the Indians, . . . do service for Communists, and the whites . . . for those red-blooded American patriots bent on rooting out the Communist conspiracy at home and standing up to its menace abroad." He cites *Cheyenne Autumn* as portraying the fairly obvious comparison between the persecution of the Indians and the German extermination camps. In more recent films he offers comparisons with America's counterculture and parallels *Soldier Blue* and *Little Big Man* with Vietnam and My Lai. What French and others see in the contemporary films is a manipulation of the Indian image to present the political ideologies of the filmmakers.

In this country it will be a long time before the major studios have many American Indians as employees or technical advisers. And financial backing for Native American film companies is sadly lacking. The film version of N. Scott Momaday's *House Made of Dawn* is available but has been shown only to limited audiences. Based on a Pulitzer Prize–winning novel written by a Kiowa Indian, directed and produced by Harold Littlebird, and featuring many new Indian actors, this film demonstrates what can be done despite a low budget and a lack of "Hollywood" experience. Although the film may receive criticism on selected technical issues or resentment from some Native Americans who would have preferred that the religious peyote ritual be omitted, it is generally a fine film which visually presents Native American experience as something other than the usual fare of "cowboys and Indians." Perhaps Rita Keshena is right after all: we will need Native Americans "in the business" if we are to receive something other than an outside view of Indian experience. Only then, perhaps, will we see movies with "real" Indians. ■

12

While he was at York University, John Price wrote this essay suggesting that the old stereotypes are breaking down and that recent films are presenting more positive images. Price reviewed the negative stereotypes of the silent films, the continued use and expansion of those stereotypes in serials, and then what he saw as new images since 1948.

THE STEREOTYPING OF NORTH AMERICAN INDIANS IN MOTION PICTURES

JOHN A. PRICE

IN the past sixty-five years the American motion picture industry has elaborated a body of ethnic stereotypes about North American Indians. They are usually characterized as riding horses, hunting buffalos with bows and arrows or guns, and wearing tailored leather clothing and feathers in their hair or in headdresses. They are seen as having been consistently cheated by whites and therefore as consistently against whites. They are portrayed as persistently involved with warfare, fighting as tribal units under a chief, and taking the scalps of their enemies as war trophies. In more racist terms they are stereotyped as sexually desiring white women and therefore abducting them, being more adversely affected by alcohol than whites, and being humorless, taciturn, and speaking simple languages.

Some of these characterizations, such as the use of elaborate feather headdresses, are correct for about two dozen Plains tribes in the late 1800s, but they are false for the remaining over 500 other Native societies in North America. As a predominant feature in their way of life, most Indians did not regularly ride horses, hunt large game, wear tailored hide clothing, or wear feathers in their hair. By population, more Indians lived in agricultural chiefdoms and states than in the simple hunting tribes of the movie stereotypes. Instead they were fishermen and farmers. They wore robes of woven bark in the populous North Pacific Coast and of cotton cloth in the agricultural Southeast, Southwest, and in southern Mexico. This other rich and diverse North American cultural heritage should not be displaced or demeaned through such biased and narrow portrayals.

We cannot dismiss the stereotypes as unimportant film portrayals because hundreds of millions of people the world over have acquired their beliefs about North American Indians through motion pictures. They were created as entertainment, but they cumulatively built a separate reality

From *Ethnohistory* 20 (Spring 1973):153–71.

about Native cultures. The belief that there is an essence of general truth about Indians in these portrayals is pervasive and persistent in modern North America. They are, for example, difficult stereotypes to correct in university courses on American Indians. Even modern American Indians draw heavily from these films in constructing their *own* views of their cultural heritage.

This is a history of distortions in the portrayal of North American Indians and Eskimos. Concluding discussions touch on such topics as the handling of interracial sex relations, the need for Indian actors, the need to portray Native societies outside the Plains, and the need to promote documentary films.

Many of the basic film stereotypes of Indians were formed in the period of silent movies. The movie story was told by white American producers and directors to a white North American audience, assuming and building the plot from anti-Indian attitudes and prejudices. Indian life was seen as savage and at an earlier stage of development, and therefore rightly vanishing as Indians are exterminated or assimilated into white society. The central figures were usually whites while Indians were used for local color, to provide action sequences, and as villains. Cawelti (1971:38) writes, ''The Western formula seems to prescribe that the Indian be a part of the setting to a greater extent than he is ever a character in his own right.'' This sharpens the moral issues and dramatic conflicts for the white principals. Also, ''. . . if the Indian represented a significant way of life rather than a declining savagery, it would be far more difficult to resolve the story with a reaffirmation of the values of modern society.''

As Western movies became a part of the culture, writers and directors built their stories with symbols that had been established in earlier motion pictures. The genre became gradually removed from real history to become a kind of allegorical history. The Western became a milieu of fictional history with symbols for such frontier concepts as freedom, pragmatism, equality, agrarianism, and brutalization. These ideas were commonly expressed in the popular Wild West literature of the nineteenth century and were then expressed cinematographically in the early twentieth century. Because the film stereotypes were still forming during the silent era there was some diversity in kinds of Indian societies portrayed and the roles of Indians in the stories. The costuming was often more authentic than in later years and there were occasional pro-Indian movies in the earliest silents.

The Wild West shows of Annie Oakley and Buffalo Bill Cody, with their Indian actors, were included in the variety show acts that were filmed by the earliest kinetoscope motion pictures in 1894. Geronimo and Sitting Bull actually participated in some of these shows, the latter even selling autographed photos of himself for one dollar each (Friar 1970:17). D. W. Griffith's second picture was an Indian melodrama called *The Red Man and the Child*, although this was not an important film because, like others at the time, it was so rapidly and poorly made. He shot the film on the Passaic

River in New Jersey in 1908, taking about one week to make it (Fulton 1960).

Indians were leading figures on the side of right in such 1911 films as *An Indian Wife's Devotion, A Squaw's Love,* and *Red Wing's Gratitude.* In 1913 there was the moderately pro-Indian movie *Heart of an Indian.* The setting of these pro-Indian movies was usually among the eastern agricultural tribes. *Ramona,* a strongly pro-Indian story set among the Mission Indians of Southern California, was filmed at least four times. Later silents shifted more toward a villainous Indian image, as in *In the Days of Buffalo Bill* (1921), *The Vanishing American* (1925), and *Redskin* (1928).

D. W. Griffith filmed *Ramona* in 1910 when he moved to Southern California for the advantages of more sunny days for shooting outdoor movies. But even Griffith was ethnocentric about Indians. In *The Battle of Elderbush Gulch* (1913) Griffith showed the Indians' preparations before they attacked the settlers. The preparations included an emotional war dance and the eating of dogs, obviously uncivilized practices to a white audience. An early story of the problems of Indian-white miscegenation in old Wyoming was *The Squaw Man* (1913) by Cecil B. DeMille. This story of a white man who loved an Indian girl was so popular that DeMille remade the film twice, in 1918 and 1931.

DeMille's *Call of the North* (1914) had Indians wearing a realistic mix of Native and white clothing. William S. Hart, who had lived among the Sioux, is noted for his struggle for realism, even playing a halfbreed Indian chief who tried to bring white education to his people in *The Dawn Maker* (1916). Colonel Tim McCoy, as an Indian Agent to the Wind River Shoshone, was an adviser to James Cruz on his use of the tribe in the first epic Western, *The Covered Wagon* (1923). McCoy later became a prominent actor who influenced filmmaking with his knowledge of Indian history and customs. If this early tradition of authenticity had continued there could have been a florescence of great films of lasting value on the ethnography and history of the American Indian.

The classic Western movie with frontiersmen and pioneers struggling against the difficulties of the elements of nature, lawlessness, and the Indians was developed in the silent era. It was in turn derived from the popular Wild West literature of the nineteenth century. This form was particularly emphasized in the serials, along with melodramas and slapstick comedies (Barbour 1970). The serials used a technique of steadily building suspense to climaxes through speed, action, and "crosscutting" from one scene of action to the next. It was in these that a band of horse-riding Indians was used to attack the settlers in order to introduce the elements of threat and action to the routine story. Extensive dialogue was unnecessary because the threat and the action were easy to portray through the pictures, so the story captions remained extremely simple. These were easy to make because they involved little writing or dramatic entanglement. Movements could somewhat replace acting, the story pattern was easy, stock footage from past films could be incorporated, and sets were inexpensive. All shots involving a given set or a key actor were filmed at the same time, although this often confused the actors because the scenes were out of sequence and they might not know to which circumstances they were supposed to be reacting.

Indians were usually portrayed as villainous, but in the silent days they were often individualistic, intelligent, and culturally diverse adversaries. "Under the influence of a mystical Indian drug beautiful Ann Little is prepared to do as she is told by Indians, but rescue by *Lightning Bryce* (1919) is imminent." At least they were assumed to have the intellectual ability to use devious methods like drugs when abducting beautiful white women. The *Moonriders* (1920) used Pueblo Indian ruins for one setting rather than the usual Plains tipi setting. Frank Lackteen played individualistic Indian villains in *White Eagle* (1922) and *Leather Stocking* (1924). By the time of *Hawk of the Hills* (1927), it was Plains tipis and costumes as the Indians catch the beautiful white girl.

THE SOUND SERIALS

When sound movies were developed, the serials continued to be popular and the major American studios shot 235 serials, all with from ten to fifteen episodes, between 1930 and 1956. Some forty of these, or seventeen percent of the total, can be classified as Westerns. These often used two or even three directors, each specializing on different elements of the same film: one on drama and dialogues, one on action scenes such as fights, and a third on second-unit locations, such as car chases and Indian-cavalry encounters. Thus the dialogue man did not worry about Indian dialogue. If the Indians spoke at all, that was handled by the Indian-cavalry specialist, who was more interested in the photographic portrayal of action.

The director of B-Westerns actually had more artistic freedom than other directors because his product was not important or expensive enough for close supervision from the studio's management. He was given a great deal of freedom as long as his product was saleable, on time, and within the budget, but his budget was so low and his production schedule was so tight that very little creativity or historical accuracy was achieved.

Tim McCoy fought Indians in a film that was made in both silent and sound versions, *The Indians Are Coming* (1930). That was the first talking serial of any kind. It had poor pacing and synchronization and no musical score. Gradually these sound features were improved as each major studio began to produce about one Western serial every year or two, reaching peak production in 1938 and 1939. The Western serials and B-Western movies tended to use the same writers, directors, and leading characters. They were inexpensive to produce, the interior sets were cheap to make and appropriate exterior scenes were readily available in Southern California. The following are the Western serials produced by major American studios between 1930 and 1956 (Barbour 1970):

WESTERN SOUND SERIALS

1930 *The Indians Are Coming, The Lone Defender, Phantom of the West*
1931 *Battling With Buffalo Bill*
1932 *The Last of the Mohicans, The Last Frontier*
1933 *Clancy of the Mounted, Fighting With Kit Carson*
1934 *The Red Rider, The Phantom Empire*
1935 *The Roaring West, The Miracle Rider*
1936 *The Phantom Rider, Custer's Last Stand*
1937 *Wild West Days, The Painted Stallion, Zorro Rides Again*
1938 *Flaming Frontiers, Hawk of the Wilderness, The Lone Ranger, Wild Bill Hickok*
1939 *The Lone Ranger Rides Again, Overland With Kit Carson, The Oregon Trail*
1940 *Adventures of Red Ryder, Winners of the West*
1941 *Riders of Death Valley*
1942 *King of the Mounties, Perils of the Royal Mounted*
1944 *Black Arrow*
1945 *The Royal Mounted Rides Again*
1947 *Tex Granger, Jesse James Rides Again*
1948 *Dangers of the Canadian Mounted*
1949 *The Ghost of Zorro*
1950 *Cody of the Pony Express*
1952 *Blackhawk, Son of Geronimo*
1954 *Riding With Buffalo Bill*
1956 *Blazing the Overland Trail*

The serials had come primarily out of pulp fiction, although a few of the later ones came from comic strips to movie serials, such as *Red Ryder* (1940) and *King of the Mounties* (1942). In the early 1940s there was a total of forty-four different Western pulp magazines, none of them Indian oriented. The B-Western Zorro series is considered to be an ancestral form to the Lone Ranger, an Americanized version of the Spanish California Zorro. Paralleling these movie serials were the B-Western movies, an occasional big budget or A-Western, and the radio adventure series, so there was an interchange among the different forms of mass media. The Lone Ranger was on radio, in two film serials and three B-Westerns, and then in a television series and in comic books.

This material was rapidly developed for television when it initially flourished in the 1950s. Thus the serials died out in motion pictures and radio but flourished for about fifteen years on television with fifty-one different Western serials, including such titles as *Hopalong Cassidy* (1947), *The Lone Ranger* (1948), *Gunsmoke* (1955), and *Bonanza* (1959). Again, none were particularly Indian oriented.

THE 1930s AND 1940s

When sound came in, Indians were rarely given speaking lines, even in some mock-Indian language, such as Tonto's use of *kim-o-sabe* with the

Lone Ranger. In one serial of the mid-1930s (*Scouts to the Rescue*) the Indians were given a language by running their normal English dialogue backwards. By keeping them relatively motionless when they spoke, the picture could be printed in reverse and a perfect lipsync maintained.

Another feature of sound is that the character of individual heroes and villains could be more subtly developed and were less expensive to employ than massed warring Indians. This led to some decrease in the use of Indians. The stereotype had developed that Indians always fought as a tribe and that individually they were disinterested in white concerns or just too dumb to be believable villains. So the Western villain was usually a crooked white gambler, major, banker, or rancher and his gang.

The Plainsman (1937) was one of the first movies to use an Indian chief by name as the tribal leader, Yellow Hand in this case. Wild Bill Hickok, Calamity Jane, and Buffalo Bill are all in this film fighting Indians. The standard use of Indians for excitement occurred in *Union Pacific* (1939) and *Stagecoach* (1939) when they attacked the train or stagecoach, as usual without historical accuracy or even sufficient fictional explanation. Indians were simply held as hostile to whites. *The North West Mounted Police* (1940) was an important full-color fictional account of the Riel Rebellion of the Canadian Metis. Cecil B. DeMille produced and directed *The Plainsman, Union Pacific, North West Mounted Police,* and *Unconquered* (1947) (Ringgold and Bodeen 1969). The latter, set in the American Colonies, includes Indians torturing a white woman, an Indian massacre of colonists, and an attack on a fort. It was about the last fully anti-Indian movie and ironically was by one of the first men to make Indian movies (DeMille began in 1913). In World War II the Nazis, Fascists, and Japanese were the major villains, but still *Geronimo* (1940) was one of the first Indian chief biographies, portrayed unsympathetically as a naturally violent man. *They Died With Their Boots On* (1942) portrayed the Battle of the Little Big Horn with some historical accuracy but was sympathetic to General George Custer and unsympathetic to Chief Crazy Horse.

THE SHIFT TOWARD PRO-INDIAN MOVIES

John Ford directed the important trilogy on cavalry life in the 1880s of *Fort Apache* (1948), *She Wore a Yellow Ribbon* (1949), and *Rio Grande* (1950). These films viewed Indians through the eyes of a sympathetic white, like the lead actor John Wayne in *Fort Apache*. The constant striving for mutual understanding between the Indians and at least certain whites is a constant theme in the three films. The true villain now tends to be a white: a martinet colonel, a trader who sells liquor and guns to the Indians, etc. The names of Indian chiefs, bands, and tribes and the Apachean dress are accurate. You get to see glimpses of the Indian women, as well as the usual masses of male warriors. John Ford directed over two hundred feature films, mostly outdoor pictures, and his Indian Westerns have consistently been more authentic portrayals than those of other directors at the time, but he never portrayed a Native culture from the inside until *Cheyenne Autumn* (1964).

Kitses (1969:13) discussed the history of the Ford's Westerns in terms of changes of Ford's personal philosophy. "The peak comes in the forties where Ford's works are bright monuments to his vision of the trek of the faithful to the Promised Land, the populist hope of an ideal community. . . . But as the years slip by the darker side of Ford's romanticism comes to the foreground . . . we find a regret for the past, a bitterness at the larger role of Washington. . . . The Indians of *Drums Along the Mohawk* and *Stagecoach,* devilish marauders that threaten the hardy pioneers, suffer a sea-change as Ford's hopes wane, until with *Cheyenne Autumn,* they are a civilized, tragic people at the mercy of a savage community." Another explanation could be that Ford gradually acquired a more sophisticated understanding of Indian-white relations.

These Ford films and later films usually attempted rationalization of Indian behavior, although as people they often came across as simple, childlike creatures, who spoke in short, ungrammatical sentences. *Broken Arrow* (1950) carried this theme of understanding the Indians further by trying to portray Indians as people with a legitimate culture, cases of stupidity and bigotry on both sides in cultural conflict, and the difficulties of achieving peace between the Apaches under an honorable Cochise and the whites. Delmer Daves, a writer and director who had lived among Hopi and Navaho as a youth, adapted the story from the historical novel *Blood Brother.* This film brought more realism, as well as nostalgia and sophisticated satire, to the big-budget Western. Jeff Chandler had his first important success as Cochise in the film, taking a white man as a blood brother and trying to make peace with the army. Audiences were now receptive to the idea of a more noble redman who had been victimized and forced into impossible situations. Indians were no longer seen as intrinsically bad or necessarily stupid. Indian heroes were often friends to the white heroes and there were both Indian and white villains. Indians were victims of circumstances created by whites and only renegade Indians caused trouble. Indians still lost, but then that was history, wasn't it?

The wave of pro-Indian movies that immediately followed *Broken Arrow* attempted to shoot the story more from the Indian point of view, but were often poorly done, such as *Taza, Son of Cochise* (1954). Two Indian Western serials were rushed out in 1952, *Blackhawk* and *Son of Geronimo.* Other somewhat pro-Indian films that came out within four years of *Broken Arrow* were *Devil's Doorway, Across the Wide Missouri, The Savage, Arrowhead, The Big Sky, Chief Crazy Horse, Sitting Bull, White Feather, Navajo, Hiawatha,* and *Jim Thorpe: All American,* an Indian athlete's biography. There was even a television series based on an Indian policeman in New York, *Hawk. Arrowhead* (1953) had a white scout stop his Indian blood brother from a murdering rampage against whites. *Apache* (1954) attempted to show an individual renegade who tried to live alone, away from both the reservation and whites, but he was hunted and hounded by whites. *Flaming Feather* (1952) was another one in which the whites go to take back a white girl whom the Indians have. These pro-Indian films of the 1950s often dealt with the difficulties of assimilation into white society because of white prejudices, as in *Devil's Doorway* (1950), *Reprisal* (1958), and *The Unforgiven* (1960). *The Half-Breed* (1952), *Broken Lance* (1954), *The Last Wagon* (1956), *Flaming Star* (1960), and *Nevada Smith* (1966) included half-breeds who had to work out the dilemmas of their dual ancestry. Negative stereotypes were then formed about the Indian-hating, treaty-breaking cavalry officers, merchants, and Indian agents who usually ignored the Indian-wise hero.

The Unforgiven (1960) had a young Indian girl brought up as a white by whites until a stranger revealed her past, which caused conflicts among her adopted brothers and the local people. In *Flaming Star* Elvis Presley portrayed a half-breed who had to choose between his two ancestries, and an Indian hero again in *Stay Away Joe* (1966). In *McClintock* (1963) a group of Indian chiefs were released from prison to find only trouble from land-hungry whites and a stupid government agent. An old chief finally begged to be given guns so that his people could die honorably in war. In *How the West Was Won* (1963) the obsessed railway man was determined to get his tracks laid across the Indian land as fast as possible, ignoring Indian burial grounds and having treaties rewritten for his own good. The Indians retaliated by stampeding a herd of buffalo into the railroad camp. The attitude then was that the white destruction of Indians was unfortunate but inevitable because of the march of technical progress. *Cheyenne Autumn* (1964) was based on historical accounts of 286 Cheyenne who left their sterile reservation and tried to return to a traditional hunting range over 1,500 miles away, only to be pursued by a cavalry unit which had been ordered to return them to their reservation.

Duel at Diablo (1966) was the standard violent action picture with Plains Indians as the cardboard villainous force, but there is some view of how whites felt about Indians: a white scout is seeking revenge for the murder of his Indian wife, and a husband is an Indian-hater while his wife, who has been captured by Indians, mothered the chief's son. In the late 1960s intimate Indian-white relations became even more important. *Hombre* (1967) had a white hero who had been raised by Indians and *The Stalking Moon* (1968) had a white woman with an Indian baby. In *The Intruders* (1967), a half-breed is hassled when he gets out of jail and tries to return to his hometown. A sign at the edge of town said, "No deadbeats or Indians allowed." He is refused a drink in the local saloon. They would not even bury Indians in the town graveyard.

THE RECENT BREAKING DOWN OF STEREOTYPES

A few recent films have been particularly authentic and sympathetic, and they are breaking down the traditional film stereotypes of Indians. There has been a drastic decline in the number of Indian movies produced but the quality has improved for those that are made. *The Boy and the*

Eagle (ca. 1968) was an excellent depiction of a Hopi myth. *Tell Them Willie Boy Is Here* (1969) told of bigoted white justice related to conflicts in assimilation, the superior ability of a Cahuilla [*sic*] Indian to survive in the desert, and the eventual destruction of the Indian hero by a posse. The story is based on a historical incident in Southern California. *Little Big Man* (1970) and *A Man Called Horse* (1971) again dealt with violence in the Northern Plains and repeated many cinematic cliches, but they treated the assimilation of whites into Indian cultures in a sympathetic and realistic way. *The Savage* (1952), *Pawnee* (1957), and *Hombre* (1967) had earlier portrayed white men brought up by Indians, but these more recent films were more realistic. Their commercial successes were attributed in part to a careful attention to the details of Indian life. They both give many ethnographic details on the day-to-day life in Northern Plains Indian cultures by following the events in the life of a white captive. The films were still told from a white point of view but did so without white moralism or attempts to devalue Indian culture. The white heroes learned to respect many Indian customs.

Little Big Man is particularly successful in showing Indian humor. To some degree this film reversed the usual situation so that the whites became stereotypes while the Indians were interesting, individualistic, and unpredictable. General Custer was played strictly for laughs and it showed that time-honored theme of Indian Westerns, Custer's Last Stand, from an Indian point of view. This was a Western comedy.

Indians have usually been used as comic figures through extreme stereotyping or through a complete reversal of the stereotype. Thus in *My Little Chickadee* (1940) W. C. Fields had an Indian friend, Milton, who contrasted completely with Fields. Fields was short; Milton was tall. Fields was rubber faced with a bulbous drinker's nose while Milton was stern faced. Fields was fairly talkative while Milton just grunted. *McClintock* (1966) [*sic*] reversed this idea and had a young Indian who was a college graduate and smarter than the whites around him but was still unable to get ahead because he was an Indian. In *Texas Across the River* (1966) Joey Bishop played a comedian Indian. In *The War Wagon* (1967) Howard Keel played a nonchalant Indian who lived with whites when their life was better and then went back to the Indians when they accidently came across some gold.

The gradual elimination of stereotypes is an indication of the increasing sophistication of the viewing public. Still, the cliches die hard and Indians are still used for violent action by savages. Indians were seen as violent by nature, not because of neurosis or criminality. They acted as tribes; they were all the same. A white villain was an individual with characteristic traits, ideas, and emotions, but an Indian could be a villain by just being an Indian. Indian chiefs were usually portrayed as representatives of a larger body, not as individuals per se. Even *Jim Thorpe: All American* (1951) was told as an Indian's successful adaptation to white society, rather than stressing the values he drew from his ancestral culture.

Billy Jack (1971) is a half-breed, Western Pueblo, ex-Green Beret, counterculture super-hero who protects wild horses and the children of a racially mixed school on a reservation from harrassment by the local white bigots. The hatred of Indians that is portrayed is extremely overstressed, particularly for the Santa Fe area where the film was shot. As in *Little Big Man,* the whites are stereotyped and, as in *Hombre,* the hero prefers his Indian heritage. With dozens of beautiful Indian ceremonials in the local Rio Grande Basin each year to incorporate into the film, the completely false Indian rituals that were contrived for the film were unnecessary. However, this film touches some contemporary Indian problems. It became a commercial success and should influence the production of more in the same vein. It does not patronize Indians, and it finds value for life today in Indian ways of living.

Two 1972 movies that were made for television are pro-Indian. *Mystery of the Green Feather* (1972) has sophisticated cattle ranching Indians, blatant hatred against Indians, whites who claim to be part Indian in order to make land claims, anti-development pleas against the railroad and for clean air, and even that phoney story about how whites taught scalping to Indians by paying for Iroquois scalps. Bounties were paid by some early European settlers for enemy scalps, but the practice was aboriginal. *Climb an Angry Mountain* (1972) ends with an excellent funeral scene in an Indian language, probably Shastan since the movie centers on Mount Shasta in northern California. An Indian, an ex-marine who is married to a white woman, escapes from police only to head toward the snow-covered Mount Shasta in the "Indian belief" that the gods will forgive those who make it to the top. The Indian is portrayed as a nice, simple guy with an unusual cultural background which eventually leads to his self-destruction.

INTERRACIAL SEX RELATIONS

DeMille handled the problem of miscegenation during the silent era in *The Squaw Man.* In this adaptation of a play the Indian wife committed suicide and the white man took their son to England. *Duel in the Sun* (1948) had a half-breed in love with a white man. In *Broken Arrow* (1950) James Stewart portrayed a white who fell in love with an Indian woman, and *Across the Wide Missouri* (1951) was a pioneer story of love between a white man and an Indian woman. In the later film the Indian wife also died, but this time her white husband returned to her tribe to raise their son. It has usually been the Indian woman who died to provide the tragic but "inevitable" ending for a racist audience. Indian women were generally portrayed as sexually more free than white women, even being casually given to passing whites for the night, as in *The Searchers* (1956).

The reciprocal form of miscegenation, Indian man and white woman, has been less acceptable to white audiences and was not used as an acceptable arrangement until very recent films: *Duel at Diablo* (1966), *The Stalking Moon* (1968), *Little Big Man* (1970), *Billy Jack* (1971), and *Climb an Angry Mountain* (1972). In *The Searchers,* two men looked for a white woman who had been stolen by the Indians many years before. They find her happily married to a Comanche Chief. Their intent was to bring her back if possible, but if not, to kill her to save her from the completely degrading situation that they imagined she had been forced into. Something tragic almost invariably happens to these miscegenous matches so that the audience is not left with a happy mixed marriage at the end. The Indian husband is usually the one who dies, just as it was usually the Indian wife who died in the other form of interracial love affair.

THE NEED FOR INDIAN ACTORS

One of the problems in Indian Westerns has been the use of non-Indians in acting roles as Indians, such as Anthony Quinn (*They Died With Their Boots On*), Jeff Chandler (*Broken Arrow*), Burt Lancaster (*Apache, Jim Thorpe*), Audrey Hepburn (*The Unforgiven*), Chuck Conners (*Geronimo*), and Sal Mineo, Dolores Del Rio, Ricardo Montalban, Gilbert Roland, and Victor Jory (*Cheyenne Autumn*). Most of the important Hollywood stars of the 1940s and 1950s played an Indian role at least once: Douglas Fairbanks, Boris Karloff, Robert Taylor, Yvonne de Carlo, Rhonda Fleming, Paulette Goddard, Jennifer Jones, Loretta Young, and so forth.

Indian actors were rarely ever given lead roles, although they were used occasionally as tribal members. A few of the MGM silent Westerns that starred the Indian expert Tim McCoy, such as *The Covered Wagon* and *The Vanishing American,* were made on Indian reservations with Indian extras. There was even an association of Indians in silent motion pictures in Los Angeles in the 1920s called the War Paint Club. John Ford has usually used Navajos as extras since his *Stagecoach* (1939). Several of the recent films have used real Indian tribes: *Cheyenne Autumn, Little Big Man,* and *A Man Called Horse.*

Part of the problem is that real Indians do not behave according to the film stereotypes that have been developed about Indian behavior, so they must learn to "act Indian." Indians, of course, are not automatically good actors, even as Indians, but whites know so little about Indian culture and behavior that even good white actors usually do a poor job portraying Indians. An Indian Actors Guild was formed in Los Angeles in 1966 to promote the use of Native people in Native roles, to promote the training of Indians in trick riding and other horseman skills, and to promote the teaching of dramatic skills to Indians. Jay Silverheels was behind this movement and helped to form an Indian Actors' Workshop at the Los Angeles Indian Center with the help of other Indians such as Buffy Sainte-Marie, Iron Eyes Cody, and Rodd Redwing (Chissell 1968).

Chief Thundercloud was in *Wild Bill Hickok* (1938) and then played Tonto in the first serial version of the radio show *The Lone Ranger* (1938), which was an Americanized version of the Zorro stories. Tonto, the Lone Ranger's assistant, like Zorro's assistant, was originally considered so insignificant that the hero could be literally called the ranger who works alone. In fact, the word "tonto" means "fool" in Spanish and this pair, whether as the Zorro or the Lone Ranger team, worked in the Southwest where Spanish is spoken. Also, there is some lore about occasional "crazy" Indians who left their tribes and associated individually with whites. However, as developed by Chief Thundercloud and the show's writers, Tonto began to emerge as a major figure in the movie series. Tonto became the first major fictional Indian film hero, particularly after Jay Silverheels played Tonto in *The Lone Ranger* (1956), television's *Lone Ranger* (1940) series and then in *The Lone Ranger and the Lost City of Gold* (1958). Jay Silverheels is a tall, handsome and intelligent Iroquois who has played Indian roles in over twenty-nine motion pictures, including *The Prairie* (1947), *Fury at Furnace Creek* (1948), *Broken Arrow* (1950), *War Arrow* (1953), and *Indian Paint* (1967). While many politically active Indians have since criticized Silverheels for playing a role that was clearly subservient to a white man, he in fact developed Tonto into one of the most intelligent and individualistic Indians to be portrayed on serial television.

Silverheels (1968:9) discussed the problem of recent Indian criticisms of Indian actors in comic television commercials. In one spoof selling housing insurance, six Indians attacked a peaceful suburban house. "Suddenly painted Indian riders attack the dwelling, yelling and shooting fake arrows, and throwing tomahawks at the building. One Indian slips on a roller skate and takes a fall. The Indians ride out of the scene; they have left a man tied. The narration accompanying this scene concerns insurance, never at any time is ridicule implied toward the Indians." Indians in Minnesota protested that the commercial degraded the Indian image. It was withdrawn from further showing on television, and the Indian actors lost out on some of the royalties they would have received if it had been shown. The commercial, of course, capitalized on film stereotypes about Indians, but by showing them in a ridiculous light they helped to dispel them. In another one, Silverheels is shown stuffing pizza rolls in his pocket. Again he was criticized. His reply was that this kind of criticism "promotes and strengthens the image that projects the Indians as being stoic, undemonstrative, incapable of showing emotion and entirely lacking a sense of humor."

Iron Eyes Cody, a Cherokee, has portrayed Indians in over thirty-five motion pictures. Rodd Redwing (a Chickasaw known for his trick gun handling), John War Eagle, and Chief Yowlachie have made many appearances. Recently, Chief Dan George came to prominence in *Little Big Man* and showed how much better a good Indian actor could do in an Indian role than most white actors have done.

THE NEED TO PORTRAY SOCIETIES OTHER THAN HORSEMEN OF THE PLAINS AND SOUTHWEST

Over 2,300 feature-length Western films and serials had been produced by 1967 (Eyles 1967). About 400, or seventeen percent, of these included significant Indian portrayals. The frequency of tribal names in the titles of motion pictures shows the predominance of the horsemen of the Plains and Southwest in Indian movies: Apache—15, Cheyenne—6, Comanche—6, Navajo—3, Mohawk—2, Seminole—2, Sioux—2, Iroquois—1, Mohican—1, Osage—1, Pawnee—1, and Yaqui—1. The Mohawk, Iroquois, Mohican, and Seminole are clearly outside the tradition of horsemen of the Plains and Southwest. The remaining eighty-five percent of the tribal names mentioned in motion picture titles are of Plains-Southwest horsemen societies. Also, one sees the predominance of Native societies with a historical reputation for violence, particularly Apache, Cheyenne, and Comanche. Societies with a more passive, nonviolent reputation are almost never portrayed, such as Hopi in the Southwest, Washo or any other Great Basin society, and any subarctic society.

Just following the success of *Broken Arrow,* which apparently popularized the Apaches, the 1950s saw *Apache Drums* (1951), *Apache War Smoke* (1952), *Apache Country* (1952), *Battle at Apache Pass* (1952), *Apache* (1954), *Apache Ambush* (1955), *Apache Warrior* (1957), and *Apache Territory* (1958). Geronimo, an Apache, has in turn been the most frequently portrayed Indian chief, most sympathetically in *Geronimo* (1962).

In the context of long-range history this particular selection of societies is ironic because the Plains Indian cultures were not fully aboriginal, did not evolve until after whites introduced the horse, and were not similar to most other American Indians. No American Indians rode horses before Columbus and most still did not hunt from horseback in the middle 1800s. Most American Indians did not depend upon large game as their primary source of food but were in fact agriculturalists. Most American Indians lived in permanent houses, not in temporary hide tents. Most American Indians did not wear tailored hide clothing, but woven robes. Plains-Southwest horsemen were even less typical of Indians than the frontiersmen were typical of Europeans because there was far more cultural and linguistic diversity in aboriginal North America than in Europe.

The selection of the Plains-Southwest horsemen as the source for the majority of stereotypes about Indians is understandable in the context of the vitality of those Indian cultures in recent historical times. The Indian military resistance to the occupation by force of Indian territory by white society was significant and still of recent memory in the Plains and Southwest. Cultural adjustments related to this traumatic period reverberated in both Indian and white societies for decades after. This white conquest and occupation probably had to be justified and rationalized to white society through the literature, the Wild West shows, and finally through motion pictures. Perhaps the extreme stereotyping soothed the guilty conscience of the nation, as time and again it was shown how white, European, Christian manifest destiny must conquer the forces of paganism and barbarism. The Plains and Southwest Indian cultures themselves rebounded after the military period to become the major source of Native cultural revitalization at the same time that extremely negative stereotyping was being developed for white audiences. This was particularly true of the social and religious pan-Indian movements, such as the Ghost Dance, Sun Dance, Peyotism, and powwow dancing.

Motion pictures have ignored most of that spectacularly rich cultural diversity of some 560 different languages and societies in North America. Instead, they have portrayed over and over the same dozen or so Plains-Southwest tribes that acquired enough military prowess to give the whites a brief resistance: Blackfeet, Cheyenne, Comanche, Apache, etc. Motion pictures have virtually ignored the state societies of Mexico and Central America (Maya, Mixtec, Aztec, etc.), the agricultural chiefdoms of the Southeast (Natchez, Creek, Cherokee, Choctaw, etc.), the marine chiefdoms of the Northwest Coast (Haida, Kwakiutl, Tsimshian, etc.), the agricultural pueblos of the Southwest (Hopi, Zuni, Taos, etc.), and hundreds of other interesting societies, to focus instead on elaborately fictionalized accounts of Indian military harassment of the struggling pioneers.

In fact, the whole horse-riding, buffalo-hunting complex was a brief cultural florescence that was created indirectly by whites. The horse was introduced into the New World by the Spaniards and it diffused northward, initially from the settlements around Santa Fe in the 1600s. This diffusion process went on through the 1700s, gradually providing more and more of the Indians of the Southwest and Plains with the great economic and military advantages of the use of horses. Societies that had gathered plants and did some hunting on foot, such as the Blackfoot and Comanche, had much greater success on horseback. The Ute decreased their plant-gathering orientation and increased hunting. Some societies, such as the Arapaho, even abandoned horticulture to take up the rich complex of buffalo hunting on horseback. People could be more mobile, could carry more things, and could build bigger tipis. They could locate herds, keep up with the herds, chase down buffalo on horseback for the kill, and carry large quantities of food and skins back to camp.

This new wealth and new way of life brought on many changes in Plains Indian life, attracted peripheral societies into the Plains, promoted rapid population growth, promoted warfare and other competition between tribes, and gradually reduced the buffalo population. The whites then entered the Plains, found some brief military resistance from Indians, and added their contribution to bringing the buffalo close to extinction. The story material is as good in dozens of other areas. If the fixation on Indian-white conflicts is necessary for a sufficiently violent story there is much good material in Spanish-Indian or French-Indian conflicts in other areas. The real needs, however, are to describe Native cultures in their own terms, in time periods other than the late 1800s, and in areas outside the Plains and Southwest.

ESKIMOS AND THE DOCUMENTARY MOVIE

Indian movies have generally been successful as popular entertainment and as financial productions, but for their quantity they have done little to advance the art or science of films. For example, they have not won Academy Awards, unless we count *How the West Was Won* (1963). Discussions about artistic creativity or the development of new techniques never seem to mention Indian films, although there have been occasional comments about their content as depictions of historical events or of frontier life. The historical judgment on the cinematographic creativity in over 2,300 Westerns is that it was a mass media within which the industry learned to use the American natural landscape, learned to use apparent visual movement to build excitement, and learned to synchronize the sounds of outdoor action, such as horses' hoofbeats and gunshots.

Eskimo cultures have largely escaped the stereotyped portrayal of Indian cultures and Academy Awards have been won for *Eskimo* (1934) and *The Alaskan Eskimo* (1953). Films on the Eskimo are particularly noted for their creativity in the field of documentary ethnocinematography, a tradition that is very careful about the use of stereotypes. There seem to be several reasons for this. Eskimos retained much of their traditional culture into the modern era, making it available for direct photography. Because of the extremely different environmental setting of the Arctic, there has been much interest in the Native solutions to the problems of cultural adaptation, even in the modern period. By contrast, the life of nearly one million Indians who live on or near reservations in the United States and Canada has virtually never been portrayed in popular feature films. Eskimos were never a significant threat to whites and, like all "band" rather than "tribal" Native societies, never warred against whites.

Another reason for the relatively realistic portrayal of Eskimos is the documentary precedent set early by Robert J. Flaherty's *Nanook of the North* (1922). This was one of the most important movies ever made, setting standards that are still difficult to meet today. Flaherty was raised in northern Michigan and northern Ontario and knew many Ojibwa Indians as a youth, even learning some of the Ojibwa language (Calder-Marshall 1963). He went to Upper Canada College in Toronto, traveled extensively in Northern Canada by canoe, and worked as a geologist in the Hudson Bay area. He made a film of the Eskimos in the Belcher Islands in Hudson Bay, but the negative was destroyed in a fire. He was dissatisfied with it anyway, particularly its disconnected portrayal of the Natives in one relatively unrelated scene after another.

He built continuity and integration into his next film by focusing on the annual round of activities of the head of a family, Nanook, from Port Harrison in northeastern Hudson Bay. He came into the community, became well acquainted with the Natives, worked without a script, and allowed the incidents that happened in the course of his filming to determine the content of his film. He let the story develop out of the lives of the people in their daily struggle for survival in a harsh environment: walrus hunt, harpooning a seal, visit to trading post, etc. He not only avoided building negative stereotypes by honest cinematic reporting, but through intimate portrayal he showed the humanity of the Eskimo. The film was completed in 1921 after sixteen months of filming. The word "documentary" was first written in English by a film critic in relation to *Nanook of the North*. After that, Flaherty went on to work on several other documentaries, including a picture on the Acoma Pueblo Indians in 1928 that he never completed.

CONCLUSION

A review of the history of the portrayal of Indians in motion pictures shows (1) the initial development of the film stereotypes of Indians in silent films; (2) the extreme emphasis on these stereotypes in the serial and B-grade Westerns of the 1930s and 1940s; and (3) then the gradual elimination of the stereotypes in big budget movies of the 1940s and 1950s. The decline of Indian stereotyping seems to have begun during World War II when the Germans, Italians, and Japanese replaced the Indians as the major villains. After World War II John Ford's more realistic Westerns, *Broken Arrow,* and a host of imitators handled Indians in more sympathetic, although still fictional, ways. A few films of the 1960s and 1970s have even approached the documentary quality of Flaherty's *Nanook of the North: Cheyenne Autumn, The Boy and the Eagle, Tell Them Willie Boy Is Here, Little Big Man,* and *A Man Called Horse.* This same period has seen a florescence in the production of true documentaries. The best documentary and educational films on Canadian Indians are described in *Films on the Indian People of Canada,* Information Division, Department of Indian Affairs and Northern Development, Ottawa. A general catalogue that includes the best on United States and other Indians is *Films for Anthropological Teaching* by Karl G. Heider, American Anthropological Association, 1703 New Hampshire Avenue, N.W., Washington, D.C. 20009. The following are the major long documentaries.

MAJOR NORTH AMERICAN NATIVE DOCUMENTARIES

1922 *Nanook of the North* (Eskimo of Port Harrison)
1920s *Before the White Man Came* (Crow Indians)
1959 *The Exiles* (bar culture Indians in Los Angeles)
1960 *Circle of the Sun* (Blackfoot Blood Indians)
1962 *The Annanacks* (Eskimo of George River)
      Basketry of the Pomo (three films)
1963 *Totem Pole* (with Kwakiutl dance and music)
1964 *Pomo Shaman*
1966 *Tahtonka: Plains Indian Buffalo Culture*
      Washoe (ceremonies for girls's puberty and pinenut harvest)

1967   *Okan, Sun Dance of the Blackfoot*
       Navajo Film Themselves (seven silent films)
1969   *To Find Our Life: The Peyote Hunt of the Huichols of Mexico*
1970   *Tepoztlan and Tepoztlan in Transition*
       Netsilik Eskimo Series (ten parts)
1972   *Caesar and His Bark Canoe* (Cree construction)
       Cheenama the Trailmaker: An Indian Idyll of Old Ontario
       (new release of an old silent on the Ojibwa)

REFERENCES

Barbour, Alan G.
    1970 *Days of thrills and adventure.* New York, Macmillan.
Calder-Marshall, Arthur
    1963 *The innocent eye: the life of Robert J. Flaherty.* London, W. H. Allen.
Cawelti, John G.
    1971 *The six-gun mystique.* Bowling Green, Ohio, Bowling Green University Popular
          Press.
Chissell, Noble "Kid"
    1968 Indian Actors' Workshop. *Indians Illustrated,* Vol. 1, no. 5 (June), pp. 6-8. Buena
          Park, California, Talking Leaves, Inc.
Eyles, Allen
    1967 *The Western: An illustrated guide.* London, Zwemmer; New York, A. S. Barnes.
Friar, Ralph.
    1970 White man speaks with a split tongue, forked tongue, tongue of snake. *Film Library
          Quarterly,* Vol. 3, no. 1, pp. 16-23ff. New York, Film Library Information Council.
Fulton, Albert R.
    1960 Motion pictures; the development of an art from silent films to the age of television.
          Norman, Oklahoma, University of Oklahoma Press.
Kitses, Demetrius J.
    1969 *Horizons West.* London, Thames and Hudson.
Ringgold, Gene, and DeWitt Bodeen
    1969 *The films of Cecil B. DeMille.* New York, Citadel Press.
Silverheels, Jay
    1968 Lo! The image of the Indian! *Indians Illustrated,* Vol. 1, no. 6 (July–August), pp.
          8-9. Buena Park, California, Talking Leaves, Inc. ●

In Ralph and Natasha Friar's article "White Man Speaks With Split Tongue, Forked Tongue, Tongue of Snake," they express dismay because, despite all the right things being said by directors and actors, Indians are still being stereotyped and are still being played by whites and Mexicans. This article is a condensed review of some of the ideas presented in their *The Only Good Indian . . .: The Hollywood Gospel*, a comprehensive treatment of the historical basis for the Indian stereotypes. It is clear that they are saying that "everything changes and yet everything remains the same."

13

WHITE MAN SPEAKS WITH SPLIT TONGUE, FORKED TONGUE, TONGUE OF SNAKE

RALPH E. FRIAR and NATASHA A. FRIAR

A few years ago we were watching a group of young American Indian boys, armed with toys made in Japan, playing cowboys and Indians on the Pine Ridge Sioux Reservation in South Dakota. But none of the boys wanted to be Indians! One of the lads, almost in tears, was yelling that he did not want to be an Indian because the others kept beating him up and he was always losing the game. This was not surprising, no one wants to be a loser. The Indians really did lose and Hollywood has never for one moment let us forget it. Although most of us do not share the tragic plight of that little Sioux boy, Hollywood's misrepresentation of the native Americans has affected us and is affecting all our children. Hollywood started playing cowboys and Indians almost as early as the cameras started cranking and film's stereotypical Indian has been part of our culture for over half a century.

William S. Hart, who attempted to portray the West as authentically as he could on the screen, did so because of his first reaction to films: "I saw a Western picture. It was awful," he said. Having lived among the Sioux, he was referring to the Hollywood idea of the West, a West which never existed. The Indian Wars, however, did exist and offered ample grist for Hollywood's mill. The Indian Wars may be just a polite way of referring to genocide or a war of extermination. "The only good Indian is a dead Indian" was no idle phrase; the white man and his government wanted the land and took it by any means possible. Many tribes were involved in this death struggle to protect themselves, their homes and their lands. To name all the tribes would result in an almost endless list; to point out only a few

From *Film Library Quarterly* 3 (Winter 1969–1970):16–23. Reprinted by permission.

would be an insult to the memory of the many thousands who died. The important thing to remember is that each tribe had its own individual culture, customs and traditions; each was like a nation unto itself. For Hollywood there seemed to be only two tribes—the Apache and the Sioux. Their popularity was probably a result of the widespread notoriety given them and their leaders during the Indian Wars, and the infamous exhibition and exploitation of Geronimo and Sitting Bull in Buffalo Bill's Wild West show. Everyone came to gape or sneer at these dastardly creatures they had so often read about. But soon the "red devils" became matinee idols and Sitting Bull sold autographed photos of himself at a dollar a shot.

Hollywood feels that constant use of these two tribal names brings instant recognition and appeal, and the costume houses stock more of their tribal costumes than any other. This, of course, is nonsense for Hollywood has perpetuated what can be best described as the "instant Indian kit," suitable for any and all Indians. So it makes no difference which tribe is depicted in a film; the costumes make them all look alike. This, in part, prompted Dr. Frederick J. Dockstader, head of the Museum of the American Indian and, himself an Indian, to say: "The war-dancing, feather-bonneted, horse-riding Indians we usually see in movies and on TV are impersonations of the Plains tribes. Most American Indians lived, dressed and danced differently. This is like using Irishmen and Irish customs to portray all Europeans—and is probably responsible for most of our popular misconceptions about Indians."

The most popular film subject involving the Sioux has been the Custer massacre. Twisting history to suit Hollywood's fancy started as early as 1909 with *Custer's Last Stand* and continued as late as 1968 with *Custer of the West*. In the interim some of the other films were: *The Massacre* (1912), *Custer's Last Fight (1912), The Scarlet West* (1925), *Flaming Frontier* (1926), *They Died With Their Boots On* (1942), *Little Big Horn* (1951), *Sitting Bull* (1954), *Chief Crazy Horse* (1955), *The Great Sioux Massacre* 1965). Even so bloody a battle could not escape the hands of Hollywood comedy hacks. A burlesque farce, *Colonel Custard's Last Stand,* was filmed in 1914 using such names as Chief Standing Cowski instead of Sitting Bull.

Hollywood's blatant disregard for historical fact is typified in *Custer of the West* and *Sitting Bull.* In the former, Custer actually meets with the Indians just before the massacre to try to talk them out of it. In the latter, J. Carrol Naish, playing the title role, comes to the fort to save Dale Robertson from execution and meets President Grant. Their dialogue ends with Grant saying; "To peace," and Sitting Bull replying, "To friendship." This scene took place after thousands of Indians had just wiped out Custer and his men. Then, in typical Hollywood fashion, Naish rides off into the sunset. The massacre itself, in both films, was treated as if that well-known illustration made famous by a beer company had come to life.

However, in *Chief Crazy Horse,* the massacre was no more than a handful of Indians killing a few soldiers. Hollywood's version of history can be so distorted that Bosley Crowther in reviewing *Sitting Bull* for the *New York Times* was moved to write: "One could work up a pique at this picture for playing so loosely with facts merely to be on the currently popular side of racial theme. Such a happy and easy solution—while it may have been most desirable—is a wicked deception of youngsters, who are likely to be the principal patrons of this film."

Not only did the Native Americans always lose but they were depicted as inept, stupid or cowardly fighters. In *Tomahawk* (1951), a supposedly sympathetic portrayal of the Indian, a horde of Sioux is wiped out by a few soldiers using breech-loading rifles. In *Bugles in the Afternoon* (1952) another horde of Sioux is held to a stand-off by three white men. The continual defeat of the Indians is, of course, historically untrue for they were among the greatest light cavalrymen in the world. Most Indians know this even if Hollywood does not. Perhaps this explains Bosley Crowther's comment in the *Times* on *Tomahawk:* "For John War Eagle, who plays the big chief, we would like to say one word. He stands aloof from the whole thing and that is precisely as he should." And Howard Thompson comments in the *Times* on *Bugles in the Afternoon:* " . . . this film should be given back to the Indians. And judging by the expressions of the contributing Sioux, they want no part of it."

Because the Indians never win, it would be hoped that some gratification might be realized from their beating Custer at the Little Big Horn. But even this is denied us. Prior to 1950, native Americans were still being depicted as cruel, bloodthirsty, inhuman savages. So we have Anthony Quinn as Crazy Horse in *They Died With Their Boots On* (1941) becoming an evil wizard of ugh. And we have Errol Flynn as Custer who is really too nice a guy to get it at the end.

THE "ENLIGHTENED" ERA BEGINS

After 1950, Hollywood started its cycle of sympathetic Indian films. The Indians were now seen as misunderstood and mistreated. The chiefs were wise, noble, proud, grand and all the things a good Boy Scout should be. We have J. Carrol Naish as Sitting Bull being a wise, patient, benevolent patriarch (Jean Hersholt with feathers), and Victor Mature as Crazy Horse, a noble, proud, religious Indian nut who keeps having visions and hearing celestial soundtrack music. Savage or sympathetic, one Indian stereotype replaced another and the Indians still lose in more ways than screen battles. They have even lost the right to play themselves. Oh, you might find a few extras in the background for atmosphere, but that is about all. Every other race and nationality have played Indians and the front office always demanded stars to portray the leading Indian characters. Even though Hollywood has learned that a so-called star playing a role badly is not much box office insurance, non-Indians are still cast as native Americans. Obviously a Tony Curtis, Ira Hayes in *The Outsider* (1962), or a Rock Hudson who played the title role in *Taza, Son of Cochise* (1954) does not an Indian make.

Suppose Hollywood were going to film the life story of Martin Luther King. Let's kick around the casting. Who do we get to play Dr. King? Well, we need somebody who shows great strength. How about Burt Lancaster? He is very good at strength. Besides, how much harm can it do? Would it change history that much? Sounds ridiculous? No more so than Mr. Lancaster playing Jim Thorpe, without anyone raising a fuss. Who else might be good for the part? Well, we need somebody who can portray great inner resolution. How about Charlton Heston? He is good at great inner resolution, especially when he plays an Indian. Now can you imagine our casting the part of Mrs. King in this way?

Of course no Hollywood producer would be insane enough to have a white actor play a black, yet this happens constantly with Indian roles. Just a few non-Indian actors who have played Indians are: Don Ameche, Joey Bishop, Chuck Connors, Richard Dix, Vince Edwards, Doug Fairbanks, Sr., Thomas Gomez, Sessue Hayakawa, Victor Jory, Boris Karloff, Martin Landau, Tom Mix, Ramon Navarro, Hugh O'Brian, Elvis Presley, Gilbert Roland, Woody Strode, Robert Taylor and Robert Wagner. Some actresses are: Anne Bancroft, Cyd Charisse, Yvonne de Carlo, Rhonda Fleming, Paulette Goddard, Audrey Hepburn, Jennifer Jones, Susan Kohner, Virginia Mayo, Mabel Normand, Mary Pickford, Donna Reed, Sylvia Sidney, Lupe Velez and Loretta Young. The list could go on *ad nauseum, ad infinitum.* And even when Hollywood does condescend to cast Indians, they are usually misused. They are made to act as Hollywood thinks they should, always folding their arms, for example, because somebody once thought it looked Indian. Today, with the so-called enlightened treatment and sympathetic attitude toward minorities in the mass media, no one would dare play blackface. Yet just about anyone plays redface. The worst ally and the best enemy the Indians could have is a sympathetic friend.

HOLLYWOOD INFLUENCES INDIANS

The promulgation of the big lie, repeated often enough and loud enough until it becomes truth, has done much to corrode the Indians' cultures. Instead of their influencing Hollywood, the reverse has come true. The beaded headband is purely a Hollywood invention so commonly associated with the Indian that even native Americans must now wear it. Indians have also adopted Hollywood costuming with all its feathers and fake Hong Kong beadwork. Organizations specializing in Indian lore have developed phony "Mickey Mouse" costumes in which many Native Americans now dress in order to appear Indian. It is our theory that the headband was popularized during the Wild West show and Hollywood's early days in order to prevent the Indian wigs from falling off. The fact that Indian styles have become a fad has not helped either. High and low fashion have further bastardized traditional Indian dress. Yes, the Indian has been rediscovered for the umpteenth time, and this time everybody is now on the side of the noble savage. Hollywood, too, has climbed aboard the repainted

Wild West bandwagon. But if you scrape away a little of that paint, you might find the same old wood rot.

STILL ANOTHER STEREOTYPE

With the "tell-it-like-it-is" Westerns, we may be confronted soon by a new stereotype—the "real" Indian. On May 12 and October 6, 1968, the *New York Times* ran articles on *Willie Boy* (working title), a new "Indian antihero" in a film written and directed by Abraham Polonsky. The two Indian leads are being played by Robert Blake and Katharine Ross, both white. All the publicity releases mention this being a real film about real people with Katharine Ross saying: "I didn't want to make her a Hollywood Indian." But the fact that she is white does make her just that—another Hollywood Indian. In *Life,* February 7, 1969, Shana Alexander in "The Sad Lot of the Sioux," says "Our latest Indian madness has not escaped Hollywood's round and avid eye, and some movie people are now spending four million dollars on the most authentic Indian movie ever made, *A Man Called Horse.*" At the moment, its one claim to fame is that it is probably the first film to have a titled white, Dame Judith Anderson, playing an Indian.

The *New York Times Magazine,* October 5, 1969, published an article about Garson and Ruth Kanin in which Mr. Kanin said: "The change in the audience has made it far more interesting to work in films. My next big project, the most difficult and complex thing I've ever attempted, is a movie of the resistance of the Nez Percé tribe to the indignities of the American government, told from the point of view of the Indians. For years it was felt by motion-picture executives that the American public wouldn't accept it, the winning of the West having been part of the visceral myth of our culture. Now I have faith that we've reached a point in our emotional and patriotic development when we can accept a more truthful account of our history." In the *Times* of the same date, Ralph Nelson, who will direct *Soldier Blue,* said: "John Gay's script depicts a mass slaughter of Indians by the U.S. Cavalry in 1870. I'm not usually one for violence on the screen, but this will be as savage, perhaps more savage than *The Wild Bunch.* It has to be, because it is based on fact, and we all feel that it is necessary to emphasize the violence in order to stir a national consciousness of the violence that was done to the Indians—a violence that is still being done."

In the October 1, 1969, *New York Times* there was an item: "U.S. Indian Has Friend In New Film." The book *Little Big Man* is being filmed on the Crow Reservation. Dustin Hoffman stars in the story which, in part, is about the Custer massacre. "I was interested in this picture," Mr. Hoffman explains, "because it presents the Indian in a different light. I've seen a lot of movies but never one that's presented the Indian fairly. Most of them go along with the 'Indians are savages' theme. They really have a lot of culture.

"When they went into battle they didn't go in to win, but as a matter of honor—honor—sometimes just to touch the enemy with a coup stick. This is why they kept losing. In Custer's last battle, the Indians won because Crazy Horse and Sitting Bull made the Indians fight like white men—to win.''

The film's producer, Stuart Millar, agrees. ''It's time,'' he said, ''movies caught up with contemporary attitudes about the history of the West, including attention to the significance of genocide.''

It would appear that all these quotes have come from the same publicity man's typewriter. Mr. Hoffman has really not learned much Indian lore, nor have the rest of the production people. Crows are playing the Cheyenne and Sioux who were their hereditary enemies. It has been said that the Crows sold out or cooperated with the white man when they acted as scouts for Custer. The Sioux had all the more reason to be their enemies. The animosity between the two tribes has been so strong that even today there are those among the tribes who do not associate with each other.   ●

Philip French, a producer for the British Broadcasting Company since 1959, viewed the Indian's portrayal during the 1960s and 1970s as a political phenomenon. He suggests that the "Indian in the contemporary allegory can stand for the Negro when the implications are social or for the Communist when the implications are political." French concentrates on films of the 1950s and 1960s, seeing them as reflecting two traits, "the role of the Indians as an external force in uniting Americans" and "the cultural clash between pioneer and redskin." He sees the films as mirroring American society whether they are "declarations in favor of the American melting pot" or "expressing deep fears about the possible breakdown of American society in the face of an underlying drive toward anarchy and disintegration."

14

THE INDIAN IN THE
WESTERN MOVIE

PHILIP FRENCH

IT is now almost a commonplace to speak of 1950 as the watershed year in which the Western movie took on a new depth, seriousness and resonance. And this change was most marked in the treatment of the Indian. One French critic has even referred to 1950 as being "a little like the 1789 of the genre's history." In that year two major exponents of the genre, Anthony Mann and Delmer Daves, directed their first Westerns. Mann's picture was *Devil's Doorway,* in which a Shoshone brave, symbolically named Broken Lance (Robert Taylor), returns from distinguished service in the Civil War to find himself an alien in his own Wyoming home. "Under the law you're not classed as an American citizen—you're a ward of the American government," he's told, and at the climax of the picture he dons his old army uniform to die a defeated man, though saying to a sympathetic lady lawyer with whom a tentative romance has been suggested, "Don't worry, Anne—a hundred years from now it might have worked."

Throughout the film Taylor is presented as an unblemished hero and is always photographed in such a manner (for example, low-angle shots against the sky or lit from behind) as to make him dominate the scene. The same is true of Jeff Chandler's appearance as Cochise, the peace-loving Apache leader in Daves's *Broken Arrow,* which also made a serious if self-conscious attempt to present Indian life with sympathy and some authen-

From *Art in America* 60 (July–August 1972):32–39. Reprinted by permission.

ticity. In this case, however, the film ends with the suggestion of permanent peace, but only after the death of Cochise's daughter. No doubt she had to die as punishment for the crime of miscegenation; she had married a cavalry scout (James Stewart), the movie's instrument of racial reconciliation.

The considerable impact of these pictures (*Broken Arrow* proved one of the year's most successful and widely discussed films) has to be seen against the then established role of the Indian in the Western. Conventionally the redskin has been one of the hazards facing those bent on taming a continent and winning the West. At best he was the noble savage of James Fenimore Cooper, sharing the same qualities of primitive grandeur that resided in the challenge of the wild terrain and harsh climate. At worst he followed a tradition established by early Victorian melodrama: he was treacherous; bloodthirsty; uncompromising; threatening rape, mutilation and death.

The depiction of Indians before 1950 was not always unsympathetic. Back in 1912, D. W. Griffith's *The Massacre* showed them as hapless victims of an unprovoked cavalry raid; James Cruze's *Covered Wagon* (1923) made clear that they were motivated by a reasonable desire to protect their hunting grounds; *The Vanishing American* (1925) sketched a history of the American Indian from early cliff-dwelling days up to the ignominious death of a World War I Indian hero (Richard Dix) back on his neglected reservation. Indeed, the historians of the genre, George N. Fenin and William K. Everson, in their book *The Western,* argue that in the early days of the silent era "the Indian was seen as a hero almost as frequently as the white man, but already there was a difference. He seemed more of a symbol, less an individual than the cowboy."

This faceless symbol became a stereotype: historically a figure to be confronted and defeated in the name of civilization, dramatically a terrifying all-purpose enemy ready at the drop of a tomahawk to spring from the rocks and attack wagon trains, cavalry patrols and isolated pioneer settlements. Unlike other racial minorities or foreigners, the Indian was unprotected by the Hays Office Code, box-office caution or political influence. There has, of course, never been a shortage of crooked traders or Indian-hating officers to provoke conflict and serve as scapegoats for the white race. But this, I think, is also part of the filmmakers' approach to their subject; for the Indian could not even serve as an individually realized villain.

The liberal, anti-racist cycle that followed *Devil's Doorway* and *Broken Arrow* has continued unabated up to the present. But if Hollywood made token amends to the Apache, the Sioux, the Cheyenne and a dozen other tribes well before Edmund Wilson made his celebrated *Apologies to the Iroquois* in 1960, the Indian stereotype has not so much been shattered as reshaped. The immediate successors to *Broken Arrow* were mostly content to repeat that apparent breakthrough, trading in an easy optimism that blithely rewrites history in terms of reconciliation and peaceful coexistence or giving a perfunctory nostalgic shrug. A few pictures attempted to go rather deeper. Particularly memorable are the opening sequences of Robert Aldrich's *Apache* (1954) where a garish white civilization is seen through the eyes of a fugitive Indian (Burt Lancaster) making his way back West after escaping from a deportation train taking him to exile in Florida. A tragic ending was planned for this picture; but the front office insisted on optimism, and this is what the makers delivered in a hopelessly unconvincing way.

So for all the fine liberal sentiment, the Indian remained one of the pawns in the Western game, to be cast in whatever role the filmmaker chose. Commercially this was inevitable, and an esthetic case can be made out (indeed frequently has been) against too radical a change in the genre's established conventions. Clearly from around 1950 the Indian in the contemporary allegory can stand for the Negro when the implications are social or for the Communist when the implications are political, though generally the identification is somewhat woolly. *Broken Arrow* obviously could be viewed as a plea for racial tolerance on a domestic level and for peaceful coexistence on an international one. The same is true of numerous other movies that followed it: during the McCarthy era Hollywood artists were often forced to turn to allegory to handle themes that the studio bosses would have rejected as too controversial in a modern setting.

Of course, the natural tendency of the Western is "hawkish," whatever the pacific intention of its individual exponents. Consequently a movie like Charles Marquis Warren's *Arrowhead* (1953), however distasteful it may seem beside its liberal contemporaries, had a charge that was largely lacking in many well-meaning pictures of its time, as well as not appearing to impose worthy latter-day sentiments onto earlier situations. The central character, an Indian-hating cavalry scout called Ed Bannon (Charlton Heston), was apparently based on a real-life scout named Al Sieber, and it is with astonishment that we realize that he is the film's authentic hero, leading a drive to put down the ghost-dancing heresy as it sweeps through Texas. The leader of the uprising is the Apache Chief Torriano (Jack Palance), who returns from an Eastern college to arouse his people. The film ends with a terrifying hand-to-hand fight in which Bannon breaks Torriano's neck and with it his influence. While I have no idea what the conscious motivations of the writer-director were, the picture strikes me as an ultra-right-wing allegory of the McCarthy period in which the Indians—and especially the college-educated Torriano bringing his heresy from the East— do service for Communists, and the whites, with their unwavering leader Bannon, for those red-blooded American patriots bent on rooting out the Communist conspiracy at home and standing up to its menace abroad.

There are relatively few Westerns of the past twenty years that take such an overtly hostile attitude toward the Indians as *Arrowhead* does. It is generally the role of the white villain to echo the 1859 sentiment of General Sheridan that "the only good Indian is a dead Indian." On the other hand,

there must be many people who would agree with the opinion expressed in a
recent *Playboy* interview by John Wayne, who has spent much of his life
fighting Indians on the screen: "I don't feel we did wrong in taking this
great country away from them. There were great numbers of people who
needed new land, and the Indians were selfishly trying to keep it for
themselves." The movies are after all an expression of the dominant
culture. Consequently the Indians are invariably viewed, whether sympathetically or not, from the point of view of the victorious pioneers and
their White Anglo-Saxon Protestant society. When serious doubts arise
about this culture, however, the Indian will be viewed in a different light; I
shall be touching later on the gradual movement in this direction.

But in passing, one should perhaps say something about the neglect in
the American cinema of the plight of the contemporary Indian. There have
been moving but evasive accounts of the sad lives of the Olympic athlete in
Thorpe (*Jim Thorpe, All American,* of 1952, with Burt Lancaster as
Thorpe) and the World War II hero Ira Hayes (*The Outsider,* 1961, starring
Tony Curtis). Occasional TV documentaries have exposed the Indians'
situation, and in 1962 there was Kent McKenzie's *The Exiles,* an unsatisfactory study of the pathetic, *déraciné* Indian poor in Los Angeles, which had
its moments but suffered from the director's inability to get his nonprofes-
sional cast to act out their lives in a convincing fashion. More recently there
has been Carol Reed's *The Last Warrior* (1970), about Indian resistance on
a deprived present-day reservation; this well-intentioned film went
disastrously astray through the unbridled performance of Anthony Quinn
doing another of his boozy, outsize, life-force figures, in this case a sort of
Arizona Zorba the Greek. This should be a growth area in the Western
genre; the material for a potential masterpiece is lurking there, waiting for
the right artist to shape it. However, the fact that Indian tribes in New Mexico are now financing movies doesn't necessarily mean that the pictures they
back will be revolutionary in character. On the contrary, current projects
suggest that they're putting their money into conventionally conservative
Western fare.

Still, my real concern here is with the treatment of Indians in Western
movies, which is a complex enough subject in itself, if admittedly trivial
when set alongside what is happening in the slums and reservations of contemporary America.

Two dominant traits during the fifties and early sixties were, on the one
hand, the role of the Indians as an external force in uniting Americans and,
on the other, the cultural clash between pioneer and redskin. In pictures as
crude as John Sturges's *Escape from Fort Bravo* (1953) and as subtle as
Sam Peckinpah's *Major Dundee* (1965), we have seen murderously divided
parties of Northern soldiers and their Confederate prisoners drawn together
in a new sense of national solidarity in the face of Indian attack. This has
become almost a cliché. The other category is more interesting: those

movies that deal with whites living among Indians and Indians (usually, but not always, half-castes) attempting to get along in white society. The major examples of this species are John Huston's *The Unforgiven* (1960) and Don Siegel's *Flaming Star* (1960), where white families stand together to protect an adopted Indian sister (Audrey Hepburn in *The Unforgiven*) and half-breed brother (Elvis Presley in *Flaming Star*) from rejection by white society or reclamation by the redskins. Thematically they are declarations in favor of the American melting pot; dramatically they are a recognition of the profound difficulties and personal tragedies involved in the process of assimilation. A far more complex approach to similar issues is to be found in Robert Mulligan's *The Stalking Moon* (1968), an extraordinarily ferocious metaphysical Western with a strong Lawrentian undertow, in which a retired cavalry scout (Gregory Peck) and an unseen Indian chief struggle for the allegiance and cultural identity of the Indian's mute, half-breed son. I mention Lawrence here because few films so directly bring up the issues he raised in his *Studies in Classic American Literature* and few pictures have so consciously exploited the naked power of the symbolic Indian.

An emphasis rather different from that of *The Unforgiven* and *Flaming Star* is revealed in pictures about white settlers embarking on expeditions to regain members of their families captured by Indians—films that are testimony to the fragility of white civilization. These pictures raise the questions: Can the prisoners, even if located, be rehabilitated? Will the seekers themselves remain the same? In the last couple of years some optimistic answers have been given to these questions. But in the fifties there was an underlying anxiety about them, and they are to be found at the center of John Ford's *The Searchers* (1956), a film of great charm and much crudity dominated by the cultural assurance of John Wayne, and the same director's *Two Rode Together* (1961), where Ford took a more pessimistic view of the effects of captivity but at the same time showed more sympathy for the captors and the culture into which the white women and children had fallen. I don't think one is reading too much into these pictures in seeing them as expressing deep fears about the possible breakdown of American society in the face of an underlying drive toward anarchy and disintegration—a feeling that the inhabitants of America have a tenuous grasp upon their continent.

One significant direction of the Western during the postwar period and increasingly in the sixties lay in setting movies at the very end of the frontier period, and thus confronting the old virtues of the West with the corrupt values of the burgeoning twentieth-century commercial civilization. This was taken to its extreme in William Fraker's *Monte Walsh* (1970), in which the aging cowhands are presented quite explicitly as victims of anonymous corporations ultimately controlled from Wall Street. In most of these films Indians in their post–Wounded Knee subjugation are notable by their absence. The only significant Western dealing centrally with the Indian during this post-frontier period is Abraham Polonsky's *Tell Them Willie Boy Is Here* (1969), which tells the true story of a Paiute outcast who in 1909 was hounded to death in a chase across Southern California by a posse of vindictive whites after the accidental killing of his prospective father-in-law. It is played out against a backgound of unyielding racial intolerance and social indifference, as well as the concurrent visit to the West by President Taft which led to insane rumors of assassination threats and of a massive Indian uprising.

The Indian as perennial outsider—as represented by *Willie Boy*—is not a new theme in the Western. One can go back to a picture that appeared in the same year as *Broken Arrow* to find the Indian presented in terms of parity with Mormons, fugitive gunfighters and traveling entertainers, as social outcasts within the implied framework of an intolerant American conformity; this picture is John Ford's *Wagonmaster*. More recently we have seen Martin Ritt's *Hombre* (1967), whose eponymous white hero (Paul Newman) has been reared as a child by Indians, has grown to manhood in white society and subsequently has elected to live as an Indian. Nothing is vouchsafed to us about his Indian background; its honesty and superiority are assumed and considered to be beyond question. When eventually he finds himself a lonely brooding figure in a decaying pioneer community, he serves dramatically as an unimpeachable moral center from which the film judges, and ultimately condemns, his white companions. In some ways he resembles Norman Mailer's concept of "The White Negro" and inevitably he has to die. *Hombre* is an extraordinary landmark in the development of the Western. An equally pronounced example, and a rather comic one, of the way attitudes toward Indians have changed over the past couple of decades is found in comparing Shelley Winters's response to the same situation in Mann's *Winchester 73* (1950) and Sydney Pollack's *The Scalphunters* (1967). In the earlier film she is a young pioneer wife trapped with a cavalry patrol by an Indian war party. As the Indians prepare for their final assault James Stewart slips her a gun. Contemplating a fate worse than death, she nods in stoic recognition and, referring to the final bullet, she says, "I understand about the last one." As a blowsy, bighearted whore in *The Scalphunters,* she quite happily quits the company of the uncouth, ill-smelling outlaws with whom she has been traveling to go off with her handsome Kiowa captors. "What the hell, they're only men," she shrugs—and reflects that the Indian chief is going to get "the damnedest white squaw in the Kiowa Nation."

Implicit in these pictures is the view that Indians are neither a deadly menace nor an alien culture that makes life uneasy for its neighbors. From this position it is a relatively short move toward seeing what can be learned from them, and only another step to viewing them as an alternative culture or counterculture. This was proposed back in 1957 in Samuel Fuller's didactic *Run of the Arrow,* which centers upon an Irish-Southerner (Rod Steiger) who fires the last shot at Appomattox and, refusing to accommodate to post–Civil War life, goes West to undergo the painful initiation that will make him a full member of the Sioux nation. Reluctantly he is won back to white civilization by a Northern cavalry officer who gives him a glib lesson in American history, and the picture concludes with the admonitory title (replacing "The End") "The end of this story can only be written by you." It is characteristic of Fuller, incidentally, that at one stage of the picture he identifies the troublesome young Sioux braves with present-day American juvenile delinquents.

Run of the Arrow anticipated by a decade several of the most ambitious works of the past few years—and a social trend among the young that has filled the avant-garde bookshops from San Francisco through London to St-Germain-des-Prés with books on Indian history. In the theater we've seen Arthur Kopit's play *Indians* (1968) and in the cinema Elliot Silverstein's *A Man Called Horse* (1969), Ralph Nelson's *Soldier Blue* (1970) and Arthur Penn's *Little Big Man* (1970). Each of these pictures, in varying ways, presents Indian life as a valid counterculture—a more organic, life-enhancing existence than white society—from which the central character of each gains a new perspective on society and a new humanity. In the case of *A Man Called Horse,* he's an English nobleman (Richard Harris) who is revitalized by a peculiarly grueling sojourn among the Sioux; in *Soldier Blue*, an American girl (Candice Bergen) becomes an incredibly articulate critic of her culture (as well as an unbelievably foulmouthed one) after her period of captivity among the Cheyenne; in *Little Big Man*, a picaresque hero (Dustin Hoffman) drifts back and forth between his adoptive Cheyenne family and a corrupt white frontier society. All three films are less inhibited in their acknowledgment of the brutal aspects of Indian life than the earlier liberal movies that argued their case for mutual respect, tolerance and peaceable relations.

Indicative of their closeness to contemporary concerns is the fact that both *Soldier Blue* and *Little Big Man* offer direct parallels with the Vietnam situation, and perhaps even with My Lai, in their presentation of cavalry massacres and the deliberate policy of exterminating Indians. Both are unsparing in their fashionable attacks on white "civilization," which they see as hypocritical, barbarous and death-seeking. There are token "good whites" to be sure, but the films' central thrust is directed against the ideology and behavior of a whole society. (*Soldier Blue* handles the material with bludgeoning crudity and *Little Big Man* with feeling and subtlety, but the general drift is much the same.) In the introductory sequence to *Little Big Man,* in which the 121-year-old narrator is encouraged to reminisce by a present-day historian, the term "genocide" is openly used to characterize the nineteenth-century treatment of the Indians. This contemporary framework makes possible what a few previous pictures have only been able to imply. In Richard Brooks's forceful *The Last Hunt* (1956), for example, we had a pathological Indian-hater (Robert Taylor) bent on exterminating the remaining herds of bison. "One less buffalo," he says, "means one less Indian." *The Last Hunt,* a box-office disaster in its days, would no doubt be welcomed now as a significant ecological Western. Again, in John Ford's *Cheyenne Autumn* (1965) there's a clear comparison made between the persecution of the Indians and the German extermination camps in the performance of Karl Malden as Captain Wessells, a rigidly Teutonic commandant of a grisly prison in which the remnant of a decimated Cheyenne tribe is briefly incarcerated. But *Little Big Man* presents the issue directly as the shame of a whole society and its almost conscious policy.

Little Big Man also manages for the first time to give a major role to an Indian actor in casting Chief Dan George as Dustin Hoffman's Indian "father," Old Lodge Skins. Previously star Indian roles and even minor speaking parts of any importance have invariably been assigned to white actors; indeed it was only a chance last-minute decision to cast Chief Dan George. The film has also gone some way toward finding a satisfactory dramatic language for the Indians, and Dan George manages to avoid the customary unctuous solemnity of movie Indians. The result is not entirely satisfactory, but a move in the right direction. The alternative, I suppose, is subtitles. In Raoul Walsh's *A Distant Trumpet* (1964), subtitles were used, and they at least give the Indians the dignity and respect that attaches to foreigners and the prestige of subtitled European movies; few filmmakers have resorted to this device since, though there is the odd case of *Texas Across the River* (1967), a feeble comedy Western, one of the better touches of which was to have the Indians speak in their native tongue and provide unintelligible subtitles in the form of Indian sign language.

Little Big Man, with its beautifully realized evocation of Cheyenne life, is perhaps the present high-water mark in the treatment of Indians in the movies, as well as being a major satirical comment on the values and appeal of the Western genre. Nevertheless it is still open to the accusation of manipulating the Indians according to the political ideas and unconscious cultural predilections of its makers. The charge has been made that the Cheyenne in *Little Big Man* are less Indians than New York Jews, and there is a good deal to be said for this view. Indeed, at the end, when Old Lodge Skins fails to bring about his ritual, ceremonial death on a hilltop outside his village, he stands up, dusts himself off and stoically observes, "Well, sometimes the magic works and sometimes it doesn't." We should of course remember that it was the belief of Joseph Smith and the Mormons that the Indians were in fact Jewish, the descendants of the lost Hebrew tribes. ●

15

Rita Keshena in "The Role of American Indians in Motion Pictures" suggests what is perhaps the only solution to the constant misrepresentation: Indian people themselves must learn the skills of the visual media and offer an alternative to the Hollywood Indian.

THE ROLE OF AMERICAN INDIANS IN MOTION PICTURES

RITA KESHENA

AMERICAN Indians have played a part in motion pictures from the time the flickering light came out of the inventor's workshop in the last decade of the nineteenth century up to the present day. It is not likely that Indians will be abandoned as a source material in the future. To understand what "part" Indians played it is necessary to have some knowledge of the way in which the motion picture industry developed.

The flickering light in the darkened room moved from the experimental stage to its present state of proficiency under a variety of names: Moving Pictures, The Picture Show, Silents, Talkies, Movies, and now, more esoterically (elevated to the rarified atmosphere of an art form), Film—or, even more elitist, Cinema. But what had begun in the clinical air of the laboratory soon took to the streets and the carnival midway, where it gained instant popularity.

The response of the early audience can only be called primitive. The first reaction was characterized by open-eyed wonder, awe, fascination, and delight. The enchanted eye of the masses was not confused by any critical faculties of evaluation, selectivity, or judgment of the content of the Magic Lantern offerings. Not then.

A minority view of the new device among literate people—intellectuals and academicians—was one of disdain and disregard. Whereas such enlightened viewers might have recognized the significance of this new form of mass communication and made use of it for serious purposes, they showed no such perceptivity. Instead they remained aloof from one of the most effective means of communication ever developed by a technological society, secure in their conviction that those dimly lighted, jerky images would remain a sideshow attraction.

From *American Indian Culture and Research Journal* 1 (1974): 25-28. Reprinted by permission.

COMMERCIAL VENTURE

Among the less informed, however, fascination with the new medium increased. The initial childlike response of excitement was heightened with every offering of the peep show, and people everywhere demonstrated an insatiable appetite to be entertained. The time was ripe for the entrepreneur. As a result, The Picture Show became a commercial venture pandering to public demand as evidenced by box-office receipts, devoting its efforts almost entirely to fanciful flights from reality in order to satisfy the need to be entertained.

What was it that satisfied the paying customers and brought them back again and again, eager for more? From its inception the motion-picture industry of this country capitalized on the naiveté of the majority society. In a frenzied rush, moviemakers began to give the public what it wanted. Comedy, romance, drama, action, violence, brutality, pathos, sex, savagery, and history were combined in varying proportions to give each plot a slightly different twist and lure the customers back to their nickel-and-dime dreams. The demand soon focused on the re-creation of a past that never existed and on a future in which good triumphed and everyone lived happily ever after. Always there emerged the dominance, righteousness, and supremacy of the Anglo American—the white man.

Nowhere did the necessary ingredients for commercially successful movies come together with greater impact, action, pageantry, and excitement than in the motion-picture history of the American West: the vast expanse of the rugged land, the hardy pioneer spirit of the early settlers, the massed defenders in cavalry blue, the lone defender in the white Stetson hat—the epitome of strength, goodness, and all-American masculinity—the cowboy; and the savages, the uncivilized red niggers, the embodiment of all that was evil. The formula was worked and reworked. Audiences clapped and cheered as the cowboys triumphed and the Redskins died.

The market for the new medium and its representations of Indians and Indian life did not diminish over the years; indeed, the public's appetite could not be satisfied. Every aspect of human experience was painted red, topped with a braided wig, and rushed out to the distributors.

STEREOTYPES

Records of the film industry reveal that thousands of films have been made about American Indians. The part that the Indian played was clearly defined. Stereotypes were established and constantly reinforced, reel after reel, year after year. Moviemakers focused on the tribes of the Sioux and the Apache, who thus became the white man's Indian, molded and cast in the white man's mind as he wanted them to be, but projected before the viewer's eye as convincingly authentic. Indians from all tribes were cast in the image of a rearranged reality. The prototype of the Hollywood Indian was treacherous, vicious, cruel, lazy, stupid, dirty, speaking in ughs and grunts, and often quite drunk.

The stories for movies were always written by white men, produced and directed by white men, and almost always performed by white men covered by Max Factor's Indian Tan. There is truth to the story that some non-Indians have played Indians so often in the movies that they have moved into the Indian community with their assumed Indian identities and become outspoken experts for the Indian world. A sadder truth is that had American Indians been employed in all the movies ever made about Indians, poverty among Indians would have disappeared. Moviemakers have even complained that they are unable to find any "real" Indians to fit the movie parts. But in making this complaint, Hollywood denies the fact that it is the "parts" and not the Indians that are unreal. In the important creative and production areas of the motion-picture industry, American Indians have been excluded entirely.

The history of Indian people in the motion-picture industry is analogous to the larger history of the American West—indeed, to that of the entire continent—a long chronicle of exploitation, distortion, denigration, debasement, denial, and deceit. When the public delighted in the representation of Indian people as savages, moviemakers obliged and collected their profits. When the public mood became more conciliatory, under the threats and acts of violence from some segments of minority communities, motion pictures began to give different representations of ethnic peoples, and American Indians were suddenly made in another image: nobility and injustice became dominant themes, and filmmakers rushed once again to give the customers what they wanted.

The white-liberal colony of Hollywood pounced on this new cause. Moreover, World War II and television changed the habits of a lot of people, who stopped going to movies so often. Besides, many of the old formulas simply didn't work anymore. It was time to change. So Jeff Chandler immortalized Cochise. John Ford, Hollywood's great Indian killer of epic proportions, eulogized the Cheyenne with the help of Sal Mineo. Richard Harris, elegant and aristocratic, was stolen by the Sioux. But what a lucky catch! He showed the Sioux how a real leader runs the show, before riding back to civilization. Candy Bergen writhed across the West to expose, among other things, the brutality of the cavalry, as naked Chicano women, cast as Indians, splattered across the screen.

In an interview, Arthur Penn told how he had entered into the Indian mind in order to create the definitive Indian film, *Little Big Man*. His prancing, mincing, homosexual character came straight from the plains of Hollywood Boulevard. The cultural patterns and sacred beliefs of the Cheyenne were traded in for low comedy and cheap laughs. "Sometimes the magic doesn't work." Crow women were characterized as depraved and perverted.

An alienated, impressionable audience swarmed in to see *Billy Jack* do his leg work and defy the establishment. All the necessary ingredients again combined to ensure box-office appeal. In an earlier time, Billy would have been cast in the face and figure of James Dean, another romanticized rebel with whom young dissident whites could identify. But Indians are, you know, like, in, and uprising. It may be of some interest to note that, since Billy never mentions his tribe, he apparently does not know where he belongs and is, therefore, undeniably illegitimate.

A Norman Jewison production, *Billy Two Hats,* starred Gregory Peck and was shot on location in Israel, with Jews playing Indians. Somehow no one was ever able to work the bugs out of that one, and it disappeared soon after release. A look at part of the background of this ill-fated film is illustrative of the way Hollywood handles the majority of motion pictures concerning American Indians. In the preproduction stage, the director, Ted Kotcheff, a Canadian Jew, was approached about the possibility of using an American Indian consultant to authenticate the Indian aspects of the film. Discussions with Kotcheff revealed that the script was in the final stages, with shooting scheduled to begin in three weeks in Israel. After briefly outlining the plot, Kotcheff said he did not know the time period ("about 1895 or so"), the setting ("somewhere in the southwest, yes, the desert"), or the tribe ("ah, yes, well, probably Apache for the woman, and of course, her older son is Cree"). The script made no reference to these things. The script did include, however, a story line at total variance with any history, tribal or white. American Indians were presented in complete distortion.

EXPLOITATION

Because of budget limitations, Kotcheff refused to consider an American Indian consultant and then noted that he was hiring several Indian actors, who could serve in the dual capacities of performing and advising. The clear exploitation of such an arrangement was not pointed out to Kotcheff at the time, but it was suggested to him that the reality of filmmaking does not permit extras to question or differ with the director, provided that they want to keep on working. Furthermore, it was highly unlikely in any event that Indians, whether actors or not, would intrude in and interfere with the actual process of filmmaking even if they did know something was inaccurate. Certainly no film director was going to check out all the Indian aspects in every scene with some Indian extras. To obtain any degree of accuracy and authenticity, the easiest solution would have been to engage an American Indian for script consultation at the outset.

The reaction of Kotcheff can only be likened to the histrionics of a Grade B Quickie, probably a musical, *circa* 1948, in the scene where the theatrical genius asserts his authority. The dialogue began on a disappointingly dated note.

KOTCHEFF [*heatedly, increasingly agitated*]: How dare you come in here and take up my valuable time to tell me that I don't know Indians and infer that I lack sensitivity or awareness about minorities. How dare . . .

There followed a long recitation of his impeccable credentials of involvement with social causes and prominent liberals, stopping just short of the banks of the Fish-In in Washington State. Emphasis was made that in this film injustice would be presented as universal in its application, since there are, in actuality, no ethnic differences in people, there is only the shared human experience. And—

KOTCHEFF [*icily*]: You have taken up enough of my time. My lunch is waiting. Get out.

The End.

The critical and commercial failure of this film may or may not have been determined by the manner in which the American Indian segment was handled. Nor is it only incidental to note that Ted Kotcheff is a Canadian Jew who learned his craft with the BBC in London: after the abysmal failure of *Billy Two Hats,* Kotcheff went on to make a film about a young Jewish hustler from Montreal that has received wide critical acclaim. The inference cannot be mistaken. One can only wonder at the response had someone suggested that an American Indian make the Montreal film—with or without a Jewish adviser.

In all the films that have been made and are being made by the film industry, issue cannot be taken with the presentation of stereotypes and historical inaccuracies alone. Motion pictures are guilty of almost total distortion of American Indians and their culture, the presentation of which has contributed harm beyond calculation to the concepts, attitudes, and beliefs that Indian people have about themselves. What may seem to some people only an innocent, entertaining motion-picture show is for American Indians a destructive weapon in the continuing War of Termination being waged against them.

PROFIT-MAKING

The profit-making and exploitative aspects of the industry cannot be overemphasized. How familiar the announcement by major producers, directors, and writers sounds, whenever a high-budget, star-studded production about American Indians is in the planning stage. Research, authentic re-creation, and the use of "real" Indians are to be incorporated into the project. Despite these preproduction announcements, the indisputable evidence of deceit is projected in the final product.

Such "lip service" is neither incidental nor a result of scholarly or humanitarian motivations. It is another aspect of the industry: publicity. In the fiercely competitive business of moviemaking and selling, the "art" of selling appears to have outdistanced the creation of movies. Firmly rooted in the marsh of fickle fantasy, the industry takes every precaution to protect its investment and show a profit. Cinema has never quite risen above the sweaty smell of the midway and the sound of the honky-tonk spielers. "Step right up" has given way to press conferences and announcements, premieres and previews, awards and film festivals. Ballyhoo and come-ons have been laundered and placed behind paneled walls and doors marked "Public Relations." But it's the same old baloney. And the continuing interest in the American Indian as a film subject is unmercifully exploited in order to heighten box-office appeal. "The End"—on and off screen— remains unchanged. Another Redskin bites the dust. Buried with him are truth, accuracy, and preproduction promises.

HOLLYWOOD

The continuing story of Hollywood and the Indians has taken a new turn with a recent announcement by Marlon Brando. (Certainly no one denies that Brando has shown concern with issues and problems in the Indian world. However ill-advised, he has attempted to focus attention on the exploitation of American Indians by the film industry. Nevertheless, it was predictable, and ironic, that his effort to that end at the Academy Awards ceremony in 1973 resulted in attacks of a personal and professional nature by his peers. The truth of his advocacy was drowned in a cacophony of catcalls.) Brando will play the role of a lawyer in a proposed new film based on the current happenings at Wounded Knee. The script is being written by Abby Mann, a Jewish writer with impressive credentials, including an Academy Award for *Judgment at Nuremberg.* But when questioned about the proposed film by the *New York Post,* Abby Mann said, "Marlon called me. I knew nothing about Indians. I was totally ignorant about them. . . ."

The *New York Times* has reported that Brando is chairman of a newly formed organization, the American Indian Development Association, which will sponsor self-help projects for Indians. Proceeds from the proposed Wounded Knee film will be donated to this organization. Brando's plan is more than commendable: it is unique. For the first time, someone in the motion-picture industry plans to enter into profit-sharing with the Indian community.

As American Indians, however, we cannot look to others to change the distorted image that has been projected for the past eighty years by a money-hungry industry. Real change will come only when Indian people become knowledgeable in the methodology of film and television. We must step out of the role that Hollywood has given us and take up positions in the important areas of creativity and production. Only then will we be able to control the way in which we are presented on film.

Given the chance to learn the required skills and techniques of the visual media, as well as the means to transfer the Indian experience into a filmic one, American Indians would be able to offer an alternative to the Hollywood Indian.   ●

John Cawelti, professor at the University of Chicago and specialist in American civilization, has written that contemporary films about Indians represent almost a complete reversal of some of the symbolic groups in the Western. The pioneers, for example, become "symbols of fanaticism, avarice, and aggressive violence, while the Indians represent a good group with a way of life in harmony with nature and truly fulfilling to the individual." Even the cavalry, long the representative of law and order, becomes the "instrument of brutal massacre."

16

REFLECTIONS ON THE NEW WESTERN FILMS: THE JEWISH COWBOY, THE BLACK AVENGER, AND THE RETURN OF THE VANISHING AMERICAN

JOHN G. CAWELTI

AT the present time, the emergence of a new attitude toward the Indian in films like *A Man Called Horse, Soldier Blue,* and *Little Big Man* seems important as the impetus behind a new vision of the meaning of the Western experience. Since the time of James Fenimore Cooper, the serious Western has often manifested a sympathetic attitude toward the Indian and has at times been openly critical of the way in which Americans have treated him. But, until recently, this sympathy has usually been focused for dramatic purposes on the tragedy of individuals.

Two main story formulas would probably cover most of the serious representations of Indians in the Western until the past decade or so: the elegy of the Vanishing American, or the Last of the Mohicans, and the tragedy of the white man who loved an Indian maiden or vice versa.

In both these stories the central point of sympathy was the plight of an individual caught in a larger clash between groups. The striking thing about the more recent Indian Westerns is that they move beyond sympathy for the plight of individuals toward an attempt at a reconstruction of the Indian experience itself. Their central plot device has been the story of the white man who becomes an Indian or who, through his experiences, becomes identified with the Indian perspective in the clash between white and Indian.

From *The University of Chicago Magazine* 65 (January–February 1973):25–32. Reprinted by permission.

THE PIONEER AS "BAD GUY"

In effect, this amounts to an almost complete reversal of some of the symbolic meanings ascribed to major groups in the Western. The pioneers become a symbol of fanaticism, avarice, and aggressive violence, while the Indians represent a good group with a way of life in harmony with nature and truly fulfilling to the individual. It is through his involvement with the Indians and their way of life that the hero is regenerated. The cavalry, symbol of law and order, becomes the instrument of brutal massacre until, at the end of *Little Big Man,* one cheers for the Indians to destroy Custer and his men because we have seen incident after incident in which the cavalry callously and needlessly slaughtered women and children.

This new Indian Western is clearly a response to that complex new fascination, particularly among the young, with traditional Indian culture, that Leslie Fiedler analyzes in *The Return of the Vanishing American.*

In its treatment of violence as an expression of aggressive drives toward destruction in the pioneer spirit, in its negative and guilt-ridden assessment of the winning of the West and its reversal of traditional valuations of the symbolic figures and groups of the Western story, this new formula has a great deal in common with another recent form which I have labeled, rather facetiously, the legend of the Jewish cowboy. The hero of this type of Western is not literally Jewish, though often played by Jewish actors like Paul Newman. Actually, I suspect that Jews are likely to be the last of the ethnic groups to insist on donning the mantle of the cowboy hero.

However, the heroes of *Butch Cassidy and the Sundance Kid* and *McCabe and Mrs. Miller* behave more like characters transported from the pages of a novel by Saul Bellow or Bernard Malamud into the legendary West than they do like the traditional Western hero. They win our interest and sympathy not by courage and heroic deeds but by bemused incompetence, genial cowardice, and the ability to face the worst with buoyancy and wit. They are six-gun schlemiels and existentialists in cowboy boots. The West they inhabit is rapidly becoming the modern industrial world and they are hopelessly out of place in the new society.

Their real enemy is not the Indian or the outlaw but the corporation. They stand for a leisurely traditional way of life which is giving way to the ruthless mechanical efficiency of the corporate society. Butch Cassidy is an outlaw who is finally driven from the country by the irresistible force of organization in the form of a superposse hired by the Union Pacific Railroad. McCabe is a small-time gambler and brothel keeper, who is eventually killed by a gang of thugs hired by a mining company which wants to take over his property.

THE CORPORATE VILLAIN

The new myth implicit in these Westerns contrasts the individualistic violence of the outlaw or Indian with the brutal streamlined force of organized society and expresses the view that the corporate violence of modern society is more dangerous and evil than the acts of individual ag-gression implicit in the Indian or outlaw's way of life. Thus many of the traditional meanings of the Western are reversed—society cannot be purged or regenerated by heroic acts because progress means destruction of humane values. The good groups are the simpler traditional societies of outlaws and Indians, but these, and the values they represent, are doomed to extinction. The true hero is not the man who brings law and order but the alienated and absurd individual who cannot fit into the new society.

PROJECTION OF TENSIONS

All three of the new Western types I have discussed—the Italian Western, the Western Godfather, and the search for a new myth—share a disillusioned and pessimistic view of society and an obsession with the place of violence in it. As the Western has always done, these new formulas pro-ject the tensions and concerns of the present into the legendary past in order to seek in the imagination some kind of resolution or acceptance of conflicts of value and feeling which cannot be solved in the present.

The Westerns of the post–World War II period seemed to reflect a general consensus of affirmation that the country, having survived the perils of depression and war, might now go forward toward the creation of a better social order. The Westerns of today, however, suggest no such con-sensus. Instead they seem to reflect a considerable variety of different emo-tional and ideological accommodations to the pessimism about society which they all share.

Three major kinds of attitude seem to have emerged: first, a sense of human depravity and corruption which seems almost to take delight in the destructiveness of violence by accepting it as an inevitable expression of man's nature; second, the fantasy of a superior father-figure who can pro-tect the innocent and wreak vengeance on the guilty, a fantasy which reflects a profound disbelief in the modern agencies of law and justice to serve their proper function (in this context, violence is the product of morally purposeful individual action in defense of the good group against the threats offered by the rest of society); and finally, the search for a new Western myth expresses the view that violence has been the underlying force in the development of American society and that all modern white Americans are implicated in guilt for their aggressive destruction of other ways of life.

The contemporary Western reflects the conflict between these differing views of our past and present. Whether any of them will eventually serve as the basis of a new consensus about our society only the further course of history can determine.   ●

4

**PHOTOGRAPHIC ESSAY ON THE
AMERICAN INDIAN AS
PORTRAYED BY HOLLYWOOD**

THE PHOTOGRAPHS in this section, reproduced here with the permission of the Museum of Modern Art/Film Stills Archive in New York, are but a limited selection of the visual images that have been presented on the screen. Early movies, relying on literary precedents from the savages of James Fenimore Cooper to the romantic figures of Helen Hunt Jackson, presented these authors' conflicting views. Soon, however, and up to mid-century, producers discovered that the savage Indian drew more crowds. With *Broken Arrow* in 1950 the pattern appeared to be changing and producers were accused of being too soft on Indians. Looking back, it is obvious that the changes were not dramatic. Indian characters continued to be played by non-Indian actors, and Tonto was still the sidekick for the Lone Ranger. In the 1970s a new type of Western emerged, called the anti-Western by some critics. The heroic Custer of *They Died With Their Boots On* was transformed into a vainglorious fool in *Little Big Man,* and early treatments of a heroic Buffalo Bill and Wild Bill Hickok were satirized in *Buffalo Bill and the Indians.* Indian life on the screen has been and continues to be artificial and unreal, yet it is these visual images that have "educated" a nation about its own history. ■

In *The Last of the Mohicans* (1920) the Indian was
portrayed as barbaric and given to excessive drinking;
his behavior was tolerable only because he was
childlike and simple. In this version of Cooper's
novel, Wallace Beery played the role of Magua.

Ramona, based on Helen Hunt Jackson's sympathetic treatment of the American Indian, was first issued in 1910. There were four subsequent versions—in 1914, 1916, 1928, and 1936. Here the young Ramona was played by Loretta Young and her lover by Don Ameche.

In the 1936 release of *The Last of the Mohicans,*
Cooper's novel was again resurrected for the screen.
White women's virtue was threatened by the ignoble
redskin.

Gary Cooper portrayed Wild Bill Hickok in *The Plainsman* (1937), a fantasy set after the Civil War in which gunrunners were selling repeating rifles to the Indians.

In *They Died With Their Boots On* (1942), the
audience was treated to a romantic view of the defeat
of Custer by Sitting Bull. Errol Flynn portrayed a
heroic Custer who valiantly gave up his life for his
country.

Buffalo Bill, the hero of the Wild West shows,
became the hero of movies as well. In 1944 Joel
McCrea and Anthony Quinn starred in *Buffalo Bill,*
another version of the heroics of the legendary hero.

The balance between civilization and barbarism was
the main theme of *Arrowhead* (1953) in which
Charlton Heston portrayed a white man and Jack
Palance an educated Indian who went on a rampage
when he returned to the reservation with an eastern
education.

In *Taza, Son of Cochise* (1954), Jeff Chandler played a
dying Cochise who passed the leadership role on to
his son who was played by Rock Hudson. Despite
professed changes in the industry after 1950, Indian
roles continued to be played by non-Indians.

In radio serials, in movies, and later in television, the Lone Ranger and Tonto have been familiar figures for the past fifty years. Ralph Friar calls Tonto an "Indian Stepin Fetchit" whose only purpose was to serve his white master.

Sal Mineo was repeatedly featured by the studios as Indian. Here he appears in *Tonka* (1958).

How the West Was Won (1963) was an epic treatment of America's idealization of its history.

Little Big Man (1971) has repeatedly done well with the critics. It provided an example of the anti-Western, exposing the disparity between the real West and the fantasized West. In this reversal of the Hollywood Western, white civilization was corrupt and hypocritical.

Ethnographic accuracy was the focus of *A Man Called Horse* (1970), but inaccuracies continue to be pointed out. The attempt to reverse roles did not solve the problem of stereotyping.

Robert Altman's *Buffalo Bill and the Indians or Sitting Bull's History Lesson* (1975) satirized the inaccurate portrayal of American Indians, returning to the legend-maker Buffalo Bill and debunking the heroes of the famous Wild West shows.

5

CONTEMPORARY REVIEWS

I N THE EARLY 1960s films began to exhibit a confusion about portraying Native Americans, and the industry's concerns have been reflected in the reviews of those movies. Increasingly reviewers have called into question the stereotypes and misconceptions about the Indians appearing on the screen. Contemporary reviews demonstrate this heightened awareness as well as the persistence of the Hollywood images.

What follows in this section is a sampling of the academic and popular reviews of a selected list of films dealing with the Native American and suggesting a number of interesting and significant changes in the portrayal of the Indian. The first three essays provide an overview of the most important contemporary films that treat the Native American. They are followed by reviews of the individual films themselves.

It becomes clear after reading the criticism on the Indian in film that reactions differ depending on the expectations of the critic or viewer. Some look for accuracy in the portrayal of cultural ways and artifacts; others are more concerned with the actors and actresses. But what they are all saying amounts to the same thing—the American Indian has been and continues to be stereotyped. The stereotypes will no doubt continue as long as the Indian is portrayed only in his adversary role in nineteenth-century America.

These recent reviews and the contemporary criticism make it clear that a reassessment of the Native

American in the movies necessitates a revision of the entire myth of the West. Pro-Indian films of the early seventies such as *A Man Called Horse, Soldier Blue,* and *Little Big Man* suggest the potential for a new way of viewing the place of the Native American in American history and American society, but Hollywood, creator and purveyor of myths, has yet to present accurate and truthful images of the Indian. The most recent hope for a change in the portrayal may be with films such as *One Flew Over the Cuckoo's Nest* in which Bromden's Indianness, although significant symbolically, is somewhat accidental. Unfortunately, what the movies most often portray are "the pretend Indians." ■

A frequent reviewer for *Film Society Review* and *The Village Voice,* Dan Georgakas in "They Have Not Spoken: American Indians in Film" discusses four of the "new" Indian films: *A Man Called Horse, Soldier Blue, Little Big Man,* and *Tell Them Willie Boy Is Here.* He too criticizes the neglect of Indians as "serious subjects in themselves." He recognizes, as does French, that the Indians often serve as substitutes for Vietnamese, Blacks, or the youth culture.

17

THEY HAVE NOT SPOKEN: AMERICAN INDIANS IN FILM

DAN GEORGAKAS

THE American Indian has been an essential dramatic ingredient in Hollywood's epic of the West, and a key element in the vision of America and its destiny embodied there. Whether we take the Indian's role as that of the abominable id—a projection of the bestiality white culture could not face in itself—or as a stand-in for the hostile "nature" that Americans thought they could overcome, it is hardly surprising that with the turmoils, reevaluations, and rebellions of the sixties a different image of the Indian should have begun to emerge in American films. Recent Indian films make a point of advertising their sympathy for the Indian point of view. Generally "real" Indians play all minor Indian roles and occasionally even major speaking parts. At first sight, no effort seems too great to obtain an aura of authenticity in regard to speech, music, customs, and history. Usually white guilt is admitted through the device of at least one rabid saliva-at-the-mouth racist ready to command a massacre of a sleeping village. This beast is contrasted to the dignified Indian spokesman who is invariably peace-minded. Such an approach is an improvement over the grunts and howls of an earlier period but only at the lowest level: the new films tell us very little about the Native Americans and even less about ourselves and our own history.

A MAN CALLED HORSE

On the surface, Elliot Silverstein's effort, which uses some five hundred Sioux actors, might seem the most authentic of the recent films. The Sioux language makes up 80% of the dialogue, the impressive Sun Dance ceremony is a central plot element, and all the action takes place within an Indian environment. The headdresses, dwellings, artifacts, masks, and ceremonial paint are as genuine as research can make them. The only trouble is that all this authenticity is an illusion and a waste. The film is a fantasy from start to finish.

The year is 1825 and Lord Morgan (Richard Harris), an English aristocrat on a hunting expedition, is captured by a Sioux band led by Yellow Hand (Manu Tupou). The Englishman is not treated as a human being but as a horse. He is given to Yellow Hand's harridan mother, Buffalo Cow Head (Dame Judith Anderson), who ties him to a stake. This is all wrong. The Sioux had a tradition of hospitality toward strangers. Anyone so odd looking as the yellow-haired pale-faced Wasichu (a term for Europeans that had no racial overtones) would be treated with great curiosity and respect, much as Lewis and Clark had been treated a decade earlier. Even if the encounter had turned hostile, there would not be torture and the kind of abuse shown for that was not the Sioux way. The idea that a man should be tied up and treated as an animal is something that might have occurred to the New England Puritans but it was as far from Sioux thinking as hunting for pleasure instead of need.

The Englishman learns the ways of the Indian slowly and Silverstein comes up with an interesting device in handling the transition. The Indians speak only Sioux and Morgan-Horse speaks only English. A captive French half-breed (a European designation, by the way) supplies minimal translations and interpretations of strange acts. This de-emphasis on dialogue makes the kind of demands on a director the silent screen once made and calls attention to the Indian trappings. One almost wishes there was no dialogue at all for almost everything the half-breed says is nonsense.

Horse's moment to impress the Sioux comes when a group of Shoshone creep up on the camp when the warriors are absent. Horse slays the intruders and is immediately elevated to human and warrior status. This dramatic turnabout would be likely, as Sioux placed importance on what individuals did and most likely would have interpreted Horse's actions as having the favor of the spirits. That Yellow Hand's daughter, Running Deer (Corrina Tsopei), falls in love with Horse is also credible as the Sioux were a romantic people and the strange white warrior who might possess special magic would be an extremely attractive figure.

But to establish full membership in the tribe, Horse undertakes the Sun Dance ceremony, and here the film is simply sacrilegious in terms of Indian beliefs. The Sun Dance was not designed to show individual courage to other men or to win a bride. The Sun Dance was the highest religious rite of the Sioux. In it, a man proved his humility and worthlessness to the spirits by mortifying his flesh. Elaborate purification rites were absolute prerequisites as a successful dance might bring a vision of use to the entire tribe. Skewers were fastened under a man's flesh and he attempted to pull loose by dancing. The pain was caused by his own acts and the onlookers pitied him and encouraged him with song and music, praying he would have an important vision. (Sitting Bull performed the Sun Dance before Custer's attack. He lost some sixty pieces of flesh but had a vision which foretold the coming triumph.) In *Horse* the ceremony is reduced to a primitive sadistic test of courage in which the vision is a delirious by-product.

Naturally, Morgan-now-Horse is successful in the Sun Dance and marries Running Deer. He sees this as another step toward his escape. His problem is cut short by a massive Shoshone raid. Again the film falls apart historically. The men of the plains never waged war in European fashion; small bands went out to steal horses or to fight small engagements more akin to duelling than war. The highest honor was to "count coup," which was to touch a living opponent still surrounded by his fighting comrades with a ceremonial stick shaped like a shepherd's staff. Killing an enemy was a less important coup. In *Horse*, the Shoshone attack like U.S. cavalry. Horse-still-Morgan saves the day when he lines up the tribal youth in English archery rows and their arrows cut down the Shoshone who attack like the Light Brigade itself. Yellow Hand dies in the battle and tribal leadership falls to Horse. Running Deer also dies conveniently but Horse shows his sensitivity to his new post by taking the harridan Buffalo Cow Head as his own mother. She waits for spring to die so that he can have good weather for his return to England.

Rather than a tale of Indian life, *Horse* is thus really about a white nobleman proving his superiority in the wilds. Almost every detail of Indian life is incorrect. An angry Sioux writing to the *Village Voice* complained about the treatment of the Sun Dance. He also noted that the Sioux never abandoned widows, orphans, and old people to starve and freeze as shown in the film. He points out that the cuckold husband in the film would not have lamented as shown but would have wiped out his disgrace by charging ten enemies single-handed. The writer adds that even something as simple as kissing on the lips is incorrect, for the custom did not come to the Sioux until mid-century. The list of such mistakes and inaccuracies is as long as the film itself.

Stripped of its pretentions, *Horse* parades the standard myth that the white man can do everything better than the Indian. Give him a little time and he will marry the best-looking girl (a princess of course) and will end up chief of the tribe. It is also interesting that Yellow Hand and Running Deer look very European while some of the nastier Indians are darker with flat features. Sioux features in fact did range from Nordic to Mongol and their color from white to copper red, but this case seems the usual pandering to ideas of Anglo-is-beautiful.

The Sioux were called the Vision Seekers because they placed so much importance upon receiving communications from the spirits in the form of visions. They were cheerful people, very fond of jokes, games, and romance. Above all, they liked to feast, dance, and sing. None of this comes through in *Horse.* Even the use of the native language becomes a handicap, for eloquence was another Sioux characteristic. Without their own words much of the beauty of their way of life is lost. The half-breed's silly interpretations should be compared to some of the speeches of the Sioux holy man Black Elk to see how much as been lost.

You have noticed that everything an Indian does is in a circle, and that is because the Power of the World always works in circles, and everything tries to be round. . . . The sky is round and I have heard that the earth is round and so are all the stars. The wind, in its greatest power, whirls. Birds make their nests in circles, for theirs is the same religion as ours.

SOLDIER BLUE

Ralph Nelson's version of the Indian massacres is an obvious commercial rip-off on the new sympathy for Indians. Instead of the dirty Injuns making dastardly attacks on helpless whites, it is the cavalry that makes dastardly attacks on helpless redskins. The director relies totally on explicit scenes of carnage for his argument and effect.

The film opens with a payroll detachment of cavalry ambushed by Cheyenne seeking gold to buy guns. The sole survivors are Honus Gant (Peter Strauss), a naive young soldier blue, and Cresta Lee (Candice Bergen), a woman who has just been released by the very band which has staged the ambush. The couple start the long trek back to the main army unit and encounter the gamut of wilderness perils. Cresta shows far more skills than simple simon Honus. She sweats, belches, and seduces while slowly convincing Honus that the white-men are much more murderous than the Indians.

The Indian lore in the film is spotty. One pleasant surprise is Cresta's admission that Spotted Wolf has released her because he could not make her happy. Many Apache warriors claimed they would not have sex with a woman captive until they had "won her heart." Chief Joseph of the Nez Percé stated that in his long war with the whites no women were ill treated. Such intriguing claims may yet undermine the image of the raping savage that is imperative to any racist mythology. Unfortunately, the virtue of the Indians in *Soldier Blue* is only a device to be set against the lusty soldiers who are bent on raping everything that walks.

Naturally, Honus must fight a duel with an Indian. Naturally he is victorious—for nowhere in film history does an Indian win one of these duels, though they are supposedly part of his culture. The victim in this case is one of three Kiowa who come upon Cresta and Honus. Good Honus cannot bring himself to kill the warrior after beating him, but one of the other Kiowa does the job for him out of disgust for his comrade's defeat. This is Hollywood Indian myth at its most flamboyant. War parties were almost always made up of relatives and close friends. The other Kiowa would not have killed their companion but would have waited to relate how he had wiped out the disgrace by some brave deed in another battle or duel.

Honus and Cresta are eventually separated, but they make their individual ways to the army camp. Cresta finds the colonel there is planning to massacre her former tribe and she rushes off to warn them. Honus does not believe the attack will occur until it actually takes place. The attack itself outdoes the many previous violent scenes by several tons worth of blood and torn limbs. Nothing is left to the imagination. Heads get chopped off and breasts sliced away. Blood and brains splatter in slow motion. Children are tossed about on bayonets. Women are raped, then mutilated. The mayhem is so grisly that it loses its effect, seeming more like a comic book than a genuine slaughter. The victims seem unrelated to the idyllic Cheyenne laughing and playing in the village shortly before the attack. Honus is outraged and rebels. He gets put in chains for his troubles. Cresta takes a Cheyenne child in her arms and goes into captivity with the survivors.

Nelson writes that he got ideas for his film by reading of the massacre at Sand Creek and making a connection with war crimes in Vietnam. Nothing so complex comes over on the screen. Colonel Iverson (John Anderson) is a maniac. His soldiers are beasts. Obviously these whites are insane. There is no question of land, skins, reprisals, or what Black Elk called "the yellow metal that makes Wasichus crazy." There is only an irrational kill instinct that horrifies the "real" white society represented by Honus and Cresta.

Nelson's use of violence for its own sake causes him to lose at least one important visual effect. At Sand Creek, Chief Black Kettle rode out to meet the soldiers waving a huge American flag given to him at a meeting when he was promised the land would be his "as long as the grass shall grow and the rivers run." The scene is shown in *Soldier Blue* but given the clichés surrounding everything else, the sight of the American flag trampled beneath the hoofs of advancing cavalry becomes the shallowest of social comments.

Had Nelson done his research more zealously, he could have produced an even more revolting scene as an anti-climax. The "real" Colonel Iverson was named Chivington, an intinerant preacher, and the assault troops were not regulars but civilian volunteers. When the battle was over, the victors and their preacher leader took their scalps, heads, arms, and other trophies to a large Denver music hall. There the show was stopped and the stage cleared so that the men could parade their souvenirs to the wild applause and cheering of the entire audience.

LITTLE BIG MAN

Arthur Penn takes a longer and more sophisticated road to dish out the same conclusions as in *Soldier Blue*. His Chief Old Lodge Skins says that everything is alive to the Indian but everything is dead to the whites. Thus the massacres are once more reduced to racial mania unconnected with social or economic considerations. Even the defeat of Custer becomes personal rather than social. Custer is an insane egocentric general who seems to know that his charge will fail. The Custer with one eye on the Democratic National Convention, the Custer who had political supporters drumming up votes at that convention, the Custer who counted on the public's partiality to successful generals, the Custer who had taken mineralogists, reporters, and miners into the Black Hills—that shrewd Custer is lost. We have only another insane Iverson commanding more soldier blues.

Penn chooses the form of the comic elegy, a tall tale told by 121-year-old Jack Crabb (Dustin Hoffman), the last survivor of Custer's Last Stand. The conception of Crabb is interesting. Unlike the typical Western hero who serves the interest of "progress" (expansion) in one form or another, Crabb just wants to survive. Captured by Indians, he becomes an Indian just as later he will be gunman, medicine seller, hobo, etc. He is Everyman and lives out various lives of the West with frequent returns to the Cheyenne and Chief Old Lodge Skins. It is through this character that for the first time an Indian speaks with more than grunts. The chief is played by Dan George of the Salish and is so much the ideological center of the film that it seems impossible that Penn originally wanted Sir Laurence Olivier or Paul Scofield for the role and indeed at one time had cast Richard Boone. The notion of these fine but very Anglo-Saxon actors playing the stoic and gracious chief who is the repository of Indian lore reflects a cheapness in Penn's conception. This cheapness surfaces on various occasions. When the chief is enjoying a good pipe, there is a hip suggestion that the old boy is smoking grass. His farewell speech to earth is made into a joke. Even more misleading, the chief's reference to the Cheyenne as "the human beings" leaves the idea that the whites must be something less. Actually, almost all tribes referred to themselves as "the people" or "the human beings"; the names we know them by are usually names given by their enemies. Similarly the often used "It is a good day to die" is not personal idiom but the standard phrase used by plains people to bolster their courage in a tough spot.

Penn does break through to some new ground in a scene toward the end of the film. The chief has become blind and is sitting in his tepee prepared to die because a battle is raging outside. Crabb convinces the chief he has become invisible, and the old man chortles and laughs, completely delighted with his invisibility as he walks amid the struggling Indians and soldiers. Penn also goes out of his way to explain what counting coup means and to note other Indian customs accurately.

Penn's use of a homosexual Sioux is far less successful. The homosexual is an offensive limp-wrist drag queen from a Manhattan Hallowe'en ball. The people of the plains had reverence and fear of homosexual men. They lived in special parts of the village and warriors might live with them without loss of dignity. At certain times, the homosexuals were sought out to perform specific rituals and other times they were studiously avoided. All this is lost between flittering eyelashes and a lispy come-into-my-tepee-sweetie performance.

The warrior who does everything backwards is another bastardized conception. He is the most disagreeable of the Indians and for some reason is shown as the slayer of Custer. Such men were usually charged with keeping camps cheerful with their jokes. Special backward ceremonies were also common to emphasize the power of the circle and to note the two faces of reality.

Backward warrior and homosexual aside, because Penn allows the audience to know the Cheyenne, their slaughter is far more horrible than that in *Soldier Blue,* even though the scenes are less brutal. The Indians' right to strike back militarily at the Little Big Horn doesn't have to be argued. (The parallel with Vietnam is strong. Crabb's wife has distinct Asian features and there is no trouble in imagining a chat between Uncle Ho and Old Lodge Skins.)

Yet, all too conveniently, *Little Big Man* is two movies in one. One paints a sympathetic picture of Indian life and the other is a crude burlesque of the white West. Nowhere is there a clash of real values. We identify with the Indians because they are nice. We are not troubled with problematic things like ownership of skins, minerals, and land. The Indians held the land was owned communally and could not be bought or sold. Their lives emphasized spiritual over material things. Their fights were matters of individual fame-seeking rather than politics and economics. Their communal way of living with reverence for all life made their way incompatible with the "manifest destiny" of the young American republic. Like *Soldier Blue, Little Big Man* fails to deal with these questions as it moves simplemindedly from massacre to massacre.

TELL THEM WILLIE BOY IS HERE

Based on actual events in California, *Willie Boy* marked the return of Abraham Polonsky to Hollywood after twenty years on the blacklist. The story is set in 1909 after the defeat of the Indians but at a time when war chiefs such as Joseph and Geronimo were still alive and warriors who had fought the cavalry were still alive to teach the young. In spite of this, Indian ways were dying. The Indian Bureau had outlawed use of Indian religion, language, dress, hairstyle, and customs. They penned the tribes on reservations, then whittled down their size each year. A few Indians had adjusted and become like whites. Most had fallen into despair, poverty, disease, drunkenness, and often suicide. Some like Willie Boy found new ways to rebel.

Polonsky only touches on the outlines of Willie's rebellion but we know he is not a "good Indian." Willie (Robert Blake) has been to a reformatory. He has a fight with pool-hall racists. He is taciturn and the audience quickly recognizes in him the alienated, isolated twentieth-century rebel hero. His life is rubbed out for the most trifling of circumstances. An Indian father forbids Willie to see his daughter. They meet and make love. The irate father intervenes with weapons and Willie has to kill in self-defense. He takes his woman and begins a flight that he, the girl, and the audience immediately understand must end in death.

Fate seems to be Willie's worst enemy. President Taft happens to be visiting in the area. The national press corps plays up the "Indian outbreak" and the possibility of presidential assassination. Old Indian hunters get out their knives for one more scalp. The local lawmen fall over themselves to prove the West is as lawful and orderly as the East. Posses chase the fleeing couple and in due time, Sheriff Coop (Robert Redford) takes up the hunt personally.

Polonsky goes out of his way to underline the equality of Coop and Willie. Their handprints in the mud match. The muffled sex cries of their women mingle on the screen. Coop respects his prey and would prefer not to hunt him, but like all white screen sheriffs he is better at the Indian game than the Indian. After cornering his man, the sheriff offers a rifle duel which Willie accepts even though he has no bullets—the suicide of the modern existentialist.

Actually, aside from some comments on how Willie is a great runner and woodsman, his Indianness is only a device. He might be a Black or rebel white youth. The other Indians are faceless, opinionless men. They help neither the sheriff nor Willie. When one Indian-hating sheriff is killed by Willie, they are pleased. When Coop allows them to burn Willie's dead body Indian-style, they are equally pleased. They are divided over the mysterious death of Willie's woman. One thinks she has killed herself to let Willie escape. Another thinks Willie has had to kill her himself so she would not be captured. Neither alternative is as likely as that the woman would have attempted to stay hidden and if captured would wait until the warrior came for her. Such common sense is very much in line with Indian thinking and very much out of line with Hollywood Indian mythology.

Such misconceptions are less critical than the mistaken inter-changeability of Coop and Willie. They seem so alike their roles could be reversed. But this is a contemporary myth element; it didn't hold in 1909. Willie was a lone rebel from a defeated civilization suffering profound cultural shock. Coop was one of a people still fresh from the conquest of a continent. He could offend politicians and reporters when it came to the matter of Willie's burial but not in the matter of his survival. Their duel was not the apparent man-to-man struggle seen on the screen. Coop has traced his prey through the aid of the telegraph and the train and the printed map and the Indian informers and the gangs of white men waiting at every possible escape point from the wilderness. Like the Nez Percé pursued by seven different regiments over fifteen hundred miles, Willie is not defeated by valor but by logistics. The liberal/radical Polonsky can afford to posit his antagonists as equals but it is not so.

Polonsky and the other directors have doubtless worked with as many good intentions as any Hollywood production allows, but they have only done a facelifting on the old Cowboys & Indians bit. The grunting, foul-smelling savage may never ride again, but it will be some time before the Native Americans are treated as serious subjects in themselves rather than as stand-ins for Vietnamese, Blacks, or youth culture. But their challenge to the screen remains and becomes more acute year by year: understanding the nature and depth of the crimes against the native Americans is essential to understanding where the United States has been and where it is going. The Indian has always been the white man's mystic enemy, dreaming dreams and living lives the whites have never dreamed or lived. Standing Bear of the Sioux spoke of this antagonism near the end of his life some four decades ago. His words seem as valid now as then:

The white man does not understand the Indian for the reason that he does not understand America. He is too far removed from its formative processes. The roots of the tree of his life have not yet grasped the rock and soil. The white man is still troubled with primitive fears; he still has in his consciousness the perils of this frontier continent, some of its vastness not yet having yielded to his questing footsteps and inquiring eyes. He shudders still with the memory of the loss of his forefathers upon its scorching deserts and forbidding mountaintops. The man from Europe is still a foreigner and an alien. And he still hates the man who questioned his path across the continent. But in the Indian the spirit of the land is still vested; it will be until other men are able to divine and meet its rhythm.   ●

18

Susan Rice laments the contemporary views of the Indian in what she refers to as *Cinema Rouge*—the Indian Film. She discusses *A Man Called Horse, Soldier Blue, Flap,* and *Little Big Man* as attempts to "square things with the Indians," which did not work. Only in *Tell Them Willie Boy Is Here* does she find a "meaningful" film about American Indians.

AND AFTERWARDS, TAKE HIM TO A MOVIE

SUSAN RICE

Lo, the poor Indian! whose untutored mind
Sees God in clouds, or hears him in the wind;
His soul, proud science never taught to stray
Far as the solar walk, or milky way;
Yet simple Nature to his hope has given,
Behind the cloud-topt hill, an humbler heaven;
Some safer world in depth of woods embraced,
Some happier island in the watry waste,
Where slaves once more their native land behold,
No fiends torment, no Christians thirst for gold.
To be, contents his natural desire,
He asks no Angel's wing, no Seraph's fire;
But thinks, admitted to that equal sky,
His faithful dog shall bear him company.

—ALEXANDER POPE
("An Essay on Man," 1733)

THE simultaneous praise and condescension, admiration and pity that characterize Pope's assessment of the Indian are not really that different from the portrayals we have witnessed the last year—which may be remembered in cinema annals as The Year of the Indian. Like student revolutionaries, Blacks and the Women's Lib, the media have chewed up the minority view and spat it out again, barely reconstituted. The Stanley Kramer approach to Problem Areas—middlebrow, Middle American, middle-of-the-road—has resulted in a series of cipher films; movies that neither move us, sharpen our perceptions, nor sensitize us to the subtleties of the issues at hand . . . for there are no issues at hand.

The confusion of guilt, gilt and gelt in the minds of American filmmakers is nothing new. In fact, these very attitudes have provided a treasure trove of kitsch culture, for the pretentious breast-beating of one generation becomes the Camp comedy of the next. And, ironically, the inadvertent

From *Media and Methods* 7 (April 1971): 43–44, 71. Reprinted by permission.

parody often becomes the true social document. The Black chauffeurs and servants of the 1940s horror films, the Amos and Andys and Aunt Jemimas of the same era are more telling records of white attitudes toward Blacks than the devout preachments of *The Defiant Ones, Pinky* or *Black Like Me.* Despite a raft of guilt-ridden films treating the *Jewish Question—Gentlemen's Agreement, The Last Angry Man, The Pawnbroker,* to name a few— none of them can really represent the issue they purport to treat because they beg the very Question. They are the serious-minded depositions of the victims themselves; testimonials to Jews by Jews. The strivings, desires and values of the Jewish immigrant are probably more evident in the Wasp fantasies churned out by movie studios under the control of Harry Cohn, Louis B. Mayer and Max Laemmle. Likewise, the most valuable records of American chauvinism vis-à-vis the Indian are preserved in countless tiny time capsules like *Broken Arrow* and *Son of Cochise.*

I am not suggesting that the asylums be run by the inmates. The chances of racial qualifications, aesthetic competence and social consciousness being in the same place at the same time are equivalent to contracting the right scenarist, the right cameraman and the right director. Getting a Black man to direct a film about blackness is no insurance of its success on any level. Melvin Van Peebles botched it with *Watermelon Man* by intensifying odious stereotypes out of his bitterness. Ossie Davis used humor and a natural locale with *Cotton Comes to Harlem* and succeeded at creating both comedy and social document that had something significant to say about Black life-styles in the seventies. John Boorman, who is white and British, made a very eloquent statement about white guilt and futility of attempting to assimilate romanticized ghetto hedonism in *Leo the Last.* No one could have predicted the success or failure of any of these vehicles on the basis of the conjectured sensibilities of the men who made them.

Which brings me to the subject of the Indian Film (*Cinema Rouge*)— what is wrong with it and what might be done about it. Last year, American filmmakers flanked the Indian on several sides. The subject has been treated comically, romantically, mythically, contemporaneously and historically. In attempting to reexamine these films now, two things occur to me. The first is that all but two of them have almost faded from my memory, leaving only a bitter aftertaste. The two I can recall— *Tell Them Willie Boy Is Here* and *Little Big Man*—I will revive briefly for the purposes of this overview.

A Man Called Horse was the first certifiably self-conscious film by a major company that set out to "present the Indian in a new light." Like *Little Big Man,* this film employs a transracial operation to get inside the soul of the noble savage. Richard Harris plays a British scout who is captured by a tribe of American Indians and schooled in their ways. His point of view is the aesthetic vehicle through which we are expected to peer at the Indian and life on the reservation. Unfortunately, the character Harris plays is vacuous and so is the narrative voice. The vision served up here does not differ radically from the hackneyed varia of the familiar cowboy and Indian genre. Even the finale—the ritualized acceptance of Harris as a Brother and—lo!—his elevation to Chief—seems a not so subtle confirmation of implicit white superiority. Wouldn't acceptance have been enough?

The facet of this film that its makers prided themselves on, and the aspect of it that was purported to distinguish and elevate it, was *authenticity*. Even the drawings on the tepee were accurate. But most genuine of all was the reenactment of the ''Vow to the Sun''—a trial by ordeal which qualified the participant as a True Brave. I cannot help but believe that this sequence—a spectacularly repellent ritual depicted graphically and in every painful detail—is the film's essential reason for being. Is this bizarre anthropology supposed to be didactic? What does this kind of voyeurism do for non-Indian audiences? Does it garner respect? Or does it simply reinforce our preconceptions about primitive natures, about the untutored mind which ''proud science never taught to stray''? What bearing does the rehearsal of this gruesome ritual have on our attitude toward the contemporary Indian? Better yet, what possible effect can ''new respectability'' like this have on Indians themselves? As spurious as this scene is, I suspect that its impact is even less insulting, less pernicious than the thinly veiled suggestion of white supremacy. In the course of the film, it is implied that Richard Harris is cannier, more resourceful and, finally, sexier than the denizens of his adopted culture. The Indians need him to survive. This ironic twist undercuts any of the film's pretensions to a new humanized approach to the Indian myth.

Although I am not a subscriber to the *auteur* theory of film criticism, I think I am safe in assuming that *Soldier Blue,* a movie that I haven't seen and don't want to, follows in the tradition of bludgeoning sensibility that director Ralph Nelson has established in his former films (*Lilies of the Field, Charly, tick . . . tick . . . tick*). Like *A Man Called Horse, Soldier Blue*'s big selling point was primarily sadistic, but instead of individuated torment, *Soldier Blue* offered a whole galaxy of massacre, a slaughter that promised to be bloodier and gorier than any previously staged in film. The only still photograph I saw featured Candice Bergen cradling a severed arm. I think there are levels of self-punishment that even a movie reviewer can be permitted to bypass, and this struck me as one of them. Squaring things with the Indian by staging an epic catharsis seems to me a little like the German film industry making a series of ghastly concentration camp films, recreating all the horror and inhumanity of that period for contemporary German audiences to lose themselves in and repent for. How would we respond to that tack? With something like ''What moxie! Do you really think you can take yourself off the hook by reenacting your crimes, with guilt rather than genocide as your motive?'' Which suggests, in turn, that these movies cannot be made by the perpetrators at all; that to make sense the stage must be set by an objective hand, a spectator rather than a participant. Ralph Nelson, no matter what his stated good intentions, mixes the grisliness of slaughter with the attendant thrills. The revulsion we feel is intimately connected with fascination. And in films like this what compels us is the spectacle of blood rather than the moral stance. If, as in *Bonnie and*

Clyde and *The Wild Bunch,* our own duplicitous fascination with violence were made clear to us in the course of the action, a movie like *Soldier Blue* might be laudable. But that is far too complex a sentiment and too sophisticated a creative attitude to expect of a director of Nelson's stature.

There is very little to say about a movie like *Flap,* except that its style of fictionalizing a contemporary situation manages to romanticize it, to make it laughable. The makers of this film made their intentions explicit: "*Flap* is dedicated to the unassailable fact that the contemporary Indian has been woefully neglected in this country." When that Indian is portrayed as a buffoon, a bumbling primitive (as Anthony Quinn depicts Flap), one begins to wonder if neglect isn't preferable, which is a startling by-product for such lofty motives. The comedy of *Flap* is based almost entirely on the slurs that are commonly directed at Indians. Haven't we had enough jokes about firewater? What is missing from this film—with its failed color, high spirit and gusto—is the pathos and impoverishment of contemporary life of Indian reservations. There is not real despair here, just hokey protest. There is no need to burlesque a situation that, quite simply, cries out to be documented. Most Americans have no idea of the conditions under which the few surviving Indians live; their inability to identify as white or red. When I was in the Southwest I saw pueblos in which there lived only very old men and women and infants. The colorful Indian artifacts were J. C. Penney blankets and plastic bowls. To make this world material for comedy, to dress it up, glamorize and ridicule it is nothing less than criminal. *Flap* relegates the Indian to the position of an Uncle Tonto. Which is how it all started anyway.

I think *Tell Them Willie Boy Is Here* made the plight of the contemporary Indian much more meaningful, much more touching, even though it is set at the turn of the century. Though *Willie Boy* suffers many of the flaws that working within the framework of myth and allegory invites, it is a dignified, principled movie that evokes a thoughtful, contemplative response. In many respects, this film managed to engender a sense of pursuit and persecution without stressing *action.* Character transcended event. Robert Blake's Willie Boy is willful, intelligent, courageous. Robert Redford's reluctant Sheriff cast a new light on the Western hero and reversed the standard operating procedure between cowboy and Indian, without denying either of these characters their manhood or nobility. Both represent standard epic qualities: Redford is silent, strong, calculating; Blake impetuous, explosive, athletic. But as Abraham Polonsky wrote and filmed them, they were simultaneously adversaries and heroes; "society" was the villain. Unfortunately, Polonsky's "society" lacks depth—it is represented by a series of predictable stock characters who seem even more clichéd because they operate in a world that also houses the multi-dimensional Willie Boy and Sheriff Cooper. What is sublimely right about this film is its mood, and that is a hard thing to talk about. The reason I like it so much is that it takes a very hot subject, a very emotional theme and treats it with cool restraint. The color is soft; the editing fluid, leisurely; the score is subtle, primitive but not pounding. These are not the qualities we have come to associate with the cowboy vs. Indian genre. New styles applied to familiar material have a way of making people think differently about things they feel they know about. I respect Polonsky's film because it respects its audience. *Tell Them Willie Boy Is Here* appeals to the mind rather than the gut and it adds the dimension of humanity to myth.

And that brings me to *Little Big Man,* whose fault is its primarily visceral appeal; there isn't very much to think about although the film has the trappings of significance. The unifying device is the narrative of Jack Crabb, the only survivor of the Battle of Little Big Horn and a white man who has been shuttled between Indian and white worlds. (Oddly, Thomas Berger uses the first-person narrative unselfconsciously in the novel; in the film, it is awkward.) Crabb is not a hero in the usual sense; he is not a man of action, but a picaresque character who undergoes changes, who is buffeted about by circumstance. Penn places him in two diverse contexts: one comic, almost mock-heroic, the other panoramic and horrifying. As in *Bonnie and Clyde*, Penn attempts to mingle bathos and pathos to trigger some new insight, to reinterpret legend. *Little Big Man* aspires to fashion a revolutionary view of history with the white man as villain, the traditional myth figures (Custer and Wild Bill Hickok) corrupted, and the savage Indian reemerging as true aristocrat and philosopher. Like many revolutionary statements, this one is counterproductive by its own excess. The comedy fails and the genocidal massacres are confusing, even repetitive. And like so many of its forerunners, *Little Big Man* does not so much depict the Indian as translate him from the point of view of the white man. Chief Lodge Skins refers to his race as ''human beings,'' but nothing in the film gives us real insight into these human dimensions. The greatest failure of *Little Big Man* is that it does not deliver any new data concerning Indian civilization, culture and ethic. Despite its pretentions, it is another adventure story, another perpetuation of the standard Indian myth.

To succeed, must these films be made by Indians themselves? I think not. Flaherty did a reasonable job on Eskimos, albeit with a documentary approach. What is perverse in the American film industry is its extremes. The director hurdle is not the only one to leap over. I am convinced that if one of the major companies were to undertake a biography of Buffy Sainte-Marie they would get Judy Collins to star in it. While I think that Dustin Hoffman is a reasonable choice for *Little Big Man* (on the other hand, I don't think you have to lose your grip over Chief Dan George—A REAL INDIAN—in the same film. I don't want to be arch, but what evidence do we have that this is, in fact, a *performance*? Pasolini uses nonprofessionals in his films, but I doubt they would garner Best Supporting Actor Awards on the basis of their believability. This may be a story for another time, but it seems to me that several instances of performance are necessary before one can judge an actor. The brouhaha over Dan George seems to me to be another installment in the Big Parade of Guilt; the wide-screen version of Take an Indian to Lunch. Was it really *that* great, that touching, that demanding, that fluid a performance? Is a craggy face, a substantial presence a performance, or is it set decoration?) That was a long parenthesis. As I was saying, Hoffman seems right. But aren't the economics that motivate the choice of an "ethnic" like Anthony Quinn (who has been variously Italian, Greek, American and Tiresome) as the drunken Indian in *Flap*, Katharine Ross as the Indian maiden in *Willie Boy*, and Dame Judith Anderson as the village eldress in *A Man Called Horse* a little undermining? In a sense, doesn't this neat Anglo-Saxon overlay negate the high principles of the filmmakers and doesn't it work in a subtle, racist way on the sensibilities of the people who see these movies? Isn't this a means of making "Indian" films not only sellable but *acceptable* to mass audiences? Aside from being exploitive, I think these tactics are self-defeating in that they are admissions that the *issues* themselves are not enough to interest the paying public. The portrayal of social justice, such as it is, must be buttressed by production values, such as they are. And this is the factor responsible for the specious effect of these movies: in the name of moral restitution, they simply reshape the stereotypes and caricatures of Indians that Hollywood fostered in the first place.

It wouldn't surprise me at all if the first significant feature film about the Indian— a film that treats the history, the myth and the man—be made by a non-American. It may take a foreign sensibility to represent us to ourselves.   ●

Richard Schickel discovers the depiction of Indians in some
current American movies including *Ulzana's Raid* and *The
Stalking Moon* to be far more interesting and provocative
than that contained in the more highly touted *Little Big Man*
and *Soldier Blue* which try to prove a doubtful thesis about
white man's impulses toward genocide. The conflict between
the Indians and their white foes seems to him to have been an
inevitable one and one that offers rich possibilities for filming. He calls for filmmakers not to fall mute at a time when
there are increasing opportunities to explore beyond a superficial excitement. As film critic for *Life* and *Time* and the
creator of the television series *The Men Who Made the
Movies,* Schickel is familiar with the trends as well as the
history of his subject.

19

WHY INDIANS CAN'T BE VILLAINS ANY MORE

RICHARD SCHICKEL

I was happily watching *Ulzana's Raid*—a modest
and excellent cavalry-and-Indian Western—on its network television
premiere the other night when it occurred to me that it is probably a movie
of far greater historical significance than its producer-director, Robert
Aldrich, or its star, Burt Lancaster, intended it to be when they made it in
1972. I don't mean merely that it came out better than most genre pieces do
(though it did) and I'm not predicting that it will develop a cult following.
No, the gloomy thought that stole over me as I watched grizzled scout Lancaster guide a troop of cavalry in pursuit of a renegade (and mercilessly
sadistic) Apache band was that it is probably the last movie of its kind that
will ever be made.

Indeed, as of this moment, *Ulzana's Raid* is precisely that—the last
movie in which the soldiery and the savages had at one another, with no lib-
eral-minded questions asked. Nor do I know of any plans (or secret desires)
to make such a movie. It is simply—and really quite suddenly—all over for
one of the classic screen forms, a form that can trace its history back at least
as far as D. W. Griffith's *The Battle of Elderbush Gulch* in 1913, an epic
form that was central not merely to the careers of many of the directors one
most admires but to the entire experience of growing up a moviegoer in
every decade since the teens of this century.

As a matter of fact, I do not believe it possible today to make a film
that even implies the historical existence of the concept of the white man's
burden, let alone one that seems to endorse it. Certainly it would be out of

From *New York Times* (February 9, 1975), Section 2, pp. 1 and 15.
Copyright 1975 by The New York Times Company. Reprinted by permission.

the question to make a movie in which whites are seen to do if not just, then justifiable, battle with persons of a non-Caucasian persuasion. If such conflicts are ever again seen on screen they will be used to "prove" that we—the whites—have been, since the beginning of time, in every clime, genocidal in our racism. (Ralph Nelson's *Soldier Blue* and Arthur Penn's distortion of Thomas Berger's *Little Big Man* are two films that seemed determined to illustrate that dubious thesis.) In short, not only would *Fort Apache* be impossible to place in production today, so would *Gunga Din* and *Four Feathers* and *Zulu* and literally hundreds of other entertainments we once thought of as innocent and, broadly speaking, historically accurate.

One does not have to look much further than *Ulzana's Raid* to see why, in the seventies, such films are, as it were, beyond the paleface. The tracking party here is under the nominal command of a callow lieutenant, a minister's son (Bruce Davison), who, at the beginning of the mission, tries to understand why the veterans among his party are so callous—and vicious—in their attitude toward the enemy.

After he's followed Ulzana's trails for a while—and found nothing but murder, rape and torture of the vilest variety—he switches his line of inquiry. Why, he keeps asking, are the Apaches so entirely lacking in humane virtue? Again, the answers are less than satisfactory: a harsh land has bred a harsh "life-style" (as we would now put it): an Indian acquires "power" from a fallen foe and the more slowly and painfully he dispatches him, the better his chances of soaking up each restorative drop of the stuff. This point of view, of course, seems nonsensical to the minister's son (and to us, who can only see these particular renegades as psychopathic children).

If *Ulzana's Raid* stops short of suggesting that it was our Christian duty to either kill or convert such madmen, it certainly implies—as most Westerns (and Far and Middle Easterns) of its type have—that the white invaders represent order, the savages a peculiarly unsettling kind of anarchy. Thus, a moral dimension is added to the white audience's natural identification with its on-screen representatives.

It is, to the modern liberal, an intolerably intolerant message. We are painfully aware of the century and more of maltreatment the Indians have endured on their reservations, the colonial repression suffered by others throughout the world who have not had the good luck to share our color. In this context, isn't *Ulzana's Raid*—or anything resembling it—deplorably regressive, even reactionary? So it would seem.

Still, one can't help but wonder if this Mafia-like policy, which insists that we (the whites) only kill each other, is really healthy. Movies (and television, too) must offer their audiences a high percentage of action drama; it is the only imperative the nature of these media dictates. Therefore, in the past couple of years we have had an extraordinarily large number of police dramas, in which the "others"—the villains—are ethnically and racially indistinct, or at least "uncontroversial" (remember that connection was *French*). More recently, we have had the villainless (and dismal) disaster movies, in which either nature or inanimate things cause all the trouble, and in which the minority-group actors are always precisely as brave as whichever WASP has top billing.

In a way, of course, the refusal to see an Indian or a Black or an Oriental in anything less than a favorable light is as much a put-down as the old implicit suggestion that they are all basically volatile children. Total goodness is also less than human—and less than thought-provoking, too. In fact, *Ulzana's Raid,* like 1969's *The Stalking Moon,* which also featured an Apache of no redeeming social value by modern standards, seems to me a vast improvement on those Westerns in which Indians were not permitted to be responsible for their own actions, their brutal behavior being "explained" as retribution for the trickery of whiskey peddlers or gun traders or what have you.

In these newer films, however, the Indians are at least permitted the dignity—and the mystery—of their otherness; their brutality makes no sense to us, but, obviously, it did to them, and perhaps it's best to leave it at that. These films at least suggest, if they do not fully explore, the true dimensions of the tragedy enacted on our western plains in the nineteenth century. What was going on out there was not a conflict analogous to some Balkan border dispute, to be settled by drawing lines on a map at a peace conference attended by people operating on essentially similar assumptions. It was, it seems to me, a truly unavoidable cultural conflict, a conflict between civilizations so disparate that it is impossible to imagine how a peaceful compromise might have been arranged between them—even if the theater of war had been more narrowly confined, more neatly divisible, than it was.

I don't wish to be held responsible for whatever crimes the white man committed in the course of that ancient, extended guerrilla conflict any more than the modern Indian wants to be held responsible for his ancestor's depredations. (It ought to go without saying that one does feel responsible for doing what one can to end current injustices.) I think we have to assume, however, that the white audience will have no difficulty understanding that times have changed, that there is no analogy to be made between Ulzana ravaging innocent people and one of his descendents demanding restitution of the land or the rights that our forefathers ripped off his forefathers.

I think all of us are capable of confronting our shared history frankly, of reaching a purely aesthetic judgment of the quality with which that history is symbolically represented in a fictional form. What is stupid is silence, the cowardly avoidance of what remains one of the richest sources of spectacle available to film, the bloody but authentically tragic conflict between the races as it was enacted on "frontiers" all over the globe in the last century.

As things now stand, we have fallen mute at precisely the moment when some filmmakers, like Robert Aldrich with *Ulzana's Raid,* were beginning to perceive, however crudely, that there were possibilities within this material not just for the superficial excitement of melodrama but for a somewhat more interesting ambiguous and resonant drama.   ●

In this review V. F. Perkins describes the way the studios reduced the impact of *Cheyenne Autumn* by eliminating the moral development of the film and substituting action so that it could be released as an "epic" film. The basic theme of the film, an "attempt to impose an inhuman discipline on a deep, anarchic emotion," is developed in the metaphor of the Indians being forced to submit to the orderly patterns of an alien culture which results in the near destruction of the native population. Ford, in his treatment of the Western myth, exposes its falseness and moral destructiveness as a guide for cultural action. Mr. Perkins is a film scholar and author of *Film as Film*.

20

CHEYENNE AUTUMN

V. F. PERKINS

JOHN FORD'S name traditionally heads the list of artists who have managed to integrate themselves into the Hollywood machine and function successfully as creative filmmakers, within its commercial structure. Ford himself has never seen it that way. As early as 1936, he made a public statement of his discomfort: "It's a constant battle to do something fresh. First they want you to repeat your last picture. . . . Then they want you to continue whatever vein you succeeded in with the last picture. You're a comedy director, or a spectacle director, or a melodrama director. You show 'em you've been each of these in turn, and effectively, too. So they grant you range. Another time they want you to knock out something another studio's gone and cleaned up with. . . ."

His film reveals with depressing clarity the nature and extent of the restrictions which the industrial system places on personal communication. Its relative, and glorious, failure demonstrates the contradictions inherent in the commercial machine and exaggerated by its current *modus operandi.*

The story of the Cheyenne nation's fifteen hundred mile trek from the government reservation in Oklahoma back to its Yellowstone homeland had long fascinated Ford as a potential movie subject. He made several unsuccessful attempts to set it up as a medium budget production. Eventually the only way to convert the project into reality was to turn it into a blockbuster.

Beyond a certain figure, every extra dollar on the budget represents an additional strain on the executive's nerves. Every scene has to be double-checked for consumer appeal. The temptation to "improve" the work of the men actually making the film seems to become irresistible. In return for

From *Movie* 12 (Spring 1965): 36–37.

their huge investment, Warners doubtless anticipated another "great Western in the classic Ford tradition." Ford delivered a film designed to question that tradition and to destroy the legend which, of all people, he himself has been most instrumental in creating. Whereas the budget was supposed to have guaranteed an action-packed epic, Ford centered the film on the moral development of a hero too human to be heroic; few of the most important scenes involved more than two or three characters.

Thus betrayed, Warners set about bringing the film into line with every philistine's image of what a blockbuster ought to be. Where Ford wanted something much more intimate and evocative, Alex North was called in to provide a self-consciously epic score. The picture was cut for action, many of the more personal sequences being jettisoned in order to build up the movie's spectacular aspects. Scenes that Ford had intended for drastic pruning (particularly those with Karl Malden which now appear overemphasized) were retained. Others, more vital to Ford's conception, landed on the cutting-room floor: Sal Mineo's important role was reduced to skeletal dimensions. One sequence, mentioned in the synopsis and essential to the plot, is quite absent from the film as released.

Cheyenne Autumn thus joins the list of the cinema's great ruins; we are more profitably employed examining its greatness than lamenting its mutilation. There's no need, at this stage, to detail its demonstrations of Ford's genius: those of us who had imagined that we could see legitimate objections to his method were silenced, and finally, by *Donovan's Reef*. Each scene, discounting the excesses allowed to Malden, is realized with precision and intimacy, the direct emotional appeal embedded in the details of the action. The pattern and meaning so firmly established in the organization of the scenes has not been allowed to emerge fully from the organization of the narrative. But, as in Minnelli's *Two Weeks in Another Town* or Ray's *King of Kings,* the power and beauty of the separate sequences contradicts, where it does not excuse, the incoherence of the total structure. On the train out of Shinbone, the aging senator Ranse Stoddard, the legendary *Man Who Shot Liberty Valance,* contemplated the transformation of the Western landscape: "Look at it, Hallie. It was once a wilderness. Now it's a garden." The central question remained open: Were we to admire or to regret the transformation? In *Liberty Valance* Ford developed an exciting tension between a story that celebrated the submission of the Old West to the rule of law and order, and a style that evoked nostalgia for the primitive nobility of its untamed frontiers. This ambiguity, essential to the entire Western legend, is resolved in Ford's own terms by *Cheyenne Autumn.*

The central subject here is the attempt to impose an inhuman discipline on a deep, anarchic emotion. For the Cheyenne, the determination to repossess their native land is unreasoned because unquestionable: a necessity that operates beyond the reach of logic and to which the desire for comfort, for life itself, is subordinated. Disaster is provoked by the inability or the refusal of others to acknowledge the force of their determination. The action of the film constitutes a series of destructive efforts to cultivate the wilderness of human feeling and make it submit to the orderly patterns of a garden.

Where the needs of the Cheyenne, which are felt rather than thought, can only be understood through sympathy, decisions based on calculation become invalid and destructive. True judgment of the situation is prevented in various ways: by administrative convenience; by economic interest (the dollar patriots and the land-grabbers); by abstract conceptions of duty (Widmark, initially) and order (Malden); and by the exploitable nature of the conflict. The "New York Globe" decides to give editorial support to the Indian cause, but as a means to increase circulation by adopting a different line, not through an understanding of the Cheyenne position. Among the Indians themselves, the first battle is precipitated by a young brave (Sal Mineo) eager to use the conflict to promote his courtship of another man's wife.

In the film's opening sequences the Cheyenne gather at the army out-post to await the arrival of a posse of politicians who are expected to do something to implement the promises made to the Indians. A soldier is dispatched in order to signal the approach of "those gentlemen from the East." Ford holds the shot until man and horse become a small speck in a huge landscape. Throughout the movie emphasis is placed on the distance between the men who make the decisions and the people whom these decisions most directly concern.

Cheyenne Autumn develops a theme that has frequently found expression in Ford's work: time and time again, at least from *Stagecoach* (1938) to *Donovan's Reef,* judgments not based on sympathy and personal involvement prove to be incomplete and destructive. Where most of us are accustomed to regard detachment as a prerequisite of true judgment, Ford finds the two qualities incompatible: judgment is a function of sympathy. This makes him the least Brechtian of directors. It may also explain why he has so often not just risked, but courted the accusation of sentimentality: he does not want to allow us a detached, unemotional, and so to his mind false view of his characters' experience.

The conflict between detachment and sympathy is traced in the evolution of Captain Archer (Richard Widmark) and in the tension between an obligation to carry out orders based on abstract calculation and a personal experience which convinces him that the orders are unjust. At the start of the film he is aware that the Indians have been betrayed; he wants "every big-wig in Washington" to see how miserable the reservation is. But his involvement does not go beyond a reasoned belief that something needs to be done to correct an administrative error. By traveling over the same territory and enduring the same hardships in his pursuit of the Cheyenne, he comes to understand, sympathize with, and finally share their determination. It is only when the Secretary of the Interior (Edward G. Robinson) has heard Archer's personal account and abandoned the attempt to deal with the problem by remote control from Washington that a solution becomes possible.

"This is the West, sir. When the legend becomes fact print the legend."
Thus the newspaper editor in *Liberty Valance. Cheyenne Autumn* again
complements the earlier picture by showing the less happy results of print-
ing the legend. Throughout the film the legendary reputation of the
Cheyenne as bloodthirsty savages distorts the facts and prevents the sympathetic consideration that their case deserves. It takes Archer a long time
to realize that these Indians are no longer the proud warriors of former
times but a collection of hungry wanderers who just want to go home. The
Western myth continually asserts itself as a destructive force: a cattleman
shoots down an unarmed brave who has come to beg for food because he
"always wanted to kill me an Indian" and because an Indian scalp would
enable him to silence the bragging of the old-timers.

As a portrayal of the degeneracy of the Old West, the end of its heroic
era, the Dodge City episode (which has been mistaken for a simple piece of
irrelevant fun) summarizes the movie's themes, though in a lighter vein.
Based like the main story on a true episode in U.S. history, the Battle of
Dodge City illustrates the Western legend operating, this time, to grotesque
rather than tragic effect. The citizens believe the wild tales about the scale of
the Cheyenne "revolt" and prepare to evacuate their inadequately garri-
soned town. The evacuation is led by men who, having known the West in
the old days, realize the folly of the general panic. Wyatt Earp (James
Stewart) and Doc Holliday (Arthur Kennedy) conduct the evacuation in pic-
nic spirit, but it turns into a rout when the citizens observe a single forlorn
Indian riding along disconsolately in the distance.

Earp himself may be less gullible, but he is scarcely more heroic than
the other Dodge citizens. With no more great battles to fight, no antagonists
worth more than passing attention, the aging marshal, shortsighted and ef-
fete, sits around in the saloon and plays a tetchy game of poker, content to
accept his ten percent cut of the town's gambling take. Miss Guinevere
Plantagenet attempts to revive memories of a meeting during the old days
back in Wichita, but without success. It was all, we gather, too long ago.
The heroes are dead: which is why the organization men have taken
over.   ●

John W. Turner, professor at Emory University, argues that a close examination of Thomas Berger's novel *Little Big Man* can illuminate some of the critical difficulties in the film, among them the use of the narrator, the identity problems of the central character, Jack Crabb, and the conflict between savagism and civilization which forms the core of both the book and the film. Turner believes the film fails because it lacks the closure that the story demands and that Thomas Berger supplied in the novel; the structure of the film collapses under the weight of the materials.

21

LITTLE BIG MAN:
THE NOVEL AND THE FILM

JOHN W. TURNER

IF Arthur Penn's *Little Big Man* has an identifiable flaw, it resides in the narrative structure of the film. Leo Braudy, in perhaps the most trenchant analysis to date, argues that the problems with the movie are a result of the inadequacies of Jack Crabb as a center of consciousness. To support this assertion, with its Jamesian overtones, Braudy contrasts the film with its source, a novel by Thomas Berger. In the novel, Braudy argues, the narrative voice of Jack Crabb is sufficient to suggest an *"Aura* of unity"* (my emphasis), but that when events are objectified on the screen they become disassociated from any narrative voice.[1] Thus, while Braudy recognizes Penn's attempt to retain Jack as narrator by using the voice-over of the 121-year-old Crabb on the soundtrack, he concludes that the device fails and that the movie devolves into a series of unconnected vignettes.

Thomas Berger's *Little Big Man* is the story of Jack Crabb, a man who sees himself split between loyalties to both the Indian and the white world. In the course of Jack's narrative, he travels back and forth between these two worlds. Structurally, his repeated oscillations between savagery and civilization become associated with competing definitions of the self. The fundamental contrast between savagery and civilization in the novel involves differing concepts of time. The Indian measures time in terms of the cycle of nature and believes that change is as much an appearance as a reality. White men, in contrast, believe in the linear configuration of history, where progress and change are of the essence. Berger's repeated use of these contrasting notions of time warrants an interpretation of savagery and civilization as metaphors for different concepts of the self. The Indian, or circular, self involves a transcendent awareness of one's place in a time-

From *Literature/Film Quarterly* 5 (Spring 1977): 154–63. Reprinted by permission.

less world; the civilized, or linear, self entails a more immediate view of one's place in a time-bound world.

When viewed as controlling metaphors in the novel, savagery and civilization define the binary opposition of the novel's structure. As *picaro,* Jack continually shifts his allegiances in the course of his adventures:

What I had in mind on leaving the Pendrakes [he says] was of course returning to the Cheyenne. God knows I thought enough about it and kept telling myself I was basically an Indian, just as when among Indians I kept seeing how I was really white to the core (p. 160).[2]

This pattern of shifting allegiances not only defines the deep structure of the novel but provides the key to our understanding of the novel's theme of identity. What the pattern suggests is that both civilization and savagery (in the metaphoric senses) are insufficient when held in isolation. Neither the circular-spiritual self, nor the linear-social self operates independently; rather, they exist as the polar opposites by which we define the continuum of identity. This polarity explains why Jack thinks like an Indian among whites and vice versa: he requires a balance of the historical and spiritual versions of the self.

Such an extended look at the structure of Berger's novel is not irrelevant to a discussion of the film by Arthur Penn. In fact, since several reviewers have argued that Penn's central concern in the movie is the problem of identity, it seems to me essential that we understand Berger's handling of that theme and the structure that embodies it. My purpose is not to establish the novel as the standard by which to judge the film, but to present an accurate appraisal of the raw materials Penn had at his disposal in order to understand the structural difficulties involved in re-creating Berger's first-person narrative on the screen.

Fundamentally, the narrative problem that Penn faced in transferring the identity theme of the novel to the medium of film was to find a cinematic equivalent for Berger's linear and circular metaphors, because it is these tropes, and not as Braudy argues Jack's narrative voice, that define the structural principle beneath Jack's oscillations between the two worlds. That this is a specifically cinematic problem can be seen from the fact that Penn attempts to include Berger's metaphors at several points in the dialogue, but that he can find no visual equivalent to reinforce their meanings. More simply, the problem is how to create credible Indians and a tangible Indian world, so as to validate cinematically the idea that Jack defines both poles of the conflict between savagery and civilization.

Penn's decision to use Indian actors to play the roles of the Cheyenne points to a commitment in this direction. But at several points in the film, Penn's comic sense deserts him and he undermines much of the credibility that he strives to create. One example of this loss of control is the character of Little Horse, a *heemaneh.* In the voice-over narration Jack explains the role of the *heemaneh* in Indian culture: "If a Cheyenne don't believe he can stand a man's life, he ain't forced to." While Jack's comment is faithful to the novel, Penn's visualization of Little Horse is not, since he relies on movie stereotypes of the homosexual. By presenting Little Horse as an "interior decorator" in Indian clothing, the movie collapses Berger's satiric contrast between Indian and white American attitudes toward sexual roles. Certainly, Little Horse is only a minor character in both the novel and film; but this disjunction between what is said about the Indians and what we see of them is emblematic of a tendency to collapse the complex contrasts between savagery and civilization established in the novel. More than just a simplification of the novel, what we have here is a conflict in the film between its visual and auditory components, a contradiction between what it *says* and what it *is*.

While Jack's voice-over narration continually insists that we "know the Indian for what he was," the limitations of the camera make it difficult to do so. In Jack's first stay with the Cheyenne, for example, Penn tries to represent Jack's education as an Indian. In quick succession, we see Jack shooting a bow and arrow, stalking buffalo, and learning how to follow a trail. These skills, however, are only the outward manifestations of Indian life; moreover, they constitute little more than the stereotypical image of the Indian in the conventinal Hollywood film. Thus they fail to communicate to the viewer what it means to do these things. The problem here, ultimately, is that what differentiates the two cultures is not what they do, but what they believe. And belief can only be limitedly represented in visual terms. As Jack says in the novel, Old Lodge Skins "taught me everything I learned as a boy *that wasn't physical* like riding or shooting. The way he done this was by means of stories" (p. 73, my emphasis). Whereas the movie can show us Jack's physical education, his psychological growth is significantly attenuated.

The difficulties of representing Indian beliefs on the screen are most apparent with respect to the Indians' faith in spiritual powers and mysteries. In the first four chapters of the novel Berger takes great pains to validate the miraculous. As with much of the novel, these mysterious incidents progress from the comic to the more serious. In the first case, Jack proves his "manly indifference to pain" by pulling his "arrow-out-of-arse trick." The hoax is very funny, but Jack points to its larger significance: "Maybe you are beginning to understand, when I pulled the arrow-out-of-arse trick, why it didn't occur to none of the children that I was hoaxing them. That is because Indians did not go around expecting to be swindled, whereas they was always ready for a miracle" (p. 76). Here, Jack refers indirectly to the disparity between the reader's disbelief and the Indians' absolute faith in miracles. Moreover, the comic tone provides a half-way house for the reader's acceptance of the antelope hunt in the next chapter, where Old Lodge Skins uses his "powers" to draw a magic line that brings the antelope to their destruction. Again, Berger allows Jack to mediate between the two worlds; Jack, in fact, challenges the reader's skepticism by highlighting his own doubts throughout his telling of the story. But the conviction with which he concludes carries over the reader: "If you don't like the aspect of the affair, then you'll have a job explaining why maybe a thousand antelope run towards ruin; and also how Old Lodge Skins could know this herd would be in this place, for no animal had showed a hair before he sat down on the prairie" (p. 71).

Short of trick photography, such dramatizations of the Indians' belief in man's "power to make things happen" are impossible in Penn's film. Again this may seem like a minor limitation, but it serves to suggest the difficulty of maintaining the significant contrasts between savagery and civilization established in the novel. The Indian's sense of time, his belief in the harmony of man and nature, and his reliance on the supernatural are all aspects of a mentality alien to the "naturalism" of Penn's cinematic representation.

As a result, Penn's attempts to develop the theme of identity are circumscribed by the difficulty in generating the binary opposition between savagery and civilization that structures the novel. In the movie, Jack's oscillations between the Indians and the whites acquire little significance beyond the comic mobility of the *picaro*. What is missing from the movie's structures are the images sufficient to embody the complex cultural differences between savagery and civilization. Without those images, Penn cannot devise a structure that will fully express the identity theme.

A second reason for qualifying Braudy's criticisms of the movie is that the identity theme does not encompass all of Penn's thematic concerns, anymore than it exhausts the richness of Berger's novel. As a historical novel, *Little Big Man* dramatizes the conflict between savagery and civilization which was enacted on the American Plains and which culminated in the Battle of Little Bighorn. This story, with its epic scope, seems naturally suited for cinema, where narrative breadth is readily available. Moreover, for Arthur Penn, Berger's story of the West held particular interest because of the inherent theme of American violence. In fact, from the middle of the movie on, the historical concerns tend to displace the identity theme altogether.

Penn's handling of the history is reasonably successful, although one could quibble with his handling of a number of small details. There is, for example, no justification for changing the fact that in the novel it is the Cheyenne, and not the Pawnee as it is in the movie, who kill Jack's family. While slight, this change could be interpreted as representative of a larger tendency to sentimentalize the Cheyenne and vilify the whites. Such a tendency runs counter to Berger's complex satire, where both ways of life receive a mixture of blame and praise. Nevertheless, despite these simplifications, Penn reproduces the essence of the historical theme: the acculturation of the Indian. Certainly, the single most effective scene in the movie—the massacre at Washita—vividly dramatizes the violence of the historical conflict. However, the very effectiveness of the scene has raised another set of questions about the structure of the movie.

Whatever else can be said, Penn handles the massacre scene extraordinarily well: sight and sound are more effectively combined in this scene than anywhere else in the movie. The setting, with its muted effect of the snow, provides the perfect visual counterpoint for the horror of the violence that follows. At the same time, the gently rising soundtrack of "Garry Owen" combines with the visual images of a dream-like advance of the soldiers to rivet the viewer's attention. We even find ourselves caught up in the visual poetry of Penn's panorama and the martial fervor of "Garry Owen," until the beauty explodes in violence. Penn's editing at this point is most expressive: by alternating shots of increasingly shorter temporal length, Penn heightens the tension of the scene, which climaxes with the death of Jack's wife, Sunshine. Jack and Sunshine hit the ground simultaneously, causing the audience to writhe with Jack in impotent horror as the visual and auditory montage culminates in the silence of Jack's agony and the stillness of Sunshine's death.

Given the violence of the Washita scene, and given the change in Jack's character, one expects a change in the remainder of the film. If the silence at the center of the massacre is to serve as a structural fulcrum, then the movie must turn to something new. What is at issue here, therefore, is a problem of tonal control. To prevent the violence of the massacre from collapsing the structure of the movie, the comedy of the second half must be tinged with darkness. The tonal control of the rest of the movie, however, is decidedly uneven. Unfortunately, what happens is that the movie reverts too often in the second half to the comedy of Jack's earlier picaresque adventures. As a result, the underlying conception of the film becomes confused and the narrative structure collapses. The problem, then, is not so much with the scene itself but with what follows it.

Disorienting tonal confusions occur at two significant points in the latter half of the narrative. The first of these, when Jack is down and out, is difficult to discuss, because the problem seems to reside less in Penn's conception than in the execution of the actor, Dustin Hoffman. Structurally, the design of the down-and-out sequence is perfect. The episode follows directly after Jack's failure to effect his revenge by killing General Custer. Jack's enforced recognition that "he is no Cheyenne brave" logically precipitates his despair. Yet, the despair is not maintained with any consistency.

While the tonal confusion here seems less a product of intention than execution, the same cannot be said of the movie's ending. Once again, given the way the massacre scene fixates our attention on the violence of the historical conflict, there is no aesthetic justification for Penn's lapse into comedy. One measure of the weakness of this comic ending is manifested in the omissions from the novel. Paralleling the earlier tendency to soften the Cheyenne character, Penn avoids any direct reference to the Indian practices of mutilating the bodies of their dead enemies. Penn also avoids the most important dramatic confrontation of the novel, which is anything but comic, between Jack and Old Lodge Skins: "Well, speak of shame, there was me. I still had not commenced to explain my presence with Custer. If indeed it could be explained, I had to try." In the movie, Old Lodge Skins inexplicably accepts Jack with open arms. And Jack does not feel compelled to explain.

But the major problem with the ending consists of the comic undermining of Old Lodge Skins. In the novel, the Indian chief wills his death. In the movie, Old Lodge Skins's gesture ends with his comic re-awakening and his statement that "sometimes the magic doesn't work." One can see parallels here with the earlier problem in the movie of handling the Indians' supernaturalism. But, more importantly, the comic ending undermines the historical sense of the movie by avoiding the ironies inherent in the Battle of Little Bighorn. Although the defeat of Custer marks the height of Indian military success, historians have recognized that the battle also marks the beginning of thm end of the Indian wars. William T. Hagan, in fact, ironically entitles his chapter on Little Bighorn, "The Warrior's Last Stand."[3] With the disappearance of the buffalo and the renewed vigor of army operations after Custer's defeat, the Indian was forced to abandon the hope that the tide of civilization could be stemmed or that his old way of life could easily be maintained. In the novel, Berger captures this ironic sense of the Indian defeated even in victory by concluding Jack's narrative of the battle with the death of Old Lodge Skins:

Though I was only thirty-four years of age, I felt in some ways older than I do now. Now it is only one man's life that is about to end; then it was a whole style of living. Old Lodge Skins had seen it all, up there on Custer Ridge, when he said there would never be another great battle. I didn't get his point immediately, and maybe you won't either, for there was many a fight afterward, and mighty fierce ones, before the hostile Plains tribes finally give up and come in permanent to the agencies (p. 444).

More than simply the death of one man, the death of the old chief symbolizes the death of a mode of life.

Penn's comic ending, therefore, not only undermines the dignity of Old Lodge Skins, but also raises questions about Penn's historicism. To a great extent, Penn seems to resist the historical implications of the conflict on the Plains. By opting for a sentimental ending, Penn undermines the effectiveness of his cinematic achievement in the Washita scene and leaves himself open to the criticisms of Pauline Kael. Kael is right about the massacre scene, but for the wrong reason. It is not that Penn should have excised his thematic seriousness; it is not even that "the film must deepen by comic means" alone, but that, having introduced a serious concern for history, Penn does not follow that theme to its tragic end as Berger does.

As a result, the movie lacks the closure that its story demands. Having entered the arena of history, Penn obligates himself to a narrative structure that rests on the opposition between the past and the present. Although Jack Crabb lives to tell his story, in the novel he knows that his story ended at Little Bighorn. In the movie, however, we miss that sense of an ending: Jack and Old Lodge Skins wander slowly back down the mountain, as if into the future. Their humorous discussion of sex furthers this sense of ongoing life. But the inconclusiveness of such an ending collapses the structure that Penn has striven to create. If Washita is to be the structural center of the movie, then it must mark the beginning of the end. What we have at the end, however, is an avoidance of closure, a relapse into comedy when it is least appropriate; the necessary somber note is totally absent.

The movie fails, then, despite all of Penn's admirable intentions and considerable craftsmanship, because he has not achieved a structure that will sustain the weight of his materials. Penn's reluctance to close off the movie's structure points to the weaknesses of his artistic conception. What vitiates Penn's achievement in the film is his failure to avoid romanticizing the past. As Leo Braudy puts it:

Penn, in fact, seems torn between preserving the past through the clarity of photographic detail and preserving the past through the romantic versions of reality that are available in myth.[4]

This tension between romance and fact is nowhere more evident than in the contrast between the grim reality of Washita and the nostalgic longing of the final scene. Moreover, this conflicting attitude remains unresolved, such that the structure of the film is impaled on the horns of its own divided loyalties.   ●

NOTES

1. Leo Braudy, "The Difficulties of *Little Big Man*," *Film Quarterly* 25 (Fall 1971):3.

2. Thomas Berger, *Little Big Man* (Greenwich, Connecticut: Fawcett Publications, Inc., 1964). Further references to *Little Big Man* are cited in the text.

3. William T. Hagan, *American Indians* (Chicago: University of Chicago Press, 1961), pp. 113–42.

4. Braudy, p. 30.

Pauline Kael, movie critic for *The New Republic* and the *New Yorker* as well as author of several books on film, criticizes *Tell Them Willie Boy Is Here* for trying to dump too much guilt onto white society for the treatment of the Indians. She sees the message of this film as suggesting that since the races cannot be reconciled we should all go up in flames together. She thinks that this apocalyptic vision accompanies one of American self-hatred which envisions the country as on the verge of collapse.

22

AMERICANA:
TELL THEM WILLIE BOY IS HERE

PAULINE KAEL

SURELY we've earned this bit of affectionate Americana; we have to have a little balance. If Americans have always been as ugly and brutal and hypocritical as some of our current movies keep telling us, there's nothing for us to do but commit genosuicide. That's what *Tell Them Willie Boy Is Here* suggests we should do. American self-hatred has reached such a point that the movies are selling it and projecting it onto the American past as well as into present-day stories. The movie of *They Shoot Horses, Don't They?* for example, a hard-boiled story turned into a macabre fantasy of the thirties, belongs to the same nightmare world as *Midnight Cowboy*. At the movies this year, I've sometimes had the feeling that audiences respond so intensely and with such satisfaction to paranoid visions because they believe that America is collapsing and that they can't stop the apocalypse, so they might as well get it to happen sooner and get their fears confirmed and have it over with. They're on the *side* of apocalypse: since they feel it's all going down anyway, it seems to make them feel better to see these movies saying that it *should* go down, that that's *right*. And now here's a movie that goes all the way—turning white Americans into a race carrying blood guilt, a race whose civilization must be destroyed. *Tell Them Willie Boy Is Here* does not, however, use the currently fashionable idioms of America-the-horrible movies; it isn't in the fractured Modern Gothic style that is as sensational and overpowering as a trip through a madhouse. It is a solemnly measured Western with the thesis explicated by symbolic characters, allusions, and heavy ironies. In a very curious, ideological way—more forties movie than late sixties—*Tell Them Willie Boy Is Here* attempts rationally to *prove* its apocalyptic message that we must all go down together in flames—because we deserve to. I think that for this message (which I find deeply questionable anyway) its technique is a mistake; when we're presented with an *argument* for the glories of Willie's self-destructive behavior, we reject it.

Onto the simple story of an Indian (Willie is well played by Robert Blake) in California in 1909 who kills another Indian, the father of his girl (she is not well played by Katharine Ross, though Lord knows what she should have done), the writer-director Abraham Polonsky has grafted enough schematic Marxism and Freudianism and New Left guerilla Existentialism and just plain new-style American self-hatred so that every damned line of dialogue in the picture becomes "meaningful." There isn't a character who doesn't make points and stand for various political forces, and the sheriff (Robert Redford) is named Coop so that his actions will symbolize the ultimate cowardice and failure of the Gary Cooper hero figures. The movie is loaded with references to fears of a presidential assassination, so we'll know that even in 1909 we were a bloody, brutal, violent, no-good nation, and the woman doctor (Susan Clark, whom I like less each time I see her, and I didn't like her to start with) who is superintendent of the reservation is a patronizing-to-Indians liberal—the ultimate villainess. Ashamed of her sexuality (like all liberals, in this schematic view) she is given such lines as—to Redford—"I use you the way you use me." (Most women in the audience will probably think, lucky you.) The movie seems to be composed of a series of obligatory scenes: Willie goes to a bar in order to encounter racists and be insulted; the varieties of racists include Barry Sullivan, who tells us about the fun of stalking Indians and scalping them; and so on. While Willie is given a modern consciousness, the other characters are stuck with period attitudes and false postures that, in this symbolic context, make them seem like monsters, until, at the end, Redford, having shot and killed the unarmed Willie, has a big Lady Macbeth scene, trying to clean his bloody hands with sand. The picture is shot in an "artistic" style (color desaturated for barren, dusty landscapes) and is paced deliberately, so that the meanings can sink in. The numbing hopelessness of an *Easy Rider* has emotional appeal; the irrationality and the cool, romantic defeatism are infused with an elegiac sense of American failure. It's easier to dismiss the programmed ideological negativism of *Willie Boy,* which stays on a conscious (almost abstract) level while attempting to demonstrate that we are a nation with bad *instincts.* There's no *regret*—not even the facile tone of regret that made Peter Fonda's Captain America such a sham hero. And one resents being trapped in a picture that says there is no place to go but down when one doesn't believe it, even in the terms of the picture. The message is that compromise is unmanly, that it's better to die—which makes you a hero. It also says that since a Black man (the Indian pretense isn't kept up for long) can't trust any white man—not even Coop—there can be no reconciliation of the races, so he should try to bring everything down. That is the only way he can make them know he was here. A strange contradiction, because there won't be anybody around to remember. *Tell Them Willie Boy Is Here* may look impressive abroad; in this country it's not likely to be very satisfying except to Black kamikazes and to masochistic white Americans—the kind who want to believe that the corollary of "Black is Beautiful" is "White is Ugly." ●

As Los Angeles editor for *Film Quarterly,* Stephen Farber is a frequent contributor to that journal. In this review he describes *A Man Called Horse* and *Flap* (*Nobody Loves a Drunken Indian*) as films expressing the growing concern for the degradation of the Indian in the film. *A Man Called Horse* expresses something of the "grandeur, the magnificence of a savage, primitive culture," and *Flap* introduces the tragedy of Indian history, especially when seen in juxtaposition with the beauty of Indian life in *Horse.* In spite of the Hollywood trappings, both movies represent a new approach to Indian culture.

A MAN CALLED HORSE
and FLAP

STEPHEN FARBER

A MAN CALLED HORSE and *Flap* (earlier titled *Nobody Loves a Drunken Indian*) express some of the growing concern about the degradation of the American Indian. *A Man Called Horse* is a portrait of Indian culture before that degradation began—in the Dakota territory around 1825. Richard Harris plays an English lord on a hunting trip in the American wilderness, who is captured by the Sioux and forced to work for them as a beast of burden until he finally proves himself worthy to be adopted into the tribe. Some militant Indian groups have criticized the film for portraying the Indian as savage, but that objection implies that they share white America's belief in the superiority of "advanced civilization"; whereas what seems to me remarkable about the film is that it suggests the grandeur, the *magnificence* of a savage, primitive culture. The attention to carefully researched details of setting, costume, and ceremony produces some extraordinarily beautiful images, a tableau of Indian life more striking than anything seen on the screen before. Most of the film has no English dialogue at all; it consists of painstaking reconstruction of rituals of initiation, marriage, war, and death—almost an anthropological document from another time. Since the film was made by whites, there is a note of terror mixed in with the wonderment: From seeing this film, we get some understanding of how New England Puritans must have felt on confronting this strange, foreign people; to superstitious, provincial, unimaginative European settlers, these fierce, bizarrely painted and costumed natives must indeed have looked like monsters from hell. The film invokes the primal tensions in the relationship of white man and red man, the recurring conflict of the civilized and the pagan; the dignity and nobility of the Indian come across more powerfully because there is no patronizing attempt to "humanize" him to fit a preconceived liberal image. It is disappointing, then, that irritating fictional contrivances sometimes intrude on the authenticity. We are urged to empathize with Harris as he undergoes a variety of conventional dramatic crises and eventually emerges triumphant. Indian groups have rightly objected to the intimation that the white Anglo-Saxon is the natural leader of the tribe (he devises a military strategy that saves them from invasion, and thus wins their devotion, in true phony-movie fashion); this is the major blemish in an otherwise honorable effort. Harris's stilted readings and his blond wig are further distractions. Elliott Silverstein has directed competently and unobtrusively, except for a dream sequence that he claims was inserted without his approval. Silverstein and his technical staff give the film exotic flavor, but a deeper appeal too—what draws us to the Sioux, in spite of their savagery, is their movingly direct relationship to the essentials of human experience—the test of manhood, courtship and marriage, death. Particularly death, for the film is basically a tragic vision of a people soon to be destroyed by the cruelty of the elements and the advance of civilization. And it is this tragic vision, the apprehension of extreme grief and suffering unchecked by civilized defenses, that touches Harris most deeply and humanizes him.

Carol Reed's *Flap* makes a fascinating contrast; looking at Reed's images of the squalor of a contemporary Indian reservation in juxtaposition to the beauty of the Indian ceremonies recreated for *A Man Called Horse* could offer a sobering introduction to a study of the tragedy of Indian history. The film etches the milieu of the reservation in fine, stinging details—a barren landscape spotted with sleazy adobe hovels and populated by a sad-faced people wearing a tawdry melange of tribal and modern-anonymous dress. But dramatically, the film falls flat. The story is about a half-hearted attempt at revolution by a group of resentful Indians, conceived as a tragicomedy. The comedy might have been an apt way of suggesting the pathetic hopelessness and absurdity of their revolutionary movement, except that it is rarely funny, only arch and repetitive. But the tragic finale is even worse—a ridiculously contrived scene of martyrdom that shamelessly milks the liberal audience. The characters are cardboard figures in Clair Huffaker's screenplay, and they are not well cast or well played. Anthony Quinn is not too bad in the pivotal role of Flapping Eagle, but he is becoming a one-man UN gallery of irrepressible minority heroes. In one scene he even does a few steps of the little dance that has become his stock in trade since *Zorba the Greek;* at that point we know we're watching not a real Indian but another of Quinn's ethnic star-turns on behalf of the Life Force. Tony Bill, obviously cast so the movie would have "youth appeal," does not even have Quinn's facility at impersonation, and a heavy coating of Mantan hardly compensates for his lack of experience. Shelley Winters is called in for a couple of scenes as—guess what?—the brassy local hooker, a role she no longer even seems to enjoy very much. It's a shame that a film with such a fresh, vital subject has to rely on all these Hollywood trappings. But even with their weaknesses, the new approach of these two movies about Indian culture is worth some notice.   ●

24

Richard Combs finds *Ulzana's Raid* is not just about the actual raid but rather is a "dream escape" in which there is no freedom and in which all flight ends in disaster. Lacking any clear goal the sortie calls up "impossible hopes and nightmarish fears" as Ulzana pillages his way across the landscape moving ever closer to his death. Mr. Combs is a frequent contributor to *Sight and Sound*.

ULZANA'S RAID

RICHARD COMBS

T HERE is a beguiling persistence of vision about the way *Ulzana's Raid* begins, as if it were another chapter in the Aldrich chronicle of dirty missions from World War II. A small detachment of soldiers, their sympathies and leadership variously divided, is dispatched on unpleasant duty by a military officialdom anxious to cover its own tracks by frequently quoting the rulebook. The military context, with its channelled struggles for power and an arbitrary authority enforcing a clear-cut distinction between friend and foe, Them and Us, seems to be as amenable to Aldrich as to Fuller; and *Ulzana's Raid* (Fox-Rank) works over various crises of authority with a vigor and economy that leave *The Dirty Dozen* and *Too Late the Hero* standing flatfooted.

Ulzana, the "incorrigible savage" who leads a small party of Apache braves in a breakout from an Arizona reservation, is much discussed but little seen. For the pursuing soldiers, led by an inexperienced lieutenant (Bruce Davison) and a seasoned scout (Burt Lancaster), Ulzana is the enemy "you ain't going to see much of . . . except for the dead things"; and the film closes with hallucinatory tightness around that perspective, mapping out the tactics of pursuit in a kind of delirious close-order drill that keeps the soldiers ineffectually distanced from a foe who remains totally, inexplicably other. At least, almost so; the mechanics of the chase reveal that Ulzana (Joaquin Martinez) is as much of a military tactician as any white soldier, in fact one whose ruthlessness, or desperate practicality, gives him that infuriating edge. Operating as mocking shadows of their pursuers, the Indians adopt useful items of army hardware: binoculars, odds and ends of uniform, the bugle with which they lure one homesteader out to a grisly death.

Denied any overt sympathy, Ulzana's plight is defined with bitter in-

From *Sight and Sound* 42 (Spring 1973): 115–16. Reprinted by permission.

tensity through the many parallels and paradoxes that are set up as his role switches through fiendish embodiment of the enemy to cruel parody of the colonizing white men. The limitations of his raid are clearly set: with scarcely any chance of permanent freedom, his brief reign of terror is a false escape, a desperate attempt to break the monotonous spell of life on the reservation. His excursion looks rather similar to Peckinpah's getaway, or to Jeremiah Johnson's deluded search for "something different." In the way that it calls up impossible hopes and nightmarish fears, Ulzana's raid is as much a flight into interior landscapes; and just as the McCoys only escape infinite replays of the same absurd action through a dream escape to Mexico, so the hope is expressed at the beginning of *Ulzana's Raid* that the Apache may just "trail south" across the border, as if he would then cease to be a problem as surely as if he had dropped off the edge of the world.

With no final goal, and no clear intention except, as the scout insists, to burn, rape and torture, Ulzana keeps his raid going from moment to moment only on certain stringent conditions, the most important being that his braves are always properly supplied with horses. In search of the materials that will keep his power alive, he comes at one point on the homestead of Rukeyser, another "alien," who has determined not to surrender his farm and possessions to the Apache and who is driven to barricade himself inside his house in a fit of insane defiance, before being tricked into delivering himself to a lingering death.

The other sustaining factor in Ulzana's desperate sortie is his son. It is the realization of the boy's death that finally breaks the Apache's will; and the sense of connection given by the relationship is taken up in shifting father-son roles throughout the film, especially as they are distorted and institutionalized by the forms of army life. Lieutenant DeBuin passes from his real father, who believes that "it is possible to be both a Christian and a soldier," to Major Cartwright, "a creature of reaction," to the pragmatic scout Mackintosh, who is on hand to temper both DeBuin's idealism as to the Apaches' intentions, and his vengeful wrath at the evidence of their atrocities. DeBuin himself plays Christian father to the Indian scout Ke-Ni-Tay, rather like Crusoe to Friday.

Mackintosh, as the constant repository of any available practical sense, seems always to stand a little outside the main action; and Burt Lancaster perhaps weighs somewhat too heavily as chorus in the generally fine ensemble playing. Similarly his sympathetic relationship with Ke-Ni-Tay is rather glib, although it serves its purpose as the only fraternal partnership in a disrupted world (from the broken pans across the landscape at the beginning to Aldrich's liking for sudden, jarring low angles) where paternal authority can so easily become unbalanced and exploitative.   ●

Tom Milne describes *Buffalo Bill and the Indians* as a confrontation between myth and myth in which the resolution
("obligatory today") is deliberately unconvincing in the scene
where Buffalo Bill is haunted by the ghost of Sitting Bull. The
Indian acquires what Milne calls a "strange magical-religious
property" which concludes the film in enigma and nightmare.
Mr. Milne is a frequent contributor to *Sight and Sound* and
the author of *The Cinema of Carl Dreyer* and other film
books.

25

BUFFALO BILL AND THE INDIANS

TOM MILNE

IN the preface to his play *Indians*, on which
Altman's *Buffalo Bill and the Indians* (EMI) is loosely based, Arthur Kopit
notes how, during rewritings between the London and Broadway openings,
he evolved from John Ford parody toward nightmare: "This, again, was
what I had always wanted. To create an impression. Not something didactic, but something musically amorphous, and viscerally disturbing, like
a bad dream—to be thought about, after it's all over. Pieced together again,
like a puzzle."

Curiously, this serves better as a description of Altman's film than of
the play, partly because Kopit never quite surmounted the problem of how
to make the nightmare not only Buffalo Bill's (as he is gradually forced to
face the extent to which he has allowed truth to be papered over by myth)
but the audience's. By using as the still center of Buffalo Bill's mental storm
a reconstruction of the U.S. Commission's visit to Standing Rock in
1886—a parley that resulted directly in the takeover of the Great Sioux
Reservation for the benefit of white settlers, and indirectly in the assassination of Sitting Bull and the massacre at Wounded Knee four years later—
Kopit in fact reduces nightmare to all-too-understandable logic. "Ya see,"
says Buffalo Bill in an effort to expound the Indians' apparently surrealistic
logic to the Senators, "the Indian believes the earth is sacred and sees
ploughin' as a sacrilegious act." Revealing the red man's ingrained
philosophical and territorial beliefs, and matching them against the white's
expansionist needs, these scenes simply demonstrate how, in the circumstances, the twain could never hope to meet.

Altman tackles the problem rather differently, by deliberately decen-
tralizing any question of the *reality* of the Indian. As the camera pulls back

From *Sight and Sound* 45 (Autumn 1976): 254. Reprinted by permission.

at the beginning of the film to reveal that the ferocious redskin attack on a pioneer shack is merely a rehearsal for one of the Wild West show's acts, a wounded Indian extra trampled by a horse is hurried away. Subsequently, as the film bustles into the characteristic Altman flurry of sidelong jokes and overlapping dialogue while the Wild West show marshals its characters and resources, an enigmatic shot of Indians silhouetted against the forest is laconically explained as the funeral of the dead extra before it is swallowed up by the kaleidoscopic action, leaving no ripple behind. A single Ford setup of a pioneer burial carries an automatic charge; but *this,* the film implies, is alien to our culture, our understanding, our emotions.

From this point on, *Buffalo Bill and the Indians* becomes a confrontation of myth with myth. And exactly as the reception committee waiting to welcome the new guest star to Buffalo Bill's Wild West show is deceived into ignoring the meekly undersized Sitting Bull (Frank Kaquitts) in favor of his gigantic interpreter William Halsey (Will Sampson), so the audience is lured into accepting the image it expects. Massive, impassive, and every inch the fearsome Geronimo of imagination, Halsey (a fictional character replacing the John Grass of history and Kopit's play) takes the part of the proud, noble savage currently worshipped. Authorized to speak throughout for the world-weary Sitting Bull, he logic-chops the opposition to ribbons at every turn, whether provoking Buffalo Bill (Paul Newman) into displays of arrogant white superiority or picking historical holes in the hilariously inept scenario for the Little Big Horn playlet. Halsey's persona as the image created by white guilt is given a savage twist when, after Sitting Bull's death, he is seen committing the final betrayal of impersonating his Chief in the gladiatorial combat in which Buffalo Bill contemptuously vanquishes his enemy.

Sitting Bull himself, meanwhile, is presented as an amusing primitive uninterested by the great debates going on around him, instead taking a simpleminded interest in the workings of a music box or a senile delight in demonstrating that Buffalo Bill uses buckshot to facilitate his sharp-shooting act. In fact, however, what his behavior displays is simply a common, unheroic humanity. "He wanted to show the truth to the people for once," cries Annie Oakley (Geraldine Chaplin), threatening to resign because Buffalo Bill refuses to change his Little Big Horn scenario to show that the massacre was provoked by an attack ordered by Custer on squaws and children in the Indian camp. But it is Halsey who proposes this rewrite in Sitting Bull's name, to the accompaniment of a spine-chilling chant, while Sitting Bull pursues the business of living with calm, unquenchable curiosity. A point undemonstratively echoed by the distant mountains, first seen in the film's opening image as the camera pans down from them to the American flag raised over the Wild West show's stockade, and thereafter omnipresent as a sort of Shangri-la beyond the land across the river to which Sitting Bull retreats with his people to escape the confines of the Wild West show. By a happy coincidence (or perhaps calculation), since the film was shot on an Indian reservation in Alberta, these mountains are the ones

Sitting Bull must have seen when, in 1877, less interested in continuing to fight or set records straight than in being left in peace to hunt buffalo, he led his people into Canada, only to return four years later for imprisonment, exile and death because neither the Great White Father nor the Great Mother who ruled Canada could see his point of view.

So while the two myths confront each other in the center of the film's arena, finally achieving the resolution obligatory today in the (deliberately unconvincing) scene where Buffalo Bill is haunted by the ghost of the Indian he betrayed, another nightmare is quietly adumbrated in the more genuinely haunting mysteries never explained by the film, and which gradually knit together to form a subtext in which the Indian acquires a strange magical-religious property: the mysterious river-crossing no one ever sees performed but which leaves Sitting Bull as high and dry as Christ walking on the waters; the moment when Sitting Bull and six followers vanish into the mountains, afterwards smilingly telling Buffalo Bill's baffled posse only that it was "the first moon of the month"; the sudden zoom in to Sitting Bull's funeral pyre to reveal, among the bones, ashes and beads, what looks uncommonly like a Christian cross; and above all, the enigmatic theatricality of Sitting Bull's appearance in the Wild West show when he first stuns the audience by leveling his gun at President Cleveland, then maneuvers his horse into the dance promised as the climax to his act.

In an election year, and with its echoes of *Nashville,* the leveled gun has obvious connotations, fulfilling the expectations of a counterculture nourished on the Wounded Knee demonstration and the welter of literature about Indian genocide currently flooding the bookshops. But what of that mysterious dance by the horse, mockingly accompanied by a Mozart minuet as the circus music fades away and President Cleveland mulishly refuses to accept the meeting foretold in Sitting Bull's dream?

According to Indian belief at the time, the old grey, which was said to have embarked alone upon its repertoire of tricks after Sitting Bull was shot dead, was in fact performing the Dance of the Ghosts. As much as anything, it was this Ghost Dance religion, newly disseminated by the Paiute Messiah, which led to the extermination of the Sioux at Wounded Knee: partly because the white men feared that the secret ceremonies of the Ghost Dance would unite the Indian tribes (Sitting Bull's disappearance in the mountains) and because it blasphemed in taking over Christ from Christianity (the cross among the ashes); and partly because the Indians believed that no further struggle was necessary. "In the next springtime, when the grass was knee high, the earth would be covered with new soil which would bury all the white men, and new land would be covered with sweet grass and running water and trees. . . . The Indians who danced the Ghost Dance would be taken up in the air and suspended there while a wave of new earth was passing, and then they would be set down among the ghosts of their ancestors on the new earth, where only Indians would live." (Dee Brown, *Bury My Heart at Wounded Knee.*)

"History is no more than disrespect for the dead," says white surrogate William Halsey, interpreting a Sitting Bull plea for a reversal of historical guilts and responsibilities which even Buffalo Bill notices that Sitting Bull never actually uttered. Sitting Bull's History Lesson is an altogether more nightmarish threat: no less than obliteration of the white man's civilization, traditions, and even existence.   ●

6

ANNOTATED CHECKLIST OF ARTICLES AND BOOKS ON THE POPULAR IMAGES OF THE INDIAN IN THE AMERICAN FILM

"Accuracy in Indian Subjects," *Moving Picture World* 5 (July 10, 1909): 48.

    This early article discusses the exaggerated acting styles and misrepresentation of the Indians in the first films.

Alexander, Shana. "The Sad Lot of the Sioux," *Life* 66 (February 7, 1969): 14E.

    Alexander gives her reactions to the filming of *A Man Called Horse* and her views of the Sioux people who acted in the film.

Ames, Katrine, and Martin Kasindorf. "Big Will," *Newsweek* 87 (July 26, 1976): 73.

    The authors present a brief biographical sketch of Will Sampson, Creek Indian who acted in *Buffalo Bill and the Indians* and *One Flew Over the Cuckoo's Nest*. Sampson comments, "All the Indians' heroes are long dead. We don't have today's heroes like white people. Indians are a proud people, but we can't say Crazy Horse is going to win the World Series."

"A 1914 Movie Review," *Akwesasne Notes* 5 (Early Winter 1973): 14.

    This reprint from *Moving Picture World* is one of the earliest comments on the portrayal of the Indian in film and underscores the fact that from the beginnings of the industry the Indian has been a prime subject for films.

Astor, Gerald. "Good Guys Wear War Paint," *Look* 34 (December 1, 1970): 56–61.

    Astor offers an interview with Dustin Hoffman and Richard Mulligan about their roles in *Little Big Man* with comments from Arthur Penn. This article describes the film experience as "the losing of the West."

Bataille, Gretchen M., and Charles L. P. Silet. "A Checklist of Published Materials on Popular Images of the Indian in the American Film," *Journal of Popular Film* 5 (1976): 171–82.

    This is an annotated compilation of books, articles, and reviews that deal with the images of the Native American in films.

Beale, Lewis. "The American Way West," *Films and Filming* 18 (April 1972): 24–30.

    Beale criticizes Hollywood's attempt to correct the stereotype of the Indian as shifting too far in the direction of showing all Indians to be good and all whites to be evil.

Bell, Arthur. "Neigh," *Commonweal* 92 (June 26, 1970): 318.

    Bell is critical of the confused standards Hollywood exhibits toward the Indian in films which are present in *A Man Called Horse*. He quotes a press release describing the film as not just another "Hollywood version of the Indian legend but the Indian's own statement of their trials." The lead Indian woman is played by the Greek actress Corinna Tsopei.

Blakey, Carla M. "The American Indian in Films, Part I," *Film News* 27 (September 1970): 6–10.

    The first of a two-part series, this article examines several films, mostly documentaries, about Indians.

————. "The American Indian in Films, Part II," *Film News* 27 (October 1970): 6–11.

    In the second part of the series, Ms. Blakey continues to review films suitable for classroom use.

Boyd, George N. "From a Comfortable Distance," *Christian Century* 88 (October 13, 1971): 1213–14.

    The film *Billy Jack* relies on stereotypes, the romance of the first Americans, and the questionable heroics of Billy Jack, the "half-breed ex-Green Beret war hero and karate expert." Trying to have it all ways, the film fails to be convincing.

"Brando Refuses Oscar," *Akwesasne Notes* 5 (Late Summer 1973): 10.

    Discusses Brando's views of the use of Indians in films as "a perennial bad force—a malignant source of evil." The text of his speech refusing the Academy Award is included as are reactions of several journalists to the incident.

Braudy, Leo. "Difficulties of *Little Big Man,*" *Film Quarterly* 25 (Fall 1971): 30–33.

    This article focuses on the character of Jack Crabb and discusses the film as the embodiment of a sense of loss of time, of youth, and of opportunity.

Brauer, Ralph, and Donna Brauer. *The Horse, The Gun, and The Piece of Property: Changing Images of the TV Western.* Bowling Green, Ohio: Bowling Green University Popular Press, 1975.

    Includes one chapter on the portrayal of minorities in the television Western and underscores the similarity of negative portrayals on television and in the movies.

Brudnoy, David. "Film Chronicle: Hoffman, Jagger and That's It," *National Review* 23 (April 6, 1971): 381.

    "*Little Big Man* embodies and scorns the old myths of the West, ironically, sometimes parodically playing the clichés (noble savage, savage redskin, civilized white, brutal racist, and so on) against each other with devastating wit and compelling force."

Buckley, Peter. Review of *Soldier Blue, Films and Filming* 17 (June 1971): 65–66.

    Finds that the bloodshed and carnage of this beautifully made film are justified by its moral outrage about the white massacre of Indians. The reviewer found *Soldier Blue* a powerful and convincing film.

Burgess, John Andrew. "*Little Big Man,*" *Film Society Review* 6 (March 1971): 30–32.

    In a negative review Burgess says that to have sympathy for the "passing of the Red Man," we must first see the way of life that ended, and Penn fails to show us that. "The movie finally never brings us to know enough about the Indians; when they are slaughtered, we react not to tragedy but to atrocity."

Bush, W. Stephen. "Moving Picture Absurdities," *Moving Picture World* 9 (September 16, 1911): 773.

    Laments the typical depiction of the Indian, always squinting as if he needed glasses, either wholly good and the white man's friend, or totally evil and fiendish. The writer believes audiences are tiring of this stereotype.

Byron, Stuart. "A Vision of American Multiplicity," *Village Voice* 16 (August 19, 1971): 47.

    Discovers in *Billy Jack* an attempt to understand and reconcile the two facets of American culture most associated with our attitudes toward the Indians: pacifism and violence. Finds the film in the tradition of the modern Western in its use of genre clichés to comment on "historical irony and reality."

Calder, Jenni. *There Must Be a Lone Ranger.* London: Hamish Hamilton, 1974.

    Calder devotes an entire chapter to the Indian's portrayal in Hollywood movies. Most of her comments refer to films from the 1930s to the 1970s.

California Advisory Committee to the U.S. Commission on Civil Rights. *Behind the Scenes: Equal Employment Opportunity in the Motion Picture Industry.* Washington, D.C.: USGPO, 1978.

    This is a detailed study of employment statistics and affirmative action in major Hollywood studios and includes employment statistics of Native Americans.

Carpenter, Edmund. "Film, Primitive Man, and Reality," *Media Ecology Review* 2 (Summer-Fall 1973): 2-4.

    Presents a general view of indigenous peoples and their portrayal in the media.

Cawelti, John G. "Cowboys, Indians, Outlaws," *American West* 1 (Spring 1964): 28-35, 77-79.

    Cawelti sees the Westerns of novels, movies, and television as a direct elaboration of the Buffalo Bill Wild West Show and dime novels. The basic elements in the myth of the West came from the period between 1850 and 1870.

_____. "Reflections on the New Western Films: The Jewish Cowboy, the Black Avenger, and the Return of the Vanishing American," *The University of Chicago Magazine* 65 (January–February 1973): 25-32.

    Cawelti sees the films setting forth a new myth about the West, one which incorporates a contemporary and changing attitude toward the Native American. This new myth amounts to a complete reversal of the symbolic meanings ascribed to major groups in the Western. The hero is regenerated through his contact with the native inhabitants, the pioneers become the bad guys and the Indians the force for good. The cavalry, a symbol of rescue and law and order, becomes "the instrument of brutal massacre."

Chavers, Dean. "A Good Movie to Miss," *Wassaja* 4 (January 1976): 20.

    Chavers criticizes *Winterhawk* as a story of a "mysterious savage with a sixth sense." He points out the many technical errors in the film, including a comment about the run in Sasheen Littlefeather's nylons.

Churchill, Ward; Nobert Hill; and Mary Anne Hill. "Media Stereotyping and Native Response: An Historical Overview," *The Indian Historian* 11 (December 1978): 45-56, 63.

    Contains a historical overview of the stereotypes of the Indian in the American film plus an analysis of similar stereotyping in other media.

Clark, Joan. "Some Wrongs Righted on Film: Vanishing American: Part I," *Film Library Quarterly* 3 (Winter 1969-70): 27, 47.

    Ms. Clark reviews four films good for classroom use: *The Ballad of Crowfoot, The End of the Trail, Mass for the Dakota Sioux,* and *Now That the Buffalo Are Gone.*

Combs, Richard. *"Ulzana's Raid,"* *Sight and Sound* 42 (Spring 1973): 115-16.

    Combs describes the films as the story of a renegade Apache who rebels against the monotonous spell of the reservation by going on a senseless rampage of rape, torture, and death.

Corliss, Richard. "Red Hot and Medium Cool," *National Review* 22 (January 13, 1970): 41-43.

". . . The Indian has finally made it onto the list of Liberal Causes just behind Blacks, Homosexuals, and Women. [*Tell Them*] *Willie Boy* [*Is Here*] skips the facile moralizing that would convert the Indian into a totem of white guilt; the leading character is . . . something more: an individual, and not as the collective hero, whether benign or rabid, or a long-silent minority."

deMontigny, Lionel H. "A Critique of the Film *Trial of Billy Jack*," *Wassaja* 3 (January–February 1975): 2.

In this review of the "Indian's answer to Kung Fu," deMontigny describes the film as "the same old stuff about Indians being an 'oppressed minority' and the usual mixture of pagan rituals."

Denby, David. "Americana: *Little Big Man*; *Love Story*." *Atlantic* 227 (March 1971): 106, 108–9.

If "Penn had been able to resist impressing certain ideologies of the present onto the past, he might have made a great movie." His portrayal of the Indian is bent on doing two things: "To do away with mumbo jumbo, the ignorant superstition, and the racist fears that have almost always characterized movie portraits of Indians" and "to end the hypocrisy of those liberal Westerns which have shown Indians being betrayed by treacherous whites, only to frighten the audience in the end with the Indians' aroused savagery—which justifies their slaughter."

Dench, Ernest Alfred. "The Dangers of Employing Redskins as Movie Actors" in *Making the Movies*. New York: Macmillan, 1915, pp. 92–94.

In an early piece about Indians employed as actors, Dench says, "The Red Indians who have been fortunate enough to secure permanent engagements with the several Western film companies are paid a salary that keeps them well provided with tobacco and their worshipped 'firewater.' "

Denton, James F. "The Red Man Plays Indian,' *Colliers* 113 (March 18, 1944): 18–19.

The Navajos are portraying the plains tribes in *Buffalo Bill* and find the transition both difficult and comical. The Indian actors are described as being primarily interested in the money they are earning with little or no concern for the historical accuracy of the film.

DiMino, Angelo V. "Stop Stereotyping Indian Studies: Filming Seneca History," *Instructor* 82 (November 1972): 100–3.

A short essay on how some fifth grade students shot their own movie of Seneca life and history.,

Ducheneaux, Franklin. "The American Indian: Beyond the Stereotypes," *Today's Education* 62 (May 1973): 22–24.

Ducheneaux discusses the dual image of the Indian, "noble savage or the bloodthirsty, dirty redskin" as well as newer mass media images. He then gives a more realistic portrayal of Indians in today's society.

Elrod, Norman, and Alexander Weber. "Indian Film Seminar in Switzerland," *Wassaja* 3 (July 1975): 15.

The authórs comment on some of the films shown in Switzerland from the perspective of evaluating images in terms of class struggles as the basis for racial problems.

"Entertainment," *News Week* 15 (February 26, 1940): 29.

Sees *Northwest Passage* as an exciting and suspenseful film that is close to a documentary account of the attack and merciless slaughter of the Abenaki Indians.

Erens, Patricia. *"Jeremiah Johnson*: The Mountain Man As Modern Hero," *Velvet Light Trap* 12 (Spring 1974): 37–39.

Discovers in *Jeremiah Johnson* an interesting reversal of the usual western prohibition against a white living among the Indians and provides a contemporary, upbeat theme in which the Indian way of life is an important counterculture symbol.

————. "Images of Minority and Foreign Groups in American Films: 1958–73," *Jump-Cut* 7 (May–July, 1975): 19–22.

Contains an introductory note to an annotated bibliography of source materials dealing with minority groups in the film. The author makes a convincing argument for studying films such as the Western, which of course involves the Indian.

Everson, William. *A Pictorial History of the Western Film.* New York: Citadel Press, 1969.

Everson includes little on the Indians except a few comments about the reliable theme—"stirring up the Indians"—which appeared over and over in the Western movie.

Ewers, John C. "The Static Images" in *Look to the Mountaintop,* edited by Robert Iocopi. San Jose: Gousha Publications, 1972, pp. 107–9.

Reviews the stereotypes of the American Indian in various media.

"The Exiles," *Time* 94 (December 19, 1969): 76–77.

Praises Abraham Polonsky for his "hard, gritty" portrayal of racial persecution in *Tell Them Willie Boy Is Here.*

Farber, Stephen. "Short Notices: *A Man Called Horse* and *Flap.*" *Film Quarterly* 24 (Fall 1970): 60–61.

A Man Called Horse is a film with a mixture of terror and wonderment. "From seeing this film, we get some understanding of how New England Puritans must have felt on confronting this savage, foreign people; to superstitious, provincial, unimaginative European settlers, these fierce, bizarrely painted and costumed natives must indeed have looked like monsters from hell."

Fenin, George N. "The Western—Old and New," *Film Culture* 2 (1956): 7–10.

Dealing primarily with the Western myth with the focus on the cowboy, he treats the Indian as part of the sagebrush which along with the bison had to be cleared from the plains before the white culture could inhabit them. There is a brief mention of Hollywood's efforts at historical accuracy in portraying the Native American in the fifties.

Fenin, George N., and William K. Everson. *The Western: From Silents to the Seventies.* New York: Grossman Publishers, 1973.

The authors trace the image of the Indian from early films to the present, pointing out the various images of the "senseless bloodthirsty savage" and the "dignified original American." They comment that the Indian was "alternately villainous and misunderstood, but he rarely emerged as a human being."

"Following the Films," *Scholastic* 36 (February 26, 1940): 36.

Describes the actions of Roger's Rangers in *Northwest Passage* as courageous and daring against savage Indians who had terrorized New England villagers.

Folsom, James K. " 'Western' Themes and Western Films," *Western American Literature* 2 (Fall 1967): 195–203.

Folsom elaborates on the "good" Indian and the "bad" Indian and reminds us of the cinematic cliché—a wagon train in a circle around the campfire with children playing and the men keeping guard; an owl hoots, but we all know it's really an Indian and an attack is soon to come.

French, Philip. *"Little Big Man," Sight and Sound* 40 (Spring 1971): 102–3.

In spite of many fine things, including several parodies of famous Westerns, Penn's film tends to dilute the charge against white America by focusing the guilt for the near genocide of the Indian on one crazy individual, George Armstrong Custer.

_____. "The Indian in the Western Movie," *Art in America* 60 (July–August 1972): 32–39.

This article concentrates on the image of the Indian in films since 1950, the "watershed year" for Western movies.

_____. *Westerns: Aspects of a Movie Genre.* London: Seker and Warburg, 1973.

French sees 1950 as the year that marked a change in the treatment of the Indian in the Westerns; he traces the images from early films such as *The Massacre* through the sixties noting always that the Indian is used as "more of a symbol, less an individual" than are other characters in the Western movie.

Friar, Ralph. "White Man Speaks With a Split Tongue, Forked Tongue, Tongue of Snake," *Film Library Quarterly* 3 (Winter 1969–1970): 16–23.

In this article Friar condenses the material and ideas presented in the longer study of the Indian in film, *The Only Good Indian . . . : The Hollywood Gospel.* He discusses some of the more significant films and comments on Kopit's play *Indians*—a production which reverses the earlier images and results in equally inaccurate stereotyping.

Friar, Ralph E., and Natasha A. Friar. *The Only Good Indian . . . : The Hollywood Gospel.* New York: Drama Book Specialists, 1972.

This book is the most complete study of the Indian in film. The Friars append a lengthy list of films that include Indians and lists categorizing the various ways in which Indians functioned in the movies. They also provide several stills and miscellaneous material such as promotional information for the films. They bring in related material such as popular literature, songs, and Wild West shows—all of which influenced the portrayal of the Indian in the Hollywood movie.

Georgakas, Dan. "They Have Not Spoken: American Indians in Film," *Film Quarterly* 25 (Spring 1972): 26–32.

Mr. Georgakas takes a serious look at the flaws in *A Man Called Horse, Soldier Blue, Little Big Man,* and *Tell Them Willie Boy Is Here.*

Gillett, John. *"Cheyenne Autumn," Sight and Sound* 34 (Winter 1964-1965): 36-37.

This positive review discusses Ford's increasing disenchantment toward "the myths he helped to create," but laments Ford's "division of feeling" toward the significance of this statement about Indians in this film.

Gilliatt, Penelope. "Back to the Trees," *New Yorker* 46 (May 9, 1970): 118.

A Man Called Horse is a film of Indian life painstakingly well researched: "The torture scenes, for instance, are obviously scholarly in their misbegotten way."

Gow, Gordon, *"Cheyenne Autumn," Films and Filming* 11 (December 1964): 27.

Finds *Cheyenne Autumn,* perhaps Ford's most profound film, a study of mutual inadequacies in the conflict between whites and Indians in the old West which has been set against the vastness of Monument Valley where men of all colors are dwarfed and need to bid for human dignity.

_____. Review of *A Man Called Horse, Films and Filming* 17 (October 1970): 45-46.

Gow sees the film as clouded in part because of the Sioux language dialogue and in part because of the mixture of trappings from both the old and new Westerns.

_____. Review of *Little Big Man, Films and Filming* 17 (June 1971): 63.

Gow feels *Little Big Man* is endowed with a sophisticated hindsight as it reviews history, sometimes satirically, sometimes seriously, with the seriousness apparently saved for the Indians and Dan George who do much to reverse the Western myth in the movie.

Handleman, Janet. "Report on the FLIC-EFLA Minorities Film Workshop," *Film Library Quarterly* 4 (Winter 1970-71): 7-9.

This brief article concentrates on an analysis of Bert Salzman's *Geronimo Jones* with references to *Ballad of Crowfoot* and *You Are on Indian Land.*

Handzo, Stephen. "Film: *Soldier Blue,"* *Village Voice* 15 (September 10, 1970): 61.

Handzo notes that "during periods of national masochism the Indian is rediscovered." He sees *Soldier Blue* as a "Theater of Cruelty Western based on proto-My Lai."

Harmon, Jim, and Donald F. Glut. *The Great Movie Serials: Their Sound and Fury.* Garden City, New York: Doubleday, 1972.

Although the book deals with all the serials, it does make references to the portrayals of the Indians in such old favorites as *The Miracle Rider, The Lone Ranger,* and *The Last of the Mohicans.*

Harris, Helen L. "The Bi-Centennial Celebration," *The Indian Historian* 7 (Fall 1974): 5-8.

Harris uses *The Reader's Digest*-produced film *Tom Sawyer* as an example of a misinterpretation of Mark Twain as well as American history to portray an uncivilized Injun Joe with an obsession for revenge.

Harrison, Louis Reeves. "The 'Bison-101' Headliners," *Moving Picture World* 12 (April 27, 1912): 320-22.

Praises the reality and accuracy of a recent spate of films on the "struggles between the primitive red man and the all-conquering white race." Describes the Indians as scattered over what is now the United States "subject to the ravages of relentless killing and torture—cruel, crafty, and predatory—with no universal language, no marks of gradual enlightenment and incapable of contributing anything of value to human evolution" when the Europeans arrived. Constantly exposed by their peaceful occupations to the indiscriminate slaughter by the Indians, these Europeans, nevertheless, subdued them and now provide for their well-being in a manner still "unenjoyed by white citizens."

Hartman, Hedy, "A Brief Review of the Native American in American Cinema," *The Indian Historian* 9 (Summer 1976): 27–29.

This brief article includes the American Indian Movement's list of criticisms about Indian portrayal in Hollywood movies as well as comments about some of the best (*Nanook of the North*) and the worst (*Northwest Passage*) of the films made with Indian content.

Hartung, Philip T. "Strange Heroes," *Commonweal* 35 (December 5, 1941): 180.

Sees *They Died With Their Boots On* as a distortion of history to suit the fancy of scriptwriters. Some of the film is dull and some exciting, but basically the film is too long for its limited content.

Hatch, Robert. "Films," *Nation* 223 (July 31, 1976): 93–94.

The film makes two basic assertions: the white man gave the red man a dirty deal and the Wild West was a fantasy concocted to conceal how dirty that deal was.

"Home of the Brave," *Time* 95 (May 11, 1970): 103.

The reviewer feels that director Elliot Silverstein "capitalizes on honesty" in his portrayal of the Indians in *A Man Called Horse.*

Hunt, Dennis. Review of *Tell Them Willie Boy Is Here, Film Quarterly* 23 (Spring 1970): 60–61.

The film is a "reminder to white Americans that they are bigoted bastards who have been brutally mistreating the Indians"; the film is an exercise in white "self-flagellation."

"Indians Grieve Over Picture Shows," *Moving Picture World* 10 (October 7, 1911): 32.

Makes the point that contemporary Indians are peacefully engaged in farming, and while they are avid movie fans, it is greatly disturbing to them to be so unjustly pictured in films.

"Indians and the Media: A Panel Discussion," *Civil Rights Digest* 6 (February 1973): 41–45.

This is a condensed transcript from a panel discussion that focused on communications as they relate to the Indian people of the United States.

"Indians War on Films: Delegation at Washington to Protest Against Alleged Libels in Moving Pictures," *Moving Picture World* 8 (March 18, 1911): 581.

A Chippewa delegation joined other tribes in an "uprising" against the use of whites dressed up as Indians in moving pictures. The groups denounced these films as having an untrue picture of the Indian.

Johnson, William. "New Light on the Past: *Cheyenne Autumn*," *Senior Scholastic* 85 (November 4, 1964): 30–31.
    The author says Ford tries to show both sides of the winning of the West and in his films he pays tribute to the Cheyenne's heroic trek.

Kael, Pauline. "Americana," *New Yorker* 45 (December 27, 1969): 47–50.
    Sees *Tell Them Willie Boy Is Here* as a film full of American self-hatred where the treatment of Indians is used symbolically to an excessive degree to represent American treatment of racial minorities.
_____. "The Current Cinema," *New Yorker* 46 (December 26, 1970): 50–52.
    Finds Arthur Penn's *Little Big Man* a film one wants to like but can't because the pieces just do not fit together, partly because it is "messagey" and partly because the slaughter is too reminiscent of Vietnam. Chief Dan George, "part patriarch, part Jewish mother," doesn't quite come off and neither do the hip comic bits with the Indians.
_____. "The Current Cinema," *New Yorker* 48 (December 30, 1972): 50–51.
    Finds *Jeremiah Johnson* something of a muddled movie wth low-key performances by both the Indians and Redford. Kael finds Johnson's final gesture to the Crow chief a way for the moviemakers to unload white guilt for past actions toward the Indians.
_____. "The Current Cinema," *New Yorker* 52 (June 28, 1976): 62.
    Describes Robert Altman's film *Buffalo Bill and the Indians* as about the making of a frontier legend fed by wish and created by theatricality. It is also about making idols and how the audience shapes roles: Buffalo Bill as frontier showman and Sitting Bull as vanishing American.
"Kalem Indian Stories Popular," *Moving Picture World* 6 (June 25, 1910): 1099.
    This short article lauds Kalem directors for their background knowledge and the authenticity portrayed in their Indian films. Predicts that an upcoming film, *Cheyenne Raiders*, will be as popular as previous ones because of such thrills as real leaps to death over real precipices into unseen life nets below.
Kaminsky, Stuart M. *"Ulzana's Raid,"* *Take One* 3 (January–February 1972): 36–37.
    This critic sees Aldrich, the director, as trying to "fathom the Apache ever since 1954 when he made a film *Apache*." We gain respect for Ulzana despite the growing atrocities. "The renegade Indian Ulzana emerges not simply as a figure of brutality and terror but as a consistent and honorable human being with a set of values so radically different from our own that we may never be able to understand them."
Kaufmann, Donald L. "The Indian as Media Hand-me-down," *The Colorado Quarterly* 23 (Spring 1974): 489–504.
    Kaufmann traces the use of the Indian figure in colonial literature (drama and novels) through the dime novel and the Wild West shows into the movies. He views Indians as a "figment of history always in the making and never coming to an ethnic rest."
Kaufmann, Stanley, "Stanley Kaufmann on Films," *The New Republic* 164 (January 23, 1971): 22.

Sees *Flap* as a corny ill-made picture full of tedious movie brawls. Recognizes it as another pro-Indian, antiwhite film.

_____. *"Jeremiah Johnson,"* *The New Republic* 168 (January 6 and 13, 1973): 24.

The treatment of Indians is evaluated as good in this film. Redford's Indian wife is described as really looking like an Indian girl, not a "starlet done up in Max Factor."

_____. *"Broken Treaty at Battle Mountain,"* *The New Republic* 172 (February 1, 1975): 20.

Kaufmann calls the film "better than documentary . . . on the subject" and praises Joel Freedman's "objective sympathy."

_____. "Stanley Kaufmann on Films—Bull Sitting," *The New Republic* 175 (July 24, 1976): 22.

Altman used Buffalo Bill's Wild West Show as a metaphor for American attitudes toward nonwhites but used the bare metaphor "as a playground for his usual assumptive anti-Americanism and for the cinematic horseplay that he thinks endorses it."

Keneas, Alex. "Indian Pudding," *Newsweek* 75 (May 25, 1970): 102, 104.

"From its opening credit of the Smithsonian Institution archives to its extensive use of Sioux dialect, *A Man Called Horse* boasts an authentic vision of Indian life. Yet for all the tepee truism, its anthropological ancestor is Hollywood, where the Indian, proud but savage, became the *raison d'être* for the cavalry charge."

Keshena, Rita. "The Role of American Indians in Motion Pictures," *American Indian Culture and Research* 1 (1974): 25–28.

Keshena reviews profit making and exploitation of the American Indian by the motion picture industry.

Kitses, Jim. *Horizons West: Studies in Authorship in the Western Film*. Bloomington, Indiana: Indiana University Press, 1970.

Provides only minor references to the Indian with two exceptions: a brief mention of Sam Peckinpah's handling of the Apaches in *Major Dundee* and some sketchy discussion of the role of the Indian in the Westerns of Anthony Mann.

Knight, Arthur. "New Look at the Old West," *Saturday Review of Literature* 48 (January 16, 1965): 36.

John Ford is quoted as saying that he wanted the audience to meet the Indian face to face and get to know him and admire him in *Cheyenne Autumn*.

_____. *"A Man Called Horse,"* *Saturday Review of Literature* 53 (May 2, 1970): 52.

Review emphasizes the authenticity of the film's approach to the Indian, the documentary feeling of living with the Sioux in spite of the anachronistic intrusion of twentieth-century music.

_____. "SR goes to the Movies," *Saturday Review* 53 (December 19, 1970): 88.

Knight sees *Flap* as an honest attempt to create sympathy for the Indians.

Lacey, Richard. "Alternatives to Cinema Rouge," *Media and Mehods* 7 (April 1971): 70–71.

Discusses some of the films that the author believes have portrayed Indian people accurately: *The Exiles, Two Rode Together,* and *The Outsider.*

Larkins, Robert. "Hollywood and the Indian," *Focus on Film* 2 (March–April 1970): 44–53.

Larkins reviews several films with Indian plots that were produced since 1950, concentrating especially on Ford's Westerns.

LaRoque, Emma. "And Now a Movie: and *Tom Sawyer* Criticized," *Wassaja* 2 (March–April 1974): 14.

This article is a criticism of *The Reader's Digest* production of *Tom Sawyer,* attacking especially the inaccurate portrayal of Injun Joe and the unnecessary emphasis on that character.

"The 'Make-Believe' Indian," *Moving Picture World* 8 (March 4, 1911): 473.

Criticizes motion pictures for not accurately portraying the Indians as a "noble race of people, with their splendid physique and physical prowess." They hope a series of films of "real" Indian life will be forthcoming.

Mantell, Harold. "Counteracting the Stereotype," *American Indian* 5 (Fall 1950): 16–20.

This report of the National Film Committee of the Association of American Indian Affairs cites the Committee's input on *Broken Arrow* as an example of how American Indian consultants can change the Hollywood image.

Marsden, Michael T., and Jack Nachbar. "The Buried Hatchet: Indian Culture in Film as Victim of the Popular Tradition" in *Hand-Book of North American Indians,* Vol. 78. Washington, D.C.: The Smithsonian Institution, 1977.

This survey discusses the Indian image in film during major periods of the twentieth century.

Metoyer-Duran, Cheryl. "Media Stereotyping of American Indians: An Editorial Focus," *American Indian Libraries Newsletter* 3 (Fall 1978): 1–2.

Focuses on stereotyping on television and the issues to be dealt with if the negative representation of American Indians is to be changed.

Millstead, Thomas. "The Movie the Indians Almost Won," *Westways* 62 (December 1970): 24–26, 55.

Although suffering from the author's biases, this article is an interesting account of the 1913 filming of a movie with Buffalo Bill and the Sioux of South Dakota. The movie was to be a reenactment of the Battle of Wounded Knee and the strained relations between the Indians and the Cavalry brought in to participate almost made filming impossible.

Milne, Tom. *"Tell Them Willie Boy Is Here,"* *Sight and Sound* 39 (Spring 1970): 101–2.

Sees Polonsky's theme as the fatalistic irony whereby Willie reverts to being an Indian when accused, in effect, of the crime of being an Indian. Willie becomes as alien and unfathomable as the painted, screaming scalp hunters who used to haunt the Hollywood Western. Milne sees the characters as so pared, the setting so subjugated to the image of bleak despair, that one begins to feel less than he should.

_____. *"Little Big Man," Focus on Film* 6 (Spring 1971): 3–7.

Among other things, Milne sees the film as "a sociological treatise on the Cheyenne culture and customs, fascinating as well as thoroughly convincing for all that it might well be pure fabrication."

_____. *"Buffalo Bill and the Indians," Sight and Sound* 45 (Autumn 1976): 254.

Feels Altman has deliberately decentralized any question of the reality of the Indian, and the film becomes a confrontation of myth against myth.

Morgenstern, Joseph. "Requiem for a Red Man," *Newsweek* 74 (December 8, 1969): 121.

The writer-director, Abraham Polonsky of *Tell Them Willie Boy Is Here,* is in search of a "pattern of white America's attitude toward nonwhite minorities." He focuses on one incident of the film as a white-Indian paradigm.

"Movies," *News Week* 18 (December 1, 1941): 70.

They Died With Their Boots On is described as a cross between a Western and an epic. The major problem is that it takes too long to get to the Indians. Custer is seen as a victim of bad luck or bad judgment.

Nachbar, Jack. *Focus on the Western.* Englewood Cliffs, New Jersey: Prentice-Hall, 1974.

This anthology includes some articles that refer to the image of the American Indian in Hollywood Westerns. Katherine Esselman's article is especially good in that it traces the Indian image from early writings through the visual media.

Nelson, Ralph. "Massacre at Sand Creek," *Films and Filming* 16 (March 1970): 26–27.

In this interview Nelson explains that he made *Soldier Blue* because of the glossing over of the white American genocide of the Indians during the winning of the West.

"Noble Non-savage: Chief Dan George," *Time* 97 (February 15, 1971): 76.

This is a biographical note on Chief Dan George, a comment on his role in *Little Big Man,* and a few words about his philosophy on Indian-white relations.

O'Connor, John E., and Martin A. Jackson. *American History/American Film*: *Interpreting the Hollywood Image.* New York: Frederick Unger Publishing Co., 1979.

Includes O'Connor's essay on *Drums Along the Mohawk* in which he compares the novel and the film and the portrayal on screen of agrarian American life "menaced by barbarous Indians."

Pauly, Thomas H. "What's Happened to the Western Movie?" *Western Humanities Review* 28 (Summer 1974): 260–69.

Pauly comments on the reversals in Westerns, one of which is that the Indian has become the hero rather than the cowboy. *Little Big Man* (1970), according to the author, proved that the "Indian's main strength lay in being the tragic victim of the white man's demented thirst for land and gold and glory."

Pechter, Williams. "Equal Time," *Commentary* 51 (April 1971): 80–81.

The author sees *Little Big Man* as "an Indian-fighting Western with its conventional demonology reversed: bad white men riding against good Indians." Penn does not perceive that the problem is the demonology itself that brutalizes an audience and is the enemy of humane feeling.

_____. "Altman, Chabrol, and Ray," *Commentary* 62 (October 1976): 75–77.

Describes *Buffalo Bill and the Indians* as a moralizing tale about an American national hero who is a complete fraud, and about the confusion caused by Sitting Bull's appearance. The show business lies prevail in the end, however, as the "venal white devils" trample the noble red men underfoot in the standard American demonology.

Perkins, V. F. Review of *Cheyenne Autumn, Movie* 12 (Spring 1965): 36–37.

Perkins asserts that this film demonstrates the studio's control over a filmmaker's material. The big money controls the contents of films by demanding consumer appeal. Warner Brothers tried to convert Ford's personal film into an epic and ruined the film's impact in doing so.

Pilkington, William T., and Don Graham. *Western Movies.* Albuquerque: University of New Mexico Press, 1979.

This collection includes several essays on films portraying American Indians.

"The Plainsman," News Week 9 (January 16, 1937): 30.

Light mention is made of Indians being in the film, but the focus is on the glory of those who beat the redskin. Mentions that Indians were used in the film as though it were a completely new idea.

Price, John A. "The Stereotyping of North American Indians in Motion Pictures," *Ethnohistory* 20 (Spring 1973): 153–71.

This article traces the images of Indians from the silent film period (1908–1929) through the negative images of the serials (1930–1947) and the breaking down of stereotypes after 1948. It also discusses the more positive treatment of the Eskimos in documentary movies.

Rarihokwats. *"The Only Good Indian . . . . : The Hollywood Gospel." Akwesasne Notes* 5 (Late Summer 1973): 41.

The editor of this Indian newspaper comments about the treatment of the Indian in the movies and praises the Friars' book which examines the topic.

Review of *Massacre, The News Week in Entertainment* 3 (January 27, 1934): 33.

Finds this melodrama hard to believe at times: "If half the white man's abuses of Indians shown in this First National film are true, it is a wonder any redskins have survived at all."

Rice, Susan. ". . . And Afterwards, Take Him to a Movie," *Media and Methods* 7 (April 1971): 43–44, 71–72.

Contains a broad survey of the current revisionist films about Indians including *Little Big Man, Tell Them Willie Boy Is Here, Soldier Blue, Flap,* and

The Outsider which she finds variously mindless, embarrassing, and inadequate. She wonders if the first really intelligent film about Indians might not be made by a foreigner.

Richburg, James R., and Phyllis R. Hastings. "Media and the American Indian: Ethnographical, Historical, and Contemporary Issues, " *Social Education* 36 (May 1972): 526–33, 562.

The authors discuss the use of visual materials to teach about the American Indian and review several suitable films.

Rieupeyrout, Jean-Louis. "The Western: A Historical Genre," *Quarterly Review of Film, Radio and Television* 7 (Winter 1952): 116–28.

This essay examines two John Ford classics, *My Darling Clementine* and *Fort Apache,* from the perspective of the Western as a historical genre which is a "crystallizer" of diffuse elements from American folklore. In looking at *Fort Apache,* the author points out how Ford used the Custer legend in his story of Colonel Thursday's dedication to duty and the destruction of the Indian. The film is touted as an example of the Western epic in its purest form, i.e., purely factual.

Ronan, Margaret. "Film: Lo, the True Indian!" *Senior Scholastic* 96 (May 4, 1970): 24–25.

Ronan believes that at last in *A Man Called Horse* the Indian breaks out of his dimension of defeat and takes his place in history.

_____. "Film," *Senior Scholastic* 109 (September 23, 1976): 12.

A short review that raises the question, Is *Jeremiah Johnson* really a symbol of the Indian tragedy?

Sando, Joe S. "White Created Myths About the American Indian," *The Indian Historian* 4 (Winter 1971): 10–11.

Although not specifically about films, this article reviews the stereotypes that have become standard elements in the Hollywood Western—scalping, laziness, battles/massacres, and the influences of the missionaries and the government.

Schickel, Richard. "Critic's Roundup: *Tell Them Willie Boy Is Here,"* *Life* 67 (November 28, 1969): 18.

This brief review describes Willie as James Dean in Man-Tan and the Indian girl as being of the "wooden, or cigar-store type."

_____. "Why Indians Can't Be Villains Any More," *New York Times,* February 9, 1975, Section 2, pp. 1, 15.

Schickel uses *Ulzana's Raid* to explore the use of historical accuracy in portraying the Indian wars and concludes that those films showing brutality and savagism accurately portray the result of a cultural conflict that could never have been settled peacefully.

Schmitz, Tony. "Film Makers' Reflections on the Productions of the American Indian Artists Series," *Arizona Highways* 52 (August 1976): 4–11.

Describes the making of the American Indian Artists Film Series which depicted the working of American Indian artists for KAET, a public television station in Phoenix, Arizona.

Sheperd, Duncan. *"Ulzana's Raid," Cinema* 8 (1973): 44–45.

Aldrich's film does not "tramp over previously surveyed territory." It does not "stretch beyond the Western genre's historical limits to gain a vantage point of enlightened hindsight." It "revives the disreputable practice of stereotyping, with striking effects."

Silet, Charles L. P. "The Image of the American Indian in Film." *The Worlds Between Two Rivers: Perspectives on American Indians in Iowa.* Ames: Iowa State University Press, 1978, pp. 10–15.

Surveys the sources for film stereotypes and how such stereotypes have been perpetuated in the twentieth century.

Silet, Charles L. P., and Gretchen M. Bataille. "The Indian in the Film: A Critical Survey," *Quarterly Review of Film Studies* 2 (February 1977): 56–74.

Reviews popular images of the American Indian as they have influenced films and film criticism. Includes material from early in the twentieth century up to contemporary reviews.

Spears, Jack. "The Indian on the Screen," *Films in Review* 10 (January 1959): 18–35.

Spears discusses the stereotyped Indian villain and the noble savage as well as the oversympathetic portrayals in films since 1950.

_____. *Hollywood: The Golden Era.* New York: A. S. Barnes, 1971.

Spears acknowledges that Hollywood has had little concern for historical accuracy or honest characterization and illustrates his statement with comments about the portrayal of the Indian on the screen.

Spenser, Richard V. "Los Angeles Notes: Indians Protest Against Indian Pictures," *Moving Picture World* 8 (March 18, 1911): 587.

Indians of Northwest and Western reservations were registering objections with the Bureau of Indian Affairs against portrayals of Indian life in films. The commissioner, Robert G. Valentine, said he was also disturbed and would help the Shoshone, Cheyenne, and Arapahoe delegates to eliminate the objectionable portrayals.

Talbot, Anne. "Prejudice: Thoughts Garnered Among the Navajo," *Media and Methods* 9 (December 1972): 36–37.

This brief article lists three films about American Indians and discusses the prejudice held against the Navajos by teachers.

Terraine, John. "End of the Trail," *Films and Filming* 3 (July 1957): 9, 30.

Terraine believes the American Indian was never much of a "noble savage." "He was brave and intelligent, cruel and smelly, and he had no drawingroom manners at all."

"They Died With Their Boots On," Time 38 (December 22, 1941): 47.

This first full-length exposition of the Custer legend whitewashes Custer and bypasses history in a way not likely to please either side.

Turner, John W. *"Little Big Man:* The Novel and the Film," *Literature/Film Quarterly* 5 (Spring 1977): 154–63.

Turner argues that close examination of the novel illustrates some of the critical difficulties of the film, among them the use of the narrator, the identity problems of the central character, and the conflict between savagism and civilization.

U.S. Commission on Civil Rights. *Window Dressing on the Set: Women and Minorities in Television.* Washington, D.C.: USGPO, 1977.

This is a nationwide study of the portrayal of minorities and women in television drama, news, and employment at the networks.

_____. *Window Dressing on the Set: An Update.* Washington, D.C.: USGPO, 1979.

Updates previous report by covering years 1975-1977 with an emphasis on television's treatment of women and minorities.

Vestal, Stanley. "The Hollywooden Indian," *Southwest Review* 21 (1936): 418-23.

Vestal is critical of the movie portrayal of Indian people as "caricatures of their race" and criticizes directors for not using Indian Actors.

Vickrey, William. "Some Wrongs Righted on Film: The Vanishing American: Part II," *Film Library Quarterly* 3 (Winter 1969-1970): 46-47.

Vickrey reviews *Ishi in Two Worlds, Tahtonka,* and *Circle of the Sun.*

"Vogue of Western and Military Drama," *Moving Picture World* 9 (August 5, 1911): 271-72.

Deals with the appeal of the Westerns as man vs. nature and states that feeling toward the "red man" has changed in the last century, that he is no longer hated or feared but admired for his noble qualities and envied for his closeness to nature. This desire to do the Indian belated justice runs through early Indian films and accounts for their popularity.

Walker, Stanley. "Let the Indian Be the Hero," *New York Times Magazine* April 24, 1960, pp. 50, 52, 55.

This is a general discussion of the Indian in television Westerns and a plea that perhaps someday the Indian will be the hero rather than the victim of inaccurate portrayals.

Walsh, Moria. *"A Man Called Horse,"* *America* 122 (May 16, 1970): 538, 540-41.

The reviewer feels that the film is a small foundation stone that by indirection "dramatizes the present plight of the Indians by portraying their past culture, its virtues as well as its unappetizing features, with some dignity and integrity."

_____. "More Loathsome Films," *America* 123 (September 19, 1970): 185-86.

The author sees the film *Soldier Blue* as a "fraud and an artistic mess and largely self-defeating." It is a "film that pretends to deny violence" while appealing "to the unspeculative forms of violence."

_____. *"Little Big Man,"* *America* 124 (January 30, 1971): 97.

Penn is able to include his awareness of "the injustice and atrocities inflicted on the Indians as the west was won" in an entertaining film that avoids "hindsight self-righteousness" and "wallowing in violence while pretending to decry it."

Westerbeck, Colin L., Jr. "All-American History," *Commonweal* 92 (September 4, 1970): 441–42.

Soldier Blue is a movie about a white woman liberated after two years of captivity by the Cheyennes and is characterized by gratuitous violence and confused motives.

_____. "The Screen," *Commonweal* 103 (August 13, 1976): 528–29.

Says that in *Buffalo Bill and the Indians* Altman has taken American history and folded it back against itself as if he wanted to make an enormous Rorschach card out of it. In effect, his whole film is about the relationship between illusion and substance, fakery and the genuine article, and the difficulty of telling them apart.

Wilkinson, Gerald. "Colonialism through the Media," *The Indian Historian* 7 (Summer 1974): 29–32.

Wilkinson points out that the media paints a picture of Indian people that serves the interest of the white public and not necessarily truth or justice. A subtle and pervasive control of Indians' psychology, their image of themselves, their values, and their culture is possible through the stereotypic portrait drawn by the media. The author argues for more Indian participation in ownership and control of media.

Willett, Ralph. "The American Western: Myth and Anti-myth," *Journal of Popular Culture* 4 (Fall 1970): 455–63.

Mentions in this discussion of the myth of the West that the pre-fifties stereotyping of the Native American is now well recognized.

Wood, Robin. "Arthur Penn in Canada," *Movie* 18 (Winter 1970–71): 26–36.

This interview with the director Arthur Penn contains some interesting information on the shooting of *Little Big Man* and discusses why Penn kept the slangy language of Thomas Berger's novel for the Indians and how he was able to create the moral tone of the film.

_____. "Shall We Gather at the River: The Late Films of John Ford," *Film Comment* 7 (Fall 1971): 8–17.

Discusses Ford's inability to create a really convincing view of the Cheyenne which resulted in the artistic failure of *Cheyenne Autumn*. His self-contradiction in dealing with Indians flaws the film. The article also deals in a general way with Ford's treatment of Indians in *She Wore a Yellow Ribbon* and *Fort Apache*.

Worth, Sol, and John Adair. *Through Navajo Eyes: An Exploration in Film Communication and Anthropology,* Bloomington: Indiana University Press, 1972.

This book documents the experiences of the authors as they taught the Navajo to make films and describes the results that illustrated in part how a given culture structures reality.

Yacowar, Maurice. "Private and Public Visions: *Zabriskie Point* and *Billy Jack.*" *Journal of Popular Film* 1 (Summer 1972): 197–207.

The author believes *Billy Jack* looks back to the American Indian for its values and detaches itself from the traditional treatment of Indians in films, thus becoming a rebuttal to the traditional Western.

Zimmerman, Paul D. "How the West Was Lost," *Newsweek* 76 (December 21, 1970): 98, 100.

Describes Penn's Western, *Little Big Man,* as a traditional Hollywood horse epic in spite of loving, human moments between Indian Dan George and white Dustin Hoffman.

INDEX